10. Special equipment

What special equipment is required, and what are its space requirements? Is security a factor?
37–38, 80, 86–87, 123, 132, 159, 196, 198, 225–26, 232, 235

11. Materials

What materials need to be uniquely considered or rejected?
70–71, 73–74, 103–4, 126, 131, 148, 189, 194, 212–13, 219

12. Acoustic control

What special acoustical considerations affect the design?
127, 194, 196

13. Lighting design

What special lighting (day and artificial) considerations affect the design?
21, 75, 156, 192, 206, 208, 210, 212–14, 217, 220

14. Interiors issues

What special considerations (scale, color, texture, finishes, furnishings, special features) affect the planning of interiors?
28–29, 31, 71, 73, 88, 134–35, 140–41, 188

15. Wayfinding

What special factors determine signing systems?
178–80, 183, 188, 189

16. Preservation/modernization

What special considerations (historical authenticity, infrastructure retrofit) arise when renovating a facility of this type?
6

17. International challenges

On international projects, what special considerations influence marketing, design, presentations, document production, and field presence?

18. Operation and maintenance

How will design decisions influence the operation and maintenance of the completed facility?
12, 25, 29, 32, 184, 203, 221–22, 230

19. Key cost factors

What are the principal determinants of the total construction cost?
221–22

20. Finances, fees, feasibility

What are the typical techniques for financing this facility?
201–4

BUILDING TYPE BASICS FOR

recreational facilities

BUILDING TYPE BASICS FOR

recreational facilities

Stephen A. Kliment, Series Founder and Editor

RICHARD J. DIEDRICH

WILEY

JOHN WILEY & SONS, INC.

Published by John Wiley & Sons, Inc., Hoboken, New Jersey
Published simultaneously in Canada

Limit of Liability/Disclaimer of Warranty: While the publisher and author have used their best
efforts in preparing this book, they make no representations or warranties with respect to the accu-
racy or completeness of the contents of this book and specifically disclaim any implied warranties of
merchantability or fitness for a particular purpose. No warranty may be created or extended by sales
representatives or written sales materials. The advice and strategies contained herein may not be
suitable for your situation. You should consult with a professional where appropriate. Neither the
publisher nor author shall be liable for any loss of profit or any other commercial damages, including but not limited to special, incidental, consequential, or other damages.

For general information on our other products and services or for technical support, please contact
our Customer Care Department within the United States at (800) 762-2974, outside the United
States at (317) 572-3993 or fax (317) 572-4002.

Wiley also publishes its books in a variety of electronic formats. Some content that appears in print
may not be available in electronic books.

Library of Congress Cataloging-in-Publication Data:

Diedrich, Richard J.
  Building type basics for recreational facilities / Richard J. Diedrich.
    p. cm. -- (Building type basics series)
  Includes bibliographical references and index.
  ISBN 0-471-47260-3 (cloth)
  1. Architecture and recreation. 2. Sports facilities--Design and
construction. 3. Physical fitness centers--Design and construction. I.
Title. II. Series.
  NA2543.R43D54 2005
  725'.8--dc22
  2004011568

Printed in the United States of America

10 9 8 7 6 5 4 3 2 1

CONTENTS

CONTENTS

PREFACE

STEPHEN A. KLIMENT *Series Founder and Editor*

The search for leisure has evolved into one of this nation's greatest pastimes. Whether this leisure time is spent on a weekend round of golf, a daily visit to a fitness center, a gallop around the park astride a horse, a downhill dash on skis, or a solemn search for self-enrichment, the culture of recreation has spawned a wide range of architectural prototypes aimed at making the experience pleasant for the user and profitable for the developer.

As author Richard J. Diedrich points out in this volume in the Wiley "Building Type Basics" series, the quality of life valued by Americans, underscored by the tragedy of September 11, 2001, is spawning a lifestyle that supports all manner of community recreation centers, religion-based young people's associations, and urban and outlying club resorts. As Diedrich notes: "the organizations running these facilities have responded by offering not only swimming, tennis, and golf but also greater sophistication, expressed as wellness and fitness, spa services, and cultural enrichment."

Dining out too has grown sharply since 2001. The National Restaurant Association has projected annual increases in sales by an average of some 4 percent a year, and club business grew by 10 percent in 2002, according to the Club Managers Association of America.

To meet the architectural planning, programming, and design challenges of the desire for leisure, Diedrich, an architect who has completed a wide array of leisure architecture, has written a versatile book which, in the tradition of the "Building Type Basics" series, tackles the practical challenges architects, engineers, and consultants face as they embark on creating an attractive and financially viable leisure facility.

Diedrich divides the book into sections that take up one by one the dominant categories of leisure and leisure and recreation building concerns. The sections address:

- Recreation facilities that support participatory activities such as golf; boating, swimming, and water-related sports; racquet sports; skiing and winter sports; and equestrian sports. Structures such as arenas and stadia that serve as venues for spectator sports are the topic of a future book in this Series.
- Fitness and wellness facilities.
- Lifelong learning and enrichment centers.
- Dining and activity-related healthy dining facilities.
- Environmental issues and techniques for incorporating environmental planning into recreational structures, especially those that impact nature.

This is not a coffee-table book, lavish with color photography but meager in usable content. Rather, it is full of immediate information architects, clients, and consultants can study quickly. As architectural practices become more generalized and firms accept design commissions over a wider range of building types, the books in this series provide a convenient hands-on resource for the critical initial design phases of a project. Developers, operators, and managers of leisure properties will find helpful information as they prepare to interview architects for recreation commissions.

The format of this book has become a hallmark of the series. The "operating system" of the series volumes resides in the set of twenty questions most frequently asked about a building type, especially in the early phases of its design. The Twenty Questions cover predesign; project management; unique design concerns; site issues; security; building codes, Americans with Disabilities Act (ADA), and other codes; environmental issues; structural, mechanical, and electrical systems; communications; materials; special equipment; acoustics; lighting; special interiors issues; wayfinding; renovation and retrofitting; operation and maintenance considerations; cost issues; and financing.

For convenience, an index links the twenty questions to relevant sections in the book. The index appears on the front and back endpapers of the book.

I hope that, as you delve into this book, it serves you as guide, reference, and inspiration.

ACKNOWLEDGMENTS

This book is the result of the assistance of a remarkable number of people.

My wife, Linda, who will not settle for less than the best.

My daughters, Dawn, Lisa, and Andrea, who now challenge me as I once challenged them.

My grandchildren, without whom I may never have been aware of some of the latest concepts in recreation.

My assistant, Caroline Long, without whom this book might never have been completed.

Image Design, Inc., for their resources and support of my effort, and in particular, Jonathan Maier for information technology and Lauren Downs for graphic design.

Addison Young for his eye and hand in transforming two-dimensional drawings into three-dimensional images.

In technical support, the author is indebted to the following people, facilities, and institutions.

Stephen Kliment, series editor, and John Czarnecki for guiding a novice through this process.

Introduction: For information on participation and trends in recreation: National Survey on Recreation and the Environment (NSRE): 2000–2002. The Interagency National Survey Consortium, coordinated by the (USDA) Forest Service, Recreation, Wilderness, and Demographics Trends Research Group, Athens, Georgia, and the Human Dimensions Research Laboratory, University of Tennessee, Knoxville, Tennessee.

Aquatics: Sona and Nikhil Kumar for their hands-on teaching of the ins and outs and ups and downs of water parks. Judith LeBlein of Water Technology, Inc., for connecting me with the best in design for water recreation.

Boating: Bruce Blomgren of Brandy Marine, and Thomas J. Lehnen for bringing a lifetime of boating experience to bear as critic and contributor.

Racquet sports: James K. Lee for his writing on handball, racquetball, and squash facilities, which are otherwise a mystery to me.

Skiing and winter sports: Charles Cunniffe, architect, Aspen, Colorado; Gary Hartman, architect, Zehren Architects, Avon, Colorado; Andy White, OZ Architects, Boulder, Colorado; Steve Sewell, mountain manager, Aspen Mountain, Aspen, Colorado; Joe Whitehouse, vice president, and Todd Morgan of Intrawest for taking the time to acquaint me with winter sports facilities.

Equestrian: Eileen Wheeler, College of Agricultural Sciences, Pennsylvania State University, for her bulletin series on horse facilities. Allison Mehta of Talaria Farms, Newman, Georgia, for her gracious and insightful tour.

Extreme sports: Zack Wormhoudt, landscape architect, Santa Cruz, California, for bridging the generation gap and introducing me to skatepark design.

ACKNOWLEDGMENTS

Fitness: Chris White of WTS International, Silver Spring, Maryland, for counsel and critique. Thomas J. Lehnen for personal input as a late-blooming fitness buff. Don Jones, Celebration Health, Celebration, Florida, for fitness in a community hospital setting.

Spa: Sr. Jose Manuel Jasso Peña, Mary Elizabeth Gifford, and Phyllis Pilgram of Rancho La Puerta, Tecate, Mexico, for insight into refreshing the mind, body and spirit at a destination spa.

Enrichment: Harry Teague, architect, Aspen, Colorado, and Jeremy Swanson, director of communications, for acquainting me with the resources of Anderson Ranch, Snowmass Village, Colorado, and Jennifer Rader, consultant, for summarizing the essence of family activity centers.

Dining: The staff of Diedrich Architects and Image Design, for producing a body of work encompassing the gamut in food and beverage for recreation.

Feasibility: Ralph Stewart Bowden, consultant, for writing the chapter on the feasibility of this diverse group of facilities.

Sustainability: Aaron Revere, East-West Partners, Truckee, California, for spearheading his company's commitment to green building design; Mark A. Diedrich, architect and LEED Consultant, Kuo Diedrich, Atlanta, Georgia, for researching and writing the chapter on sustainable design.

CHAPTER 1
INTRODUCTION

According to the National Survey on Recreation and the Environment (NSRE), over 97.6 percent of Americans over the age of 16, or 207.9 million people, take part in outdoor recreation on an intermittent or regular basis (NSRE 2002). This participation rate is up from 94.5 percent in 1995. People are living longer, and thus staying active longer, and, assuming rising affluence, leisure activities are projected to continue to grow faster than the population. Although the most popular activity remains walking for pleasure, the menu of recreational pursuits is getting longer and more diverse. Some of fastest growing, such as jet skiing, were not even listed by NSRE ten years ago. Many of the slower growing pursuits have a huge base of participants, consequently their expansion is relatively more significant, in absolute numbers.

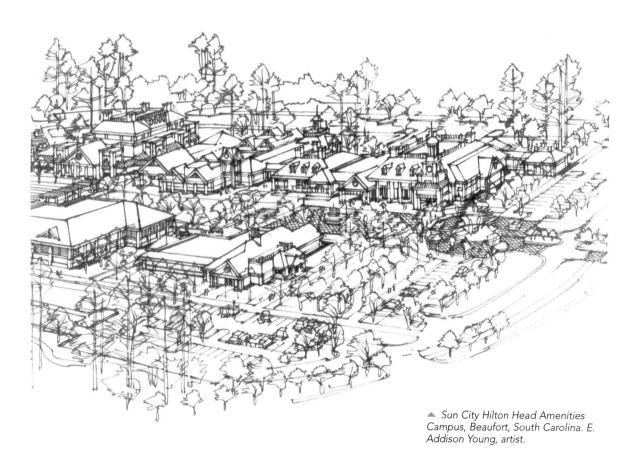

▲ Sun City Hilton Head Amenities Campus, Beaufort, South Carolina. E. Addison Young, artist.

OUTDOOR RECREATION IN THE UNITED STATES, RATES OF PARTICIPATION*		
	Participation (percent)**	Number of Participants (000)
Land Activities		
Walking for pleasure	82.3	175,381
Golf	16.7	35,588
Horseback riding (general)	9.6	20,458
Rock climbing	4.3	9,163
Water Activities		
Swimming in outdoor pool	41.6	88,650
Motorboating	24.3	51,783
Canoeing	9.6	20,458
Rowing	4.2	8,950
Kayaking	3.7	7,885
Snow/Ice Activities	26.6	56,685
Downhill skiing	8.6	18,327
Snowboarding	5.0	10,655
Cross-country skiing	3.8	8,098
Viewing/Learning Activities		
Visit nature centers, etc.	56.4	120,188
Visit historic sites	45.3	96,534
Visit prehistoric/archaeological sites	20.5	43,686

*Based on NSRE 2000.
**Of a population of 213.1 million, age 16 and older.

Trends in recreation parallel trends in society. In outdoor recreation, a growing sensitivity to the environment is mirrored in an increase in the number of people who enjoy bird watching and wildlife viewing. Technological improvements in equipment have resulted in a dramatic rise in the snowboarding, jet skiing, and kayaking participation rates. As well, the increase in numbers of people visiting nature and interpretive centers reflects an interest in lifelong learning. Pursuit of fitness and development of an environmental consciousness has increased hiking numbers while maintaining walking as the top recreational activity.

Developers of resorts and planned communities have not missed the popularity of recreational activities. Since the 1980s, the focus of land development for communities and resorts has expanded to include incorporation of recreational

RECREATION TRENDS IN THE UNITED STATES*			
Activity	Participants, 1994–1995 (millions)	Participants, 2000–2001 (millions)	Percent Change, 1994–2001
Kayaking	2.58	7.29	182.56
Snowboarding	4.43	10.53	137.70
Horseback riding	13.94	20.95	50.29
Canoeing	13.76	20.63	49.93
Handball or racquetball	11.02	15.07	36.75
Walking for pleasure	130.66	177.00	35.47
Visiting nature centers	90.93	122.28	34.48
Visiting architectural sites	34.09	44.84	31.53
Cross country skiing	6.38	8.10	26.96
Rock climbing	7.26	9.21	26.86
Golfing	29.04	35.93	23.73
Rowing	8.24	9.42	14.32
Visiting historic sites	86.43	98.62	14.10
Motorboating	45.93	52.27	13.80
Downhill skiing	16.45	18.20	10.64
Pool swimming	86.52	87.09	0.66

*Cordell 2003.

amenities and an eye to environmental preservation. The clubhouse at Marlborough Crossing, for example, a planned recreational community in Marlborough, Connecticut, is conceived as a group of buildings surrounding a New England village green.

Many recreational activities are housed in buildings or supported by building type structures. This book addresses programming, planning, and design of these facilities. Although many of the recreational facilities are sports related, this book does not attempt to define site planning or civil engineering for the playing field or sport venue except as it affects the building facilities normally used in conjunction with the activity. For instance, the principles of planning of a golf course are not addressed, but the programming, planning, and design of golf clubhouses and maintenance facilities are included. Marinas and engineering of marine structures such as docks and seawalls are not covered, but the design of boat dry-stack storage is included.

ORGANIZATION

The book is organized by type of recreational activity. Those looking to design

◀ *Marlborough Crossing community recreational amenities, Marlborough, Connecticut, include a community hall, social and dining areas, golf locker rooms, cart barn and pavilion, fitness, child-sitting, and aquatics. Diedrich LLC, architect. Landmark Partners, Inc., developer; BL Companies, planner. E. Addison Young, artist.*

▶ *The Point community recreational amenities, Lake Norman, North Carolina, housed in a Nantucket-style village, include a golf shop, locker rooms, bar and lounge, dining, private dining room, community hall, family activity center, fitness, aquatics, child-sitting. Chapman, Coyle, Chapman, architects. Crescent Resources LLC, devloper. Photo, courtesy Crescent Communities.*

one of the diverse building types can find the essence of design in one of the following sections or chapters:

Recreational sports:

- Golf
- Aquatics
- Boating
- Handball, racquetball, squash, and indoor tennis
- Skiing and winter sports
- Equestrian
- Extreme sports

There are some aspects of recreational facilities that are more universal across the variety of physical activity, including:

- Fitness and wellness facilities
- Spas and salons

Recreation that exercises the mind, encourages creativity, and raises the spirit is addressed within the chapters on:

- Lifelong learning and enrichment centers
- Dining facilities

Building-related issues like codes, acoustics, lighting, and structure are targeted at the particular building type within its chapter. There are, however, two chapters that address recreational buildings in general as well as applications pertinent to specific building types:

- Financial feasibility
- Sustainability

Common Aspects of Leisure and Buildings

Facilities supporting recreation included in this book may be looked at based on these common aspects of leisure activity.

Preparation for the activity

Golf clubhouses, bathhouses, and Nordic centers are all examples of facilities that support the participant in outfitting or equipping for the recreational activity. Interpretive centers and nature centers prepare the participant by providing the setting for learning about a particular natural environment or culture.

Positioning for the activity

Gondola stations and heli-ski lodges for downhill skiers are buildings providing access to a sporting venue.

Housing the activity

Fitness facilities, indoor racquet sports, and indoor pools house the recreational pursuit itself. Enrichment centers and lifelong learning studios and labs house the arts and crafts workshops growing in popularity today. Spas and teen centers are other facilities containing a range of leisure and recreational activities.

Housing the vehicle and equipment

Dry-stack boat storage, equestrian stables, and golf cart barns house the vehicle or animal used in the sport or recreation. Also included are spaces housing equipment and personnel dedicated to grooming and maintaining the recreational venue, as in a golf maintenance facility.

Celebrating and viewing the activity

This book is about participatory sports as recreation, rather than viewing attendance at sports events. The camaraderie built through eating and drinking, however, is an essential part of some recreational pursuits. The 19th hole in golf, après ski in downhill skiing and snowboarding, and the yacht club are all based on the appeal of watching one's peers finishing or participating in their activity, boasting of their prowess, and swapping opinions on equipment and the sporting venue.

Enabling the activity

To participate in recreation, parents may require temporary care for their children. Consequently, this book introduces planning of basic child-sitting facilities that might be found in clubhouses or a community recreation center. It does not take up the professional, licensed day-care center.

There is also programming and planning material on teen centers. These facilities not only provide recreation for the teen but also serve as a wholesome setting for after-school activity for children of working parents.

"Green" Architecture

Since a great deal of recreational activity is outside, much of it affects the natural environment. Appropriately, this book provides a chapter on sustainable design. Recreational buildings that support teaching about the environment are prime candidates for "green" architecture.

PART I

RECREATIONAL SPORTS FACILITIES

Previous page: *Livonia Community Recreation Center, Livonia, Michigan. Neuman/Smith Architects and Associates; Barker Rinker Seacat Architects. Photo by Justin Maconochie.*

CHAPTER 2
GOLF

The increase in golf participation is linked to the graying of the population; as a result, a surge in players is likely until 2010. Over that time, the large numbers of "baby boomers," those born in the years after World War II, will reach that period in life when they have the time and money necessary to pursue golf as a recreation. However, other changes in the lives of aging boomers affect this traditional leisure time. Increases in hours worked and child-rearing delayed to later in life have placed work and family demands on time that might once have been spent on golf. Due to these changes, continued increases in the number of golfers is made more difficult. In response, to show a greater family orientation, the golf industry has encouraged women and younger golfers to take up the game. Most gains in participation over the past few years are attributable to women and junior golfers (National Golf Foundation 2004). Also, there is more consideration of "nontraditional" golf, which is less time consuming and may be, as well, more family oriented. Family golf may comprise nine or fewer holes while an additional forward series of tees serves younger children. Real turf putting courses may raise miniature golf to a golf learning exercise.

Despite the expense of equipment and the course, golf is played in many cultures. Since it is played in small groups,

▼ *Cherokee Country Club, Atlanta, Georgia. Drawing by E. Addison Young.*

it is conducive to conversation, except during the golf swing. Therefore, it is a social form of recreation. Private golf clubs not only enhance the camaraderie but also provide a safe place for family activities. Golf is important for resorts and almost required by conference planners as an amenity for conference participants.

Even in times of economic downturn, golf in general rounds per occupied room is still strong at full-service resorts.

TYPES OF GOLF CLUBS

Golf clubs may be defined in the following categories:

- Daily-fee course and clubhouse
- Resort
- Private club

The Daily-Fee Clubhouse

A daily-fee course and clubhouse may be privately owned but available to the public, or it may be a municipal course, owned by the community and open to the public.

Daily-fee course clubhouses usually consist of the basics: a golf shop, restrooms and a changing area with lockers, and golf cart and bag storage. There is a food and beverage element, typically a 19th hole bar and grill with a kitchen, back-of-the-house support area, and a small administrative office.

Even within the basics, the emphasis may vary. A daily-fee course clubhouse may take advantage of the golf setting to offer catered events in a function room overlooking the golf course. Catering eliminates the need for a commercial preparation kitchen and its staff. In lieu of a commercial kitchen, a catering kitchen or offsite preparation tailored to

the specific event will suffice.

If the market warrants it, a local restaurateur may elect to take advantage of the golf course amenity with a restaurant; but the volume generated by golf play will not support a restaurant. In addition, they are different businesses, and only private clubs and resorts supply the volume of users to support the combination of restaurant and golf club.

A satellite golf clubhouse may be part of a private golf community or a resort and may serve as the base of operations for golf courses too remote to be served from the main clubhouse. Distance from the main clubhouse may be several miles if the course or courses had to be added because the original community master plan did not anticipate enough golf holes for the ultimate number of residents. The satellite clubhouse is very similar to a daily-fee clubhouse in its space allocation. In fact, the clubhouse may serve as a daily-fee facility until resident and member rounds reach capacity.

The Resort Golf Clubhouse

The resort clubhouse is made up of the same elements as a daily-fee course clubhouse but with a different emphasis on its components. The focus is the golf shop. Golf at a resort is an attraction, and well-known golf course architects who bring a cachet and a particular challenge to the game often design the course or courses. Having met the challenge of the course, the golfer is interested in logo-ware to commemorate the occasion. The golf shop that is part of a resort has a high turnover of customers who are in a "buying" mode. A resort golf shop typically exceeds $500 per sq ft in sales per year, comparable to an upscale boutique. All of the above war-

◀ *Bonita Bay East Golf Club, Bonita Springs, Florida, a satellite golf club-house, golf-side view. Diedrich Architects. Photo by Ed Chappell.*

▼ *Bonita Bay East Golf Club floor plan. Bonita Bay is a registered trademark of Bonita Bay Properties, Inc. Used by permission. Diedrich Architects.*

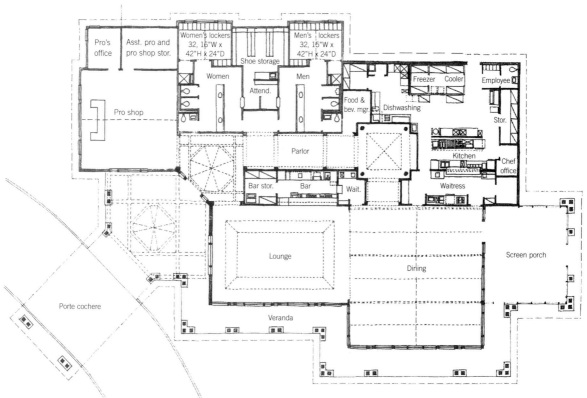

PROTOTYPICAL SPACE PROGRAMS, BY CLUBHOUSE TYPE						
PROGRAM ELEMENT	**SPACE REQUIRED (sq ft)***					
	DAILY FEE		**RESORT**		**PRIVATE**	
	Low	**High**	**Low**	**High**	**Low**	**High**
Golf shop	1000	1500	1500	3000	800	1500
Shop support	400	600	600	1600	600	1600
Locker rooms	800	1200	1200	1500	4000	12000
Dining/bar lounge	1000	3000	2100	4000	3000	10500
Kitchen	400	1200	1600	1600	1600	2500
Lobby	0	400	500	800	800	3000
Administration	400	500	600	800	900	1500
Fitness	0	0	separate facilities		1500	10000
Back of house	0	600	600	1200	1500	2500
Subtotal	4000	9000	8700	14500	14700	45100
Mech./elec./circ.	200	900	870	2180	2940	9020
Total conditioned	4200	9900	9570	16680	17640	54120
Cart storage	3000	5000	3000	5000	3000	5000
Bag storage	200	300	300	500	900	1800
Swim	0	0	separate facilities		1000	5000
Tennis	0	0	separate facilities		1000	2500
Total unconditioned	3200	5300	3300	5500	5900	14300
Total	7400	15200	12870	22180	23540	68420

*Assumes 18 holes of Golf
Copyright Diedrich LLC 2004

rants a proportionally large golf shop, emphasizing its role as a major retail outlet at the resort.

From a food and beverage viewpoint, a resort may use the golf clubhouse as another location for guest dining. Golfers, depending on the number of golf holes and capacity of the course, may provide a market for breakfast and lunch. A dinner business from golfers, however, depends on the seasonal aspects of the location. For instance, high season in a tropical resort is concurrent with the short days of winter in the Northern Hemisphere; therefore, golf play ends in late afternoon, before dinnertime. A bigger concern is the propensity of the foursome to unwind at the traditional 19th hole. This boisterous celebration may go into the early evening, and it may conflict with early dining by families and couples. As a result, dinner is not usually served at a strictly golf clubhouse. In a resort situation, however, the entire clubhouse is available as a special place for group events.

◀ *The Village Clubhouse at Kapalua, Maui, Hawaii, a resort clubhouse. Diedrich/NBA, architect. Photo by Kapalua Land.*

◣ *The Village Clubhouse at Kapalua, main level floor plan.*

▽ *The Village Clubhouse at Kapalua, lower level floor plan.*

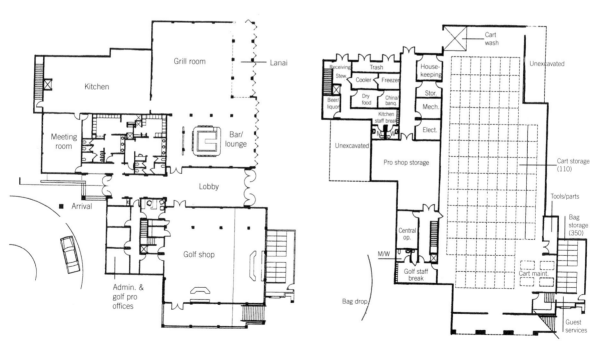

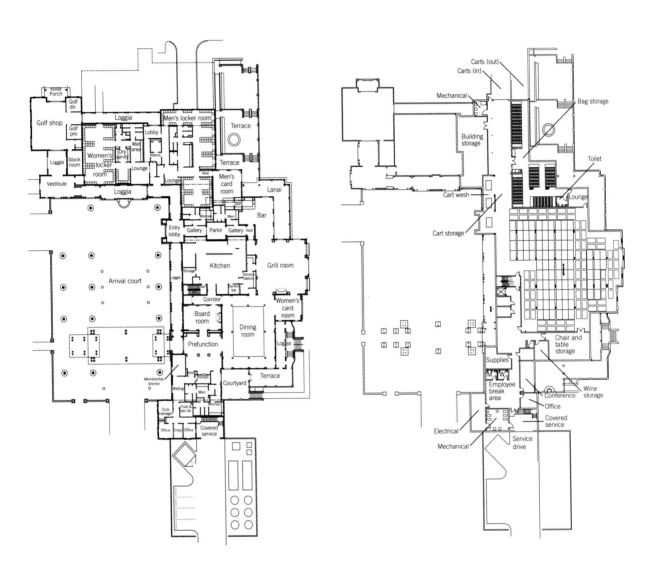

Mediterra Clubhouse, Naples, Florida, a private club. Main level clubhouse floor plan. Mediterra is a registered trademark of Bonita Bay Properties, Inc. Used by permission. Diedrich/NBA, architect.

Mediterra Clubhouse, lower level floor plan.

◀ *Mediterra Clubhouse, Naples, Florida. View of the men's vanity area. Diedrich/NBA, architect. Photo by Gabriel Benzur.*

The Private Golf Club

The private golf club generates its own set of priorities to meet the needs of its members. The most striking element is the emphasis on locker rooms. Embodying one of the social traditions of golf, the locker rooms go beyond storage of golf attire to creating the setting for fellowship. The men's locker room in a private club, in particular, usually includes a large lounge and card room. Beverage service is often available, and use of the locker room for cards or socializing is the norm.

The Golf and Country Club

A family-oriented facility that includes recreational amenities in addition to golf is the golf and country club. Traditionally offering dining, swimming, and tennis, country-club clubhouses increasingly include major fitness facilities. In ski areas, the trend is toward four seasons of activities, with a clubhouse serving cross-country skiers in the cold months and golfers in warmer months. Indoor activities often supported by a country-club clubhouse are addressed in this book and include:

- Aquatics (see Chapter 3)
- Handball, racquetball, squash, and indoor tennis (see Chapter 5)
- Fitness and wellness centers (see Chapter 9)
- Dining (see Chapter 12)

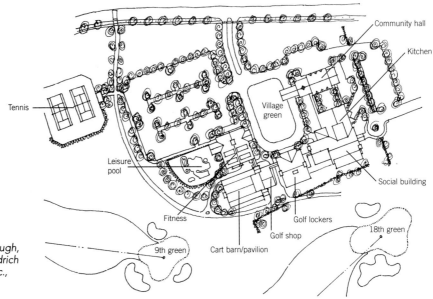

▶ *Marlborough Crossing Community Club, Marlborough, Connecticut, site plan, Diedrich LLC. Landmark Partners, Inc., developer.*

▼ *Marlborough Crossing Community Club floor plan. Diedrich LLC.*

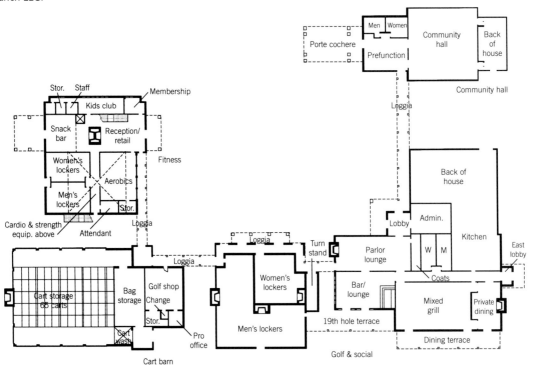

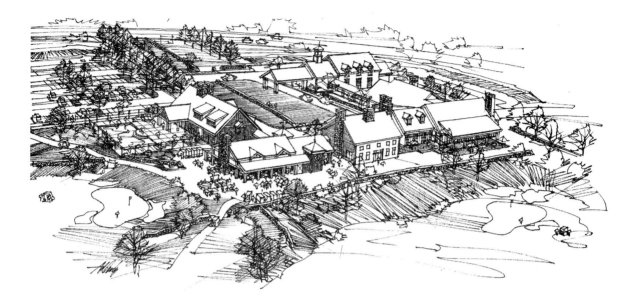

THE CLUBHOUSE SITE

Perhaps more than any other building type, the golf and country club clubhouse demands integration with its site and its recreational amenities. Given the golf course, optimizing the setting and vistas from the clubhouse is paramount. The many linked golf activities situated in the vicinity of the clubhouse include those shown in the table on page 12.

Bag Drop

The bag drop is the transfer point for the golf bag taken from an automobile and put on a golf cart. The golf cart with the bag (or bags) may then be staged for a round of golf, transferred to another cart, or stored with others in the bag storage area. Therefore, the best location for the bag drop is between an approach driveway and the cart staging area. The staging area would have direct access to bag storage.

The bag drop structure may be as simple as a railing with pegs to separate the golf bags as they are leaned against the rail. A roof element or awning may protect the bags from a rain shower. In the case of a high-volume, daily-fee course, however, the bag drop is more elaborate. Unlike a private club, the daily-fee golfers are strangers and bags may not be left at an unattended drop-off or pick-up site. Therefore, the bag drop is staffed and housed in an open, boothlike roofed structure that functions like a valet parking booth. In fact, in an upscale facility, the golfer may drop the bag and give the automobile to a valet parker at this same point.

If a resort only allows play by hotel guests, the golf bags are typically handled at the hotel check-in and then transferred with other bags directly to the golf club. Therefore, individual bag drop-off and pickup are not a significant issue.

▲ Marlborough Crossing Community Club, sketch. Diedrich LLC. Drawing by E. Addison Young.

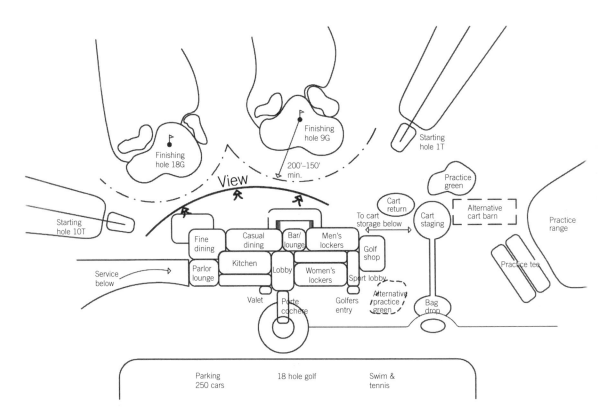

Finishing
hole 18G

Finishing
hole 9G

Starting
hole 1T

200'–150'
min.

View

Starting
hole 10T

Practice
green

Cart
return

Alternative
cart barn

Practice
range

To cart
storage below

Cart
staging

Fine
dining

Casual
dining

Bar/
lounge

Men's
lockers

Golf
shop

Practice tee

Kitchen

Lobby

Parlor
lounge

Women's
lockers

Sport lobby

Service
below

Valet

Porte
cochere

Golfers
entry

Alternative
practice
green

Bag
drop

Parking
250 cars

18 hole golf

Swim &
tennis

▲ *Typical clubhouse
site plan. Diedrich LLC.*

Golf Cart Staging

Golfers pick up their golf cart and bag at the cart staging area before going to the starting hole. Staging is ideally located next to the golf shop and cart storage. A large area of paving would enable a day's complement of golf carts to be staged at one time. In the golf course setting, however, a large paving apron negates the pastoral nature of the site. Therefore, some restraint is required in programming and planning the staging area. If the cart storage is convenient, an area of about 1,000 sq ft to stage and access 16 carts is adequate for 18 holes of golf. For tee times at eight-minute intervals, this is about one hour's worth of carts. An equal amount of cart return area is required.

Since golfers wear spikes, the staging area should be paved with a material other than asphalt, preferably an architectural paver.

A major challenge is the staging for a shotgun start (in which players may start at any hole on the course), for which 64 carts may need to be set out for a full course. The solution lies in the two-way golf cart paths normally in the vicinity of the clubhouse. Carts may be staged along the wide cart paths for a shotgun start.

Practice Green

The practice green, or putting green, is designed by the golf course architect. It is traditionally close to the clubhouse, so collaboration between the golf course architect and the clubhouse architect is critical.

The green is not only a very attractive landscape element but, when well located, a significant focus of activity. Placing the practice green near the clubhouse may serve both starting holes as well as providing access to the golf shop for golfers who wish to try out new putters.

The Practice Tee and Range

The practice range, as the largest single element of the golf course, may impact the clubhouse. It is best located within easy access of the clubhouse. A long distance to the practice tee, however, requires use of a cart, necessitating an increase in the complement of carts and additional cart storage.

Recent design of practice ranges, with target greens and features testing each golf stroke, has made the range a much more attractive vista from the clubhouse. Combined with the activity on the tee, the practice range may be the focus for a social area of the clubhouse.

Note that the range ball-picker, ball cleaning, and storage areas need to be housed near the practice tee and range. (See "Range House," page 33.)

The Starter and Starter House

The starter and starter house are vital on a resort or daily-fee course where there are periods of high volume of play by players who may not know the course. It may not be needed for a private club with 18 holes, where a club ranger may handle peak times. As the number of holes increases, however, the starter becomes more critical.

The starter house is a small, boothlike structure located near the starting holes of the course. The structure is about 8 sq ft with a counter to hold the book or computer used to record tee times. A sliding window and speaker system enables the starter to communicate with the golfers. A private club with multiple courses is also likely to have a starter house. Otherwise, start times are managed from the pro shop.

Closeness of the starting tees—one and ten—to the clubhouse speeds play; but the tees do not offer the engaging visual attraction of the greens at the finishing holes.

The Finishing Holes

One of the great traditions in golf is lounging in the 19th hole, in the clubhouse, with a cold drink, watching one's peers finish their game at the 18th green. Course architects have created great vistas in the beautifully sculpted finishing holes. A key role of the clubhouse architect is to provide a vantage point over the 18th green. But it is not that simple. Concurrent with development of the golf course, the clubhouse architect must review the proposed golf-grading plan in the area of the clubhouse and focus on its relationship to the finishing holes. The green may tilt away from the spectator, or it may be bunkered in such a way as to cut off the putting surface sight line. In fact, the prominent golf course designer Tom Fazio prefers a backdrop of natural landscape for the finishing hole. All of the above considerations point to the need for collaboration between the architects designing the golf course and the clubhouse.

Capturing the overlook of the finishing hole also affects the placement and design of such elements as terraces, balconies, and railings, all of which have to be tested not only for positioning but for uninterrupted sightlines from view-oriented interior spaces.

Arrival and Porte Cochere

If feasible, the approach to the clubhouse should be along the golf course rather than through the parking lot. At some clubhouses, such as Longue Vue, which was built in the 1920s near Pittsburgh, Pennsylvania, or the more recent Hammock Dunes Club in Palm Coast, Florida, arrival is literally through the golf course.

The casual use of clubhouses, coupled with banquet or event business, warrants two entrances. The casual golfer and the formal wedding party are more comfortable in their own setting—the casual golfer prefers direct access to the golf shop and locker room while the wedding party prefers the shelter of a porte cochere. In fact, the porte cochere is an icon of a club and allows covered drop-

▲ *Wynstone Clubhouse, North Barrington, Illinois. Golfside view, showing view-oriented dining and social area. Diedrich Architects. Photo by Hedrich Blessing.*

▶ *Hammock Dunes Club, Palm Coast, Florida. Site plan shows drive along the golf course. Edward D. Stone, Jr. & Associates, planners/landscape architects; Diedrich Architects. Rendering by EDSA.*

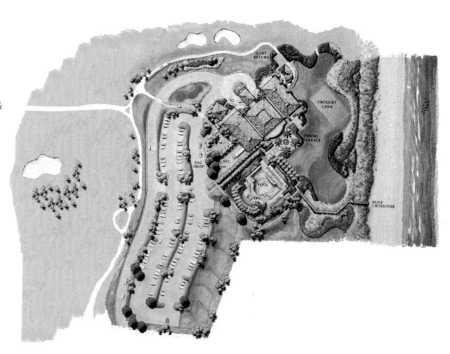

off and pickup and periodic valet service for large functions or events.

Service and Receiving Area

It is often the case that a golf clubhouse has no back door, as the golf course may wrap around 180–270° of the perimeter of the clubhouse site. With the approach-side taking the remainder of the site, finding a place for (and screening) the service area is a challenge. Typically, there is the extensive golf-related activity of bag drop, cart staging, and return at one end of the clubhouse. The planning approach, then, is to use the opposite end of the clubhouse for receiving—to avoid conflict between golf and the service area and vehicles.

The service area usually consists of two 12 ft wide truck bays, one for delivery and one for the trash compactor. Clubhouse operators differ as to whether dock height or at-grade delivery is most functional. The at-grade proponents indicate that most deliveries are unloaded from the truck's side, or the trucks have lift gates. The dock-height advocates argue that the dock is needed for delivery of building equipment during construction.

THE GOLF SHOP

The golf shop is the control center for the golf operation and its retail outlet. Control of the golf operation is generally concentrated at the golf shop desk. Golfers check in at this point, and it serves as a cash-wrap counter. Ideally, it overlooks the cart staging area. Phoned-in reservations for tee times are taken here and entered in the computerized schedule. Multiple-course resorts may have a separate room to handle the high volume of reservations and to organize outings.

▲ Porte cochere at Old Overton Clubhouse, Birmingham, Alabama. Diedrich Architects. Photo by Gabriel Benzur.

Following retail principles, the cash-wrap counter is located to guide the customer through the merchandise from entrance to check-in. Store planning and fixture design is normally done by specialists who combine planning, design, and millwork production of the fixtures.

The number of windows in the golf shop is often an issue between the architect and the golf professional. The architect looks at the golf shop as the center of the golf operation to be characterized as an open, inviting shop. Also, it usually adjoins the locker rooms, which present a more closed-in mass. Those responsible for sales from the golf shop give higher priority to wall space to display merchandise, whereas the designer wants to open the space. Ideally, a golf shop achieves a balance of these two valid goals.

Lighting, as in all retail, is important. If the golf shop has a high ceiling, the space relieves a crowded feeling of fixtures and merchandise; but the need for focused and flexible lighting must be met. Track fixtures provide flexibility, and directed

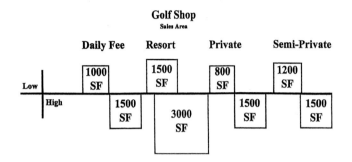

▲ Prototypical golf and country club-house. Relative program area. Diedrich LLC.

fixtures highlight the merchandise. To feature the goods, intensity of lighting must exceed the ambient natural lighting through the windows. The ideal ratio for highlighting goods is 5:1, accent lighting level to ambient lighting. In order to even approach this ratio, the natural light must be controlled through tinting, shading, or indirection.

An added feature, particularly in a private club shop, is a soft seating group, perhaps focused on a fireplace. The seating also serves as a place to try on shoes.

In a resort or daily-fee course clubhouse, the shop is adjacent to the main lobby. Featuring the shop is part of the business of golf. In a private club, the shop is usually located off a secondary "sport" lobby, also serving the locker rooms. The shop becomes more discreet, and its commercial nature less obvious.

▶ Prototypical golf shop floor plan. Diedrich LLC.

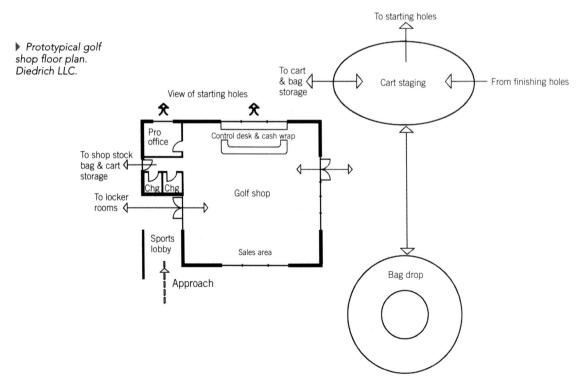

◀ *Bear's Club Clubhouse Golf Shop, Jupiter, Florida. Peacock & Lewis, architects; Image Design, Inc., interior design; Procraft, pro shop Designer. Photo by Gabriel Benzur.*

GOLF CART AND BAG STORAGE

In the United States and at many golf resorts around the world, golf carts are the chief way for the golfer to circle the course. Storing the carts in a convenient location for the operator is a basic element of a golf facility. Seventy-five carts is the normal complement of carts for 18 holes of golf; but approximately five beverage and utility carts also need to be stored. Since a full golf course normally would hold 64 carts, the additional carts would be cleaned and in process for the next players. This backup, however, means that an additional 18 holes may be served by less than even multiple of 75, that is, 140 carts for 36 holes. Other factors may affect the number of carts required. If the practice range is so remote that the golfer needs a cart to get there, additional carts will be needed. If the golf club is part of a recreational community or resort and golfers are allowed or encouraged to have their own private carts, the quantity to be stored may be less. In this case, however, the club may be in the business of maintaining members' carts so additional cart maintenance area may be required after all.

For operational efficiency, the carts should be stored so they may be easily staged near the golf shop and the course starting holes. The sequence is for the golfer to check in at the golf shop, whereupon the golf clubs are either taken out of bag storage or picked up at the bag drop and placed on a cart. The cart is then located in the staging area where golfers collect it in time to meet the tee time.

Consequently, the carts should be easily accessible for staging, stored below the golf wing of the clubhouse and connected with a short ramp to the staging area. Equally convenient is cart storage in a cart barn at grade across the staging area from the golf shop. Either approach may work, but there are pros and cons to each.

Cart Storage, Main Club Lower Level

Cart storage on the lower level saves land. This may be the overriding criterion for the clubhouse site. Golf carts, however, whether electric or gas powered, are hazardous. Gas is highly flammable and may explode. The electric battery charging process generates highly explosive hydrogen gas. This gas rises and will collect in high pockets. Therefore, the ceiling design should neither be coffered nor have cavities. Instead, a flat concrete slab is the best solution. In any case, the building code will require a several-hour fire separation between the cart storage and any adjoining spaces (next-to or above). The solution usually is a cast-in-place concrete enclosure surrounding the

cart storage. In addition, codes require the storage space to be mechanically ventilated. The size of the cart storage (approximately 5,000 sq ft) requires a personnel exit opposite the cart ramp entrance. Although a cart may make up to a 20 degree slope, cart handlers must have a separate stair, or there should be a maximum slope of 10 percent for the entrance-exit ramp.

Cart Storage, Cart Barn

Given the safety concerns, designing a cart barn as a separate building may be simpler if the land is available. The building may be more economical as frame construction and more easily ventilated and evacuated at grade. The largest issue with a cart barn hinges on its status as a light industrial building housing the cleaning and storage of vehicles. In a golf clubhouse complex, especially a private club, a cart barn needs to be designed as an integral part of the clubhouse compound. As to construction

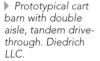
▶ Prototypical cart barn with double aisle, tandem drive-through. Diedrich LLC.

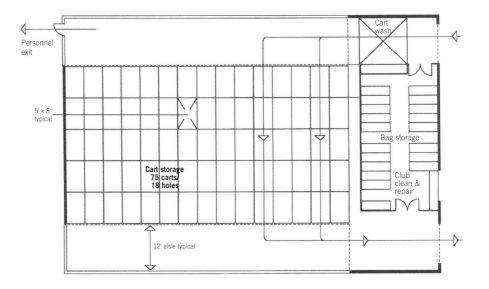

cost, architectural treatment of a cart barn may be equal or less than basement cart storage. Topography may permit or hinder either approach. In any case, the cart entrance and cart wash area must be screened. An advantage of the cart barn is that in milder climates the drive aisles may be uncovered, albeit screened. This reduces the building area from approximately 5,000 sq ft to 3,000 sq ft.

Processing Golf Carts

Processing of the carts follows this sequence:

- A cart with golf bags is picked up in the staging area (usually two golfers per cart, two carts per foursome).
- Golfers and cart circumvent the golf course.
- Cart dropped off by the golfer in a return area, usually near the staging area.
- Cart taken by staff member to wash area.

- Golf bags removed and stored in bag storage, or placed at the bag drop to be picked up.
- Cart cleaned, washed, and stored in sequence.
- Electric cart hooked up to the battery charger.
- When fully charged, the cart is driven from storage in sequence (following a sequence that ensures a fully-charged cart is pulled for staging).
- Golf bags are loaded and the cart is staged.

A drive-through pattern with two single-loaded drive aisles supports sequencing. An aisle is typically 12 ft wide and the cart-parking module is assumed to be 5 ft x 8 ft.

The area of cart storage may be saved by using only one aisle with double-loaded tandem parking. Operational efficiency will suffer, however, and the necessity of a backing-up maneuver as opposed to drive-through may lead to some cart damage.

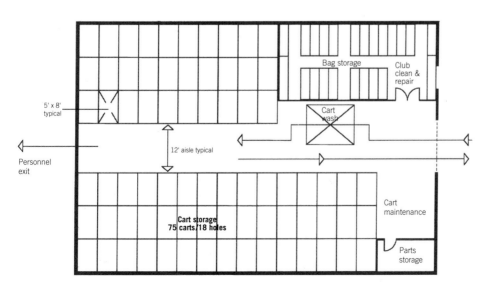

◀ Prototypical cart barn with single aisle, double-loaded tandem. Diedrich LLC.

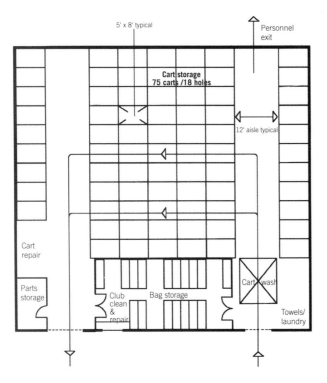

5' x 8' typical

Personnel exit

Cart storage
75 carts /18 holes

12' aisle typical

Cart repair

Parts storage

Club clean & repair

Bag storage

Cart wash

Towels/ laundry

▲ *Prototypical cart barn with double aisle, double-loaded drive through. Diedrich LLC.*

Another option double-loads two lanes with tandem drive-through. Double-loading the aisles results in a smaller area for the same complement of carts.

Golf Bag Storage

Golf bag storage works well when located next to the cart storage. By circulating carts around the bag storage, staff may load bags on carts at one end and receive bags from the cart at the cart-wash area at the other. Bags may be stored in fixed racks or rolling rack systems, which are more efficient in storing bags in a given area. If a large number of bags are to be stored, the rolling rack systems are more cost-effective.

The bag storage room in a private club also houses the club cleaning and repair area. This area consists of a counter, sink, and cabinets. If in a cart barn, a window

helps the cart staff oversee the cart staging area. A restroom meets the need for the cart and bag handling staff in this area.

Other elements in the cart storage area include equipment for the pressure washer, a washer and dryer for cart towels, and an ice machine for ice water, as well as the cart maintenance area. Although most cart fleets are now leased and heavy maintenance is usually done by the lessor, an area is set aside for day-to-day maintenance. It includes one or two cart bays, plus room to work. There is a workbench and a secure storage area for tools and parts.

If a golf facility has caddies, the caddy lounge is best located near the cart and bag storage. This area consists of a lounge with television; it also needs restrooms with shower, changing area, lockers, and hanging space for uniforms. It is important to provide acoustic separation for the caddy lounge from the member or guest area in a resort.

The Cart Barn as an Outing Pavilion

Recognizing that cart storage is a 3,000–5000 sq ft space suggests other possible uses. In Tournament Players Clubs (TPC), developed by the PGA Tour, extra height is built into the lower level cart storage area, and the space may be used as a media center for televised tournaments. An additional use of a cart barn may be as an outing or event pavilion. Likely located adjacent to the golf course, with its vistas, the cart barn with some planning may become a column-free, pavilionlike space. Cart chargers may be placed in the truss space so that the electrical connectors are tucked out of sight. The interior may be painted and

▶ *Marlborough Crossing Cart Barn–Pavilion, Marlborough, Connecticut. Example of a cart barn that can be used as a party barn and outing or event pavilion. See site plan on page 16. Diedrich LLC. Drawing by E. Addison Young.*

▶ *Bear's Club men's locker room, Jupiter, Florida, showing full-height lockers with bench seat. Image Design, Inc., interior design. Photo by Gabriel Benzur.*

work areas like the cart washing area screened. The carts may be temporarily stored on the site. The cart-barn wall, or screening wall, is planned to open out to the golf course. The cart barn may then be used as an event pavilion or party barn.

GOLF CLUBHOUSE LOCKER ROOMS

The Men's Locker Room

The programming of the locker room begins with the size and number of lockers. The most exclusive golf clubs with members who are aficionados of the game may have full-height lockers, which are often coupled with bench seats at the

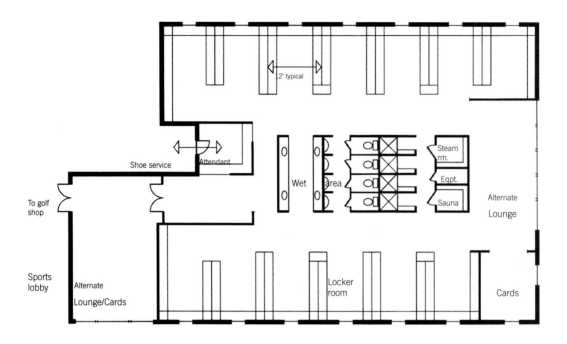

2' typical
Shoe service
Attendant
To golf shop
Wet area
Steam rm.
Eqpt.
Sauna
Alternate Lounge
Sports lobby
Alternate Lounge/Cards
Locker room
Cards

▲ *Prototypical locker room for a golf clubhouse. Diedrich LLC.*

base. This style of locker and bench identified with traditional clubs such as the original St. Andrews in Scotland, Augusta National, Augusta, Georgia, and Seminole, North Palm Beach, Florida.

Most newer clubhouses, even the more exclusive, use stacked or tiered lockers. For the men, a tiered locker 42" high provides hanging space for a jacket. An equivalent number of full-height lockers will take twice as much area, and the locker itself will cost more than stacked lockers. A potential model for the industry in upscale private clubs is the locker specified by the PGA Tour for its TPC clubhouses. It is 42" high, 18–22" wide, and 24" deep. With normal off-the-shelf lockers, which are only 22" deep, the extra depth works well for additional shoe space and hangers. Locker bays are 12' on center, resulting in 8' between lockers. Grooming stations located at the end of the locker peninsulas are conve-

nient. Windows may be located at the end of the locker bays, with wide-blade shutters providing screening.

Another advantage of tiered lockers comes into play with larger clubs that have more than 18 golf holes. With the number of members derived from the number of golf holes, even an exclusive club could have 700 members for 36 holes of golf. Seven hundred full-height lockers, plus guest lockers, however well planned, may become a maze.

For larger numbers of lockers, building planning should consider a two-story locker room. In the overall building planning some advantage to each level should be designed to avoid a caste system in locker location. For instance, at Cherokee Country Club in Atlanta, Georgia, the men's locker room has 980 lockers for 36 holes of golf. The lower level logically relates to the golf shop and golf course itself. The upper level relates to the men's card room and lounge with food service from the main kitchen. These social spaces also overlook the golf course. The most direct entrance to the locker room from the parking area is to the upper level. This entrance is defined enough that the men's social area may be scheduled for mixed gender use in the evening. In the two-story scheme, wet areas proportionate to the number of lockers are provided at each level.

A private club men's locker room will differ for a stand-alone golf club as opposed to a community club whose members live nearby. At the stand-alone club, the members may come from a distance or directly from work. They will require a change of clothes for golf and, consequently, more use of the lockers and the showers. Clubs may

▲ *Cherokee Country Club, men's locker room, showing stair and atrium lounge for two-story locker room. Design Continuum, Inc., interior design; Diedrich Architects. Photo by Ray Boule, Full Circle Productions*

◄ *Cherokee Country Club, Atlanta, Georgia, lower level floor plan. Diedrich Architects.*

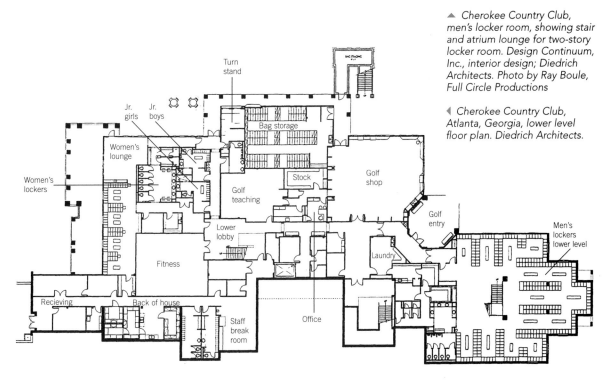

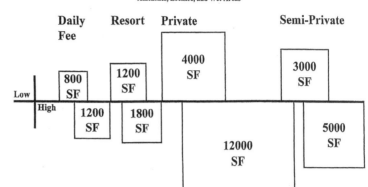

Locker Rooms
Amenities, Lockers, and Wet Areas

	Daily Fee	Resort	Private		Semi-Private
Low			4000 SF		3000 SF
	800 SF	1200 SF			
High	1200 SF	1800 SF			5000 SF
			12000 SF		

▶ Prototypical golf and country clubhouse relative program area for locker rooms. Diedrich LLC.

▼ Country Club of the North, Beavercreek, Ohio, women's locker room. Diedrich Architects; Image Design, Inc., interior design. Photo by Gabriel Benzur.

run short of showers after a shotgun outing, but it is impractical to plan for these events.

To determine the number of fixtures needed for the men's locker room, a cue may be taken from the foursomes and even spacing of tee times common to golf. For eighteen holes of golf, this dictates that four urinals and four lavatories are adequate even if one considers pre- and après-play. A lower frequency of use suggests three water closets. Larger clubs with larger numbers of players require more fixtures. A diversity factor again comes into play, so that the number of fixtures is something less than a proportionate multiple of that cited for eighteen holes. Because of the plumbing fixtures needed in each locker room and, most often, separate restrooms for the dining areas, the plumbing code almost never requires an additional number of fixtures.

The Women's Locker Rooms

Women's locker rooms today warrant qualitative parity with the men's locker room. The number or size may differ, though. Differences arise from the number of users. Tiered lockers predominate today in women's locker rooms also; but stacked, 42" lockers raise the upper locker clothes hook or hanging rod to 87", beyond the reach of most women. Therefore, 36" high lockers are used. Beyond that, the width and depth should match the men's lockers.

The foursome criterion also applies to the ladies' water closets and lavatories; but women's attitudes toward taking a shower at a club demands a different approach. Women value privacy, and therefore women's showers are rarely used at clubs. All women's locker rooms, however, require at least one shower. An effective approach in an upscale club is to create a shower and dressing room that includes a vanity in which a private enclosure is created that also meets Americans with Disabilities Act (ADA) requirements for the shower. This enclosure should allow a woman to shower and put on make-up in private. This may tie up the shower for a period, however. In any case, the women's shower should have a comfortable and private drying area.

The Locker Room Lounge

Rather than enter a locker room through a vestibule, down a hall, and past an attendant, a more gracious approach is through a lounge area. The locker room entrance sets the tone for the quality of the locker room. This is especially true for the women's facility in an upscale private club. The lounge need not be large, but it will be used for small meetings—i.e., house the women's golf committee or serve as a location for the handicap computer or the provision of coffee and juice in the morning. Approximately 300 sq ft is adequate.

Although this may also work as a ladies' small card room, the ladies' card playing should be in a social area of the club—in a private dining room or a multiuse room. Unlike the men, women do not like their card room to be part of the locker room. The overall club plan may allow the card room to be part of the lounge, but coming and going may disturb the card players.

Entry to the men's locker room through a lounge may be nice, but it is less important than in the women's locker room. Men prefer their card room to be part of the locker room and see their lounge as their secure domain. Consequently, privacy is a big issue. In any case, the choice for the lounge loca-

▲ Cassique Clubhouse, Kiawah Island, South Carolina, women's locker room. Shope Reno Wharton Associates, Architect. Jaquelynne P. Lanham Designs, Inc., interior design. Photo by Peter Vitale.

▲ *Wynstone Golf and Country Clubhouse, North Barrington, Illinois, men's grill. Diedrich Architects; Image Design, Inc., interior design. Photo by Gabriel Benzur.*

▶ *Prototypical men's and women's locker room attendant area. Diedrich LLC.*

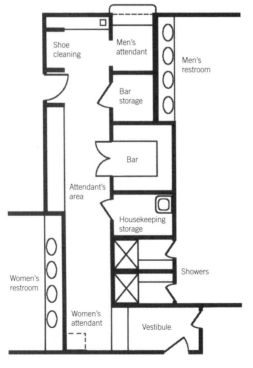

tion may be to overlook the golf course as opposed to the locker room entrance. The men would opt for seclusion with a view and access to the golf course.

The men's card room is most likely linked with their lounge; but to allow for concentration by the dedicated player, some separation from the lounge is in order.

The Locker Room Attendant

A club large and busy enough warrants separate attendants in each locker room. The men's attendant is a tradition in a private golf club; a women's area attendant may be the norm in a particular club with a strong women's golf program (e.g., a retirement community) or an attendant may be warranted where the women's locker room also serves a significant exercise and fitness area. Use of the fitness facility will generate a proportionate use of the locker room by women.

If a women's attendant is not justified, one approach is to locate the men's attendant area near the women's locker room. This will allow a blind drop to be created for the women to leave their shoes for cleaning or for the attendant to provide beverage service, if available. If there is both a women's and a men's attendant, it is best to connect the attendants' area to a towel and supply storage area and possibly to a service bar.

An attendant area includes a service counter for receipt of shoes, a screened shoe cleaning area, cubicles for shoe storage, shelving for towel storage, and a heavy-duty residential washer and dryer for laundering towels. Additional storage space is required for the vanity toiletries and housekeeping supplies.

GOLF OUTBUILDINGS

In addition to a main clubhouse, support of golf may require several strategically located outbuildings.

Course Shelters

A golf site usually includes an on-course shelter for each 9 holes, that is, between holes 4 and 5 and between 13 and 14. The shelters provide restrooms, drinking water, and protection from lightning and other weather concerns. In addition to the two restrooms, the shelter includes an open area that is roofed and sized to cover four golf carts, essentially providing a protected area for golfers in an electrical storm.

Like the other golf outbuildings, the shelters are an opportunity to extend the architecture of the main clubhouse well beyond its immediate site.

Turnstand or Halfway House

If a golf course routing plan has the ninth and eighteenth greens near the clubhouse, the course is described as "returning nines." In that case, the snack and beverage turnstand would usually be housed in the main clubhouse, for instance, through the 19th hole bar. Prompt service is important to prevent delaying the flow of golfers on the course. Often orders are phoned in from the 9th tee so that the order is ready after the foursome finishes the hole. Restrooms should be easily available at the turnstand.

If the finishing hole of a golf "nine" is remote from the clubhouse, a turnstand or halfway house is often provided. (Sometimes the snack and beverage function is handled from a beverage cart.) The turnstand is essentially a snack

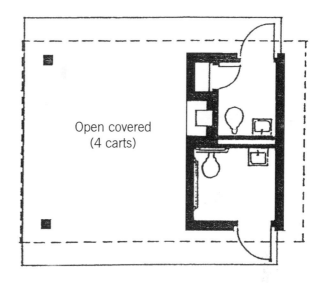

Open covered (4 carts)

▲ *Prototypical golf shelter plan. Diedrich LLC.*

bar with its array of equipment (see Chapter 12). Most often there is only window snack and beverage service and a patio, with no inside seating. Where golfers may be playing in hot or cold weather, limited inside seating in a halfway house or turnstand may be provided. Again, in the interest of the flow of the game, it is unlikely that more than two foursomes would be at the halfway house at any one time. The turnstand/halfway house will also include restrooms.

Range House

The range house stores equipment for the golf course driving range. Housed there is the range ball-picker, which is a vehicle that scours the range for golf balls. The range balls are then cleaned by machine and stored prior to distribution on the range tee. At English Turn Country Club, New Orleans, Louisiana, the range house is combined with the halfway house.

▶ *English Turn, New Orleans, Louisiana, view of turnstand exterior. Diedrich Architects. Photo by Jonathan Hillyer.*

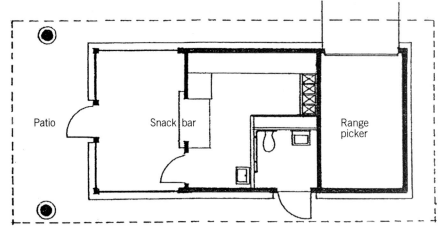

◀ *English Turn, New Orleans, Louisiana. Turnstand/range house floor plan.*

Patio

Snack bar

Range picker

THE GOLF ACADEMY

Teaching how to play golf is becoming more institutionalized and based in new technologies and golf swing physiology. The golf academy building supports teaching individuals and small groups of golfers. The academy building is usually remote, at the opposite end of the range from the normal practice tee, so that the teaching professionals may give all their attention to the academy students.

The Studio Tee

The heart of the golf academy is the studio tee where multiple cameras may record the golfer's swing. The video image is analyzed by computer software comparing the subject's swing to a classic swing or to subject's earlier attempts. The studio tee space needs to be a minimum of 25 sq ft and 13 ft high so the camera location and angle may record the moving image without distortion. The space may be an interior space with the golfer hitting into a net, or it may have one wall opening to the driving range. The area must work for either a right- or left-handed golfer. An adjoining space houses the computer and monitor and an area for the student and teaching professional to review the video.

There may be multiple studio tees, but there also will be more traditional practice tees, which need a minimum of 9 ft on center. Again the tees may be interior spaces or open to the range. A covered tee, however, is important so that lessons may be scheduled regardless of the weather.

Reception and Retail

The arrival area in an academy is like a small golf shop. Unlike the larger golf shops, there is little emphasis on soft goods and logo-ware and more emphasis on golf clubs in the academy arrival area. An important aspect of teaching golf is the opportunity for creating and selling a set of customized golf clubs; therefore, an adjoining room with equipment and a work area is appropriate.

Classroom

This is a small room designed for orientation and briefing the class group. The maximum class size is usually only seven people. A large television monitor is important for viewing videos and golf telecasts. This space may be a separate room or part of the lobby and reception area, serving as a television lounge when it is not a class time.

Fitness

The academy also focuses on training the muscle groups used in golf. Stretching and strength-training equipment and

techniques are introduced as a regimen to enhance the golfer's physical ability.

Offices, Kitchenette, Storage, and Restrooms

A staff office for teaching professionals and for the storage of teaching materials and equipment is required. A kitchenette for beverages and preparation of a light buffet for breakfast and snacks is also needed, as well as adequate storage for kitchen materials. In addition, there should be restrooms with a changing area and lockers for students and teaching professionals.

The Golf Academy Building at Berkeley Hall

Berkeley Hall, a community near Hilton Head, South Carolina, features a golf academy that has a multiuse lounge space that greatly expands building use.

Berkeley Hall provides a handsome room for class meetings and breaks and is used as an additional food and beverage venue for the golf and country club. Available for private parties in the evening after the golf day, the area with its patio is in the heart of the golf environment. This kind of space requires a small catering kitchen and storage for tables and chairs to allow changing of furnishings for different functions.

This building was built initially as the interim golf clubhouse until the main clubhouse was completed two years later.

GOLF MAINTENANCE COMPLEX

The golf maintenance complex is a compound formed by the buildings that house and support the staff, materials, and equipment needed to maintain the golf course. In a resort or recreational

▶ *Berkeley Hall Golf Learning Center, Hilton Head, South Carolina. View of hitting stations. Cowart Coleman Group, architect. Photo by Berkeley Hall.*

Hitting
stations

1.

2.

Club
customizing

3.

Studio
tee

Swing
analysis

Terrace

Office

Lounge/
classroom

▲ *Berkeley Hall, Hilton Head, South Carolina. Golf Learning Center floor plan. Cowart Coleman Group, architect.*

community, this staff would also handle all of the common grounds maintenance.

Because the buildings that make up the maintenance complex are typically preengineered metal buildings, the facility is usually located out of sight of the public. Heavy truck access is required for delivery of materials, however, and because the complex needs to be near the golf course, the complex may be in view and will need to be architecturally treated.

In any case, a good planning approach is to use the structures of the complex to surround an equipment yard. A minimum dimension of about 100 ft allows the turn-around of cumbersome equipment such as a tractor equipped with a mower.

Elements of the maintenance compound follow:

• *Office and shop:* Administrative offices, staff break room, lockers, and

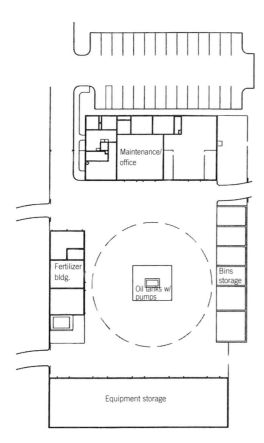

◀ Golf maintenance complex floor plan at Tournament Players Club Boston, Norwood, Massachusetts. Diedrich/Niles Bolton Associates architects.

restrooms are in this building. The shop for maintenance and repair of equipment is in the same structure. For security reasons, small handheld equipment is stored adjacent to the shop.

- *Equipment storage:* Typically built as an unconditioned basic structure, this building is used to shelter the tractors, mowers, and other driven, motorized equipment. In milder climates, the wall on the lee side, the sheltered side, of the building may be open to the yard. Although fac-

ing all buildings on the yard works well for appearance and security, a drive-through equipment storage structure more efficiently uses the building area.

- *Fertilizer and pesticide storage:* Because of the hazardous nature of materials stored in this building, it is usually a separate structure.

- *Material bins:* these are open bins for storage of materials like topsoil, sand, mulch, top dressing, and other materials needed for golf course and grounds maintenance. The bins are sometimes covered; however, because handling of the material is by front-end loader, the roof structure must be of a height to allow the equipment proper clearance.

- *Fuel island:* Centrally located for easy access by motorized equipment, the fuel pump island usually sits atop the underground fuel storage tanks.

- *Wash rack and dumpster:* Needed for cleaning of vehicles and equipment.
- *Parking:* For staff and visitors, preferably outside the compound.

The size of the structures depends on the acreage to be maintained and may be programmed with the operating staff by projecting an inventory of the equipment required.

Mirasol community recreational amenities, Palm Beach Gardens, Florida. Recreational amenities include: golf courses, golf academy, cart barn, main clubhouse of 55,000 sq ft, and aquatics, fitness, and tennis center. Diedrich/Niles Bolton Associates, architect; Jeff Ornstein, architect. Photo by C. J. Walker.

◀ *Mediterra Clubhouse, Naples, Florida. This private member golf and country club serves an active adult community, and its 36 holes of golf were designed by Tom Fazio. The Mediterranean-style clubhouse echoes the community's name and features a loggia-wrapped arrival court. The Bonita Bay Group, developer. Diedrich/NBA, architects. Photo by Ed Chappell. Mediterra is a registered trademark of Bomita Bay Properties, Inc. Used by permission.*

▼ *Mediterra Clubhouse, Naples, Florida. The golfside view of the Mediterra clubhouse reveals the concept of a large estate house added to over time. The variation in mass, height, and color breaks down the scale of the 42,000 sq ft structure in a residential community. The Bonita Bay Group, developer. Diedrich/NBA, architects. Photo by Ed Chappell.*

▶ Livonia Community Recreation Center, Livonia, Michigan, exterior view with splash pool. This municipal center includes indoor competition and leisure pools, gymnasiums, fitness center with an elevated indoor track, gymnastic area, climbing wall, kids quarters, and senior area organized around the indoor activity street. Neumann/Smith Architects & Associates and Barker Rinker Seacat, architects; Water Technology, pool designer. Photo by Justin Maconochie.

▼ Ocean Dome, Phoenix Seagaia Resort, Miyazaki, Japan. The retractable vaulted roof spans 328 ft and covers a footprint of 390,000 sq ft, the world's largest indoor water-park. The white sand beach is 459 ft long and waves over 8 ft can be generated for surfing. Mitsubishi Dome Structures, dome designer. Courtesy Seagaia Resort.

▲ *The Beach Club, Kiawah Island, South Carolina. Shingle-style architecture frames this classic beach club with casual dining and freshwater pools and deck, connected by a dune crossover to the beach on a barrier island. Robert A. M. Stern, architect. Photo by Lisa R. Adams.*

▲ Amelia Island Racquet Club and Spa, Amelia Island, Florida. Part of a spa and fitness center, this enclosed pool is housed in a glass and metal structure that engages the surrounding forest of live oak trees. In good weather, sections of the roof and walls open to the outside. NCG Architects, Inc. Photo by Paul Beswick.

◄ Bohicket Marina Village, Johns Island, South Carolina. Located between two resorts on barrier islands near Charleston, South Carolina, this marina village combines restaurants, retail, ship's store, yacht broker, dry-stack boat storage, and 90 residential units in a marina setting. The commercial structures define a plaza as a gathering place for entertainment, fishing tournaments, and watching the sun set. Diedrich Architects.

▲ Minneapolis Rowing Club Boathouse, Minneapolis, Minnesota. Exterior of boathouse, looking into rowing shell storage level. VJAA Architects.

◀ Minneapolis Rowing Club Boathouse, Minneapolis, Minnesota. Boat storage opening to mezzanine and trussed warped roof above. VJAA Architects.

▲ Arrowhead Alpine Club, Beaver Creek, Colorado. Strategically located at the base of the ski mountain, this club serves as a gateway to the ski slopes. The facility houses locker rooms, a bar and lounge, and fitness and spa amenities convenient for member skiers. Zehren and Associates, Inc., architects.

◀ Sunspot Restaurant, Winter Park Resort, Colorado. A contemporary interpretation of the traditional ski lodge vernacular defines this ski-in mountaintop restaurant. Zehren and Associates, Inc., Architects. Courtesy Winter Park Resort

◤ Vail X-Stream Action Park, Vail, Colorado. An indoor extreme sports street would be created in this unbuilt concept to expand recreational activities available in the Vail ski resort. A skateboard street, indoor whitewater kayaking, and rock climbing would entertain and remind winter visitors of the attractions of the area as a year-round resort. Zehren and Associates, architects, EDAW Planners. Illustration courtesy of HGA, Stan Doctor.

▶ Four Seasons Hotel Chicago Spa, Chicago. A chaise in a niche of upholstered walls, tea and juice, define a relaxation lounge for before or après treatment at this upscale hotel day spa. The Gettys Group, interior design. Photo by David Clifton.

◀ Rancho La Puerta, Tecate, Mexico. The sculptural doors accentuate the main entrance to the arrival lobby at this destination spa. Artist James Hubbell, whose architectural sculpture is spread throughout the spa campus, created the carved wood, wrought iron, and stained glass doors. James Hubbell, door designer. Photo by John Durant.

▲ Clay Fitness Center, New York, New York. The upscalse minimalist setting for the relaxation lounge and juice bar are the center of camaraderie and are adjacent to the weight room in this fitness center in Manhattan. Studios Architecture, architect and designers. Photo by Doug Fogelson.

◀ The Ritz Carlton Golf Club and Spa, Jupiter, Florida. The wet lounge is a focus of this upscale day spa that serves a second-home community. Peacock & Lewis, architects; Image Design, Inc., interior designer. Photo by Gabriel Benzur.

◀ Ritz Carlton Hotel Chicago Spa, Chicago, Illinois. Textured and clear glass set the theme and visually connect the lounge and indoor pool in this urban hotel day spa. The Gettys Group, interior designers. Photo by Hedrich Blessing.

▼ Sun City Hilton Head Learning Center, Beaufort, South Carolina. The life-long learning center as part of this active adult community recalls the little red school house as the place for learning in the community. The complex houses arts and crafts studios and a computer laboratory. Diedrich Architects, Inc., architects. Courtesy Sun City Hilton Head.

◀ Anderson Ranch Arts Center, Dow's Barn, Snowmass Village, Colorado. The historic barn and contemporary addition house the art gallery and administrative offices for Anderson Ranch, a center for continuing education in the fine arts. Harry Teague, Architects.

▼ Las Piedras Kuchumaa Ecological Center, Tecate, Mexico. This nature center is integrated into the granite boulders of Kuchumaa mountain and the Mexican chapparal. Drew Hubbell, architect; Enrique Cevallos and James Hubbell, designers.

Las Piedras Kuchumaa Ecological Center, Tecate, Mexico. The sculptural interior of the Las Piedras Center is striking in its mystery as its goal is to fascinate visiting school children and help them see it as a special place to learn about their native environment. Benches in the form of a rattlesnake provide seating. Drew Hubbell, architect; Enrique Cevallos and James Hubbell, designers.

▲ Country Club of the North, Beavercreek, Ohio. Bar lounge with lobby overlooking 18th green. Diedrich Architects, Inc., architects; Image Design, interior designer. Photo by Gabriel Benzur.

▶ Mirasol Country Club, Palm Beach Gardens, Florida. Golfside view of the clubhouse, showing dining, social areas, and terraces with vistas of the golf course. Golf Academy building on the left. Diedrich/Niles Bolton Associates, architects; Jeff Ornstein, architect. Photo by C. J. Walker.

▲ Virginia Hand Callaway Discovery Center at Callaway Gardens, Pine Mountain, Georgia. View across the lake used to heat and cool the center, an example of sustainable design. Hart Howerton, architect. Photo by F. Charles Photography.

▼ Wild Goose Restaurant, North Lake Tahoe, California. The main dining room with an open fire integrated into the community table. The restaurant is an example of green building design. Cass Calder Smith, architect. Photo by Eric Laignel.

CHAPTER 3

AQUATICS

Beginning in Europe, in the 1960s, indoor swimming pools evolved from regulation-sized pools that serve the competitive swimmer to free-form pools with water features that are appropriately labeled "leisure pools." In the past decade, in colder climates in North America, indoor pool complexes have begun to offer a variety of water features that rival the scope of a water park. Swimming and water play have consistently ranked high in participation on the list of recreational activities included in the National Survey on Recreation and the Environment (NSRE 2002). According to Liberty Travel's first kids vacation poll, 75 percent of kids ranked play in a swimming pool as their number one activity. Commercial hotels, municipalities, and educational institutions, like the Young Men's Christian Association (YMCA), are recognizing the appeal of indoor, water-based activities.

INDOOR AQUATIC FACILITIES

Indoor aquatic facilities addressed here include:

- Swim clubs
- Municipal recreation centers
- Health and fitness clubs
- Hotels and resorts
- Indoor water parks

▼ *Old Overton Swim Club, Birmingham, Alabama. Drawing by E. Addison Young.*

Cities have recognized that a municipal pool is usable year-round and is a well-received investment of tax dollars in recreation if features attractive to residents from toddlers to seniors are included. Indoor leisure pools have become commonplace even in small towns under 6,000 population in Canada. YMCAs, including some in the southern United States, have expanded their indoor aquatic facilities from competitive swimming and lap pools to leisure pools with water play features that appeal to families through the winter months. Universities, with an emphasis on fitness and intramural recreation, are including free-form pools and other leisure pool features in their aquatics facilities.

Hotels in summer resort destinations like Wisconsin Dells, Wisconsin, have found that indoor water park amenities have been so successful in extending the location to a year-round attraction that fifteen lodging facilities now have indoor water parks, ranging from 10,000–90,000 sq ft in area.

Some new elements of water structures appeal to all ages. Zero entry pools work for everyone, from the toddler testing the water to the senior adult or handicapped person entering for water aerobics or water play. Constant depth pools, however, are useful for water aerobics.

The James J. Harris YMCA
The Aquatic Center addition to the James

▼ *James J. Harris YMCA, aquatic center addition, Charlotte, North Carolina. FWA Group, architect.*

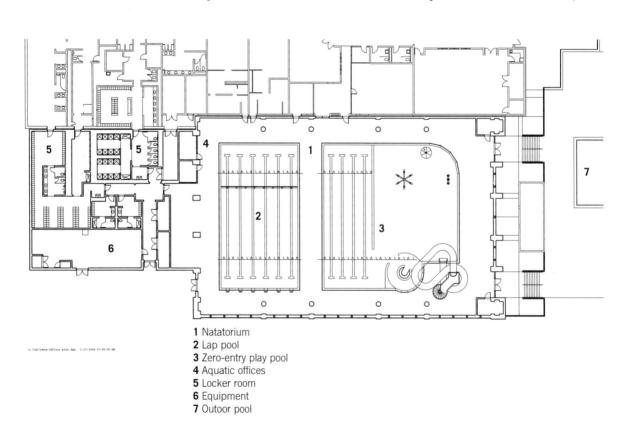

u:/tgl/ymca/cdfloor plan.dgn 1/27/2004 10:58:26 AM

1 Natatorium
2 Lap pool
3 Zero-entry play pool
4 Aquatic offices
5 Locker room
6 Equipment
7 Outdoor pool

J. Harris YMCA in Charlotte, North Carolina, is a hybrid indoor pool complex that includes the traditional 25-meter lap pool and a leisure pool. The complex totals 17,000 sq ft of natatorium and 7,000 sq ft in locker rooms and support area. The zero-entry leisure pool has several interactive water spray features, a water slide, and a lazy river.

The architectural firm, FWA Group of Charlotte, North Carolina, achieved an elegant solution to the highly corrosive atmosphere inherent in an indoor pool enclosure. The FWA project featured the building's structure, which was made of a hybrid wood glue-laminated beam and stainless steel cable truss that supports the tongue-and-groove wood decking. Not only is this a long-term solution to the moisture problem but the wood creates an unusually warm feeling for this kind of space. Emphasizing the lightness of the structure and daylighting the space, clerestory windows surround the pool area.

Aspen Aquatic Center

The Aquatic Center at the Aspen Recreation Center (ARC) in Aspen, Colorado, exemplifies the creative use of what originated as water theme park elements in a community indoor pool. The pool complex at the ARC includes the basic six-lane, 25-meter pool for competition and lap swimming. The pool is programmed for fitness in that two lanes are dedicated for lap swimming during open hours. The pool's depth transitions from 4 ft to a diving well of 12 ft for a one-meter springboard.

In contrast, the recreational pool transitions from a zero entry to 4 ft of constant depth. Elements include a two-story body slide, a lazy river, and multi-

ple spray features. The lazy river offers a varying aerobic experience, through walking with or against the current. Zero entry creates a beachlike entry, which works well for toddlers. In addition, a zero entry provides the required handicapped entry. A long high wall of glass naturally lights the pool space. During good weather, the lower half of the wall opens with a series of metal and glass overhead doors. Upon construction of a planned outdoor pool in the future, the indoor-outdoor elements of the aquatic complex will work together.

▲ James J. Harris YMCA, view of indoor aquatic center with lap pool in foreground and leisure pool in the background. FWA Group, architect. Photo by Harris YMCA.

▶ *Aspen Recreation Center, Aspen, Colorado, main level floor plan. Durrant Architects, architect of record; Hagman Architects, associate architect; Vince Davies Architects, Ltd., pool architect.*

1 Multipurpose room
2 Climbing tower
3 Lobby
4 East entry
5 Arena seating
6 Staff offices
7 Locker rooms
8 Leisure pool
9 Lap pool
10 Future outdoor pool area
11 Staff housing

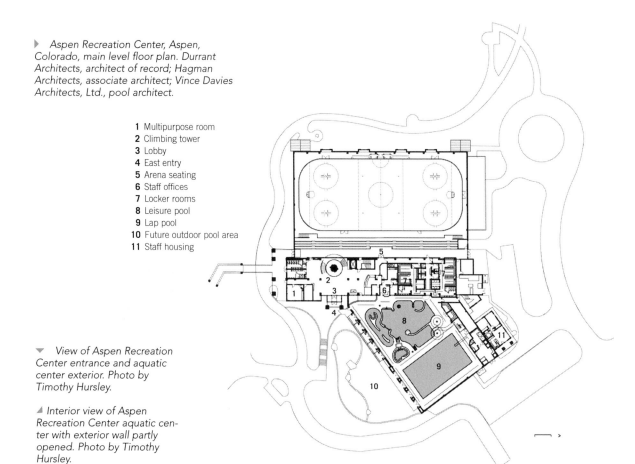

▼ *View of Aspen Recreation Center entrance and aquatic center exterior. Photo by Timothy Hursley.*

◢ *Interior view of Aspen Recreation Center aquatic center with exterior wall partly opened. Photo by Timothy Hursley.*

Livonia Community Recreation Center

The Livonia, Michigan, Community Recreation Center is a complex with a range of activities that serve the community's primarily family market. Planned as three major blocks of recreation space organized around an irregular L-shaped "street," the architecture exposes the user to windows of activity throughout the 130,000 sq ft facility.

Designed by Neumann Smith & Associates of Southfield, Michigan, in association with Barket Rinker Seacat Architecture of Denver, Colorado, the building includes aquatics, gymnasium, and administrative blocks as well as circulation streets and two high-tech pools.

The aquatics block includes:

- Leisure pool with a 250 ft long body slide that spirals out of the building's cylindrical tower, zero-depth entry, lazy river, hot tub, and sunning deck. Immediately outside the aquatics block, a splash pool and fountain is the attraction.

- Eight-lane competition and lap pool with an adjustable floor that can be made deeper for competitive swimming or shallower for water aerobics or swimming lessons. A moveable bulkhead adjusts the length, for 25 yards or meters or for water polo.

- Locker rooms, which also serve the gymnasium spaces. Included are six private changing rooms complete with restrooms for families with young children or for the elderly or handicapped who need privacy or personal assistance.

- Bleachers for 400 overlook the competition pool.

- Movement studio and multipurpose room, with windows overlooking the leisure pool.
- A soft indoor play area that is part tree house and part castle.

The gymnasium block includes:

- Main gym
- Auxiliary gym and multiuse space
- Cardiovascular and circuit weight training equipment area
- Mezzanine-level running track
- Gymnastics center

The administration and special area block includes:

- "Kid's quarters," child-sitting area that enables parents to participate in the many activities on the property. (See page 175.)

Livonia Community Recreation Center, Livonia, Michigan. View of indoor leisure pool. Neumann/Smith Architects and Associates; Barker Rinker Seacat Architects; Water Technology, pool designer. Photo by Justin Maconochie.

AQUATICS

▶ *Livonia Community
Recreation Center, Livonia,
Michigan. View of recreation
street. Neumann/Smith
Architects & Associates;
Barker Rinker Seacat
Architects. Photo by Justin
Maconochie.*

▼ *Livonia Community
Recreation Center, first
floor plan.*

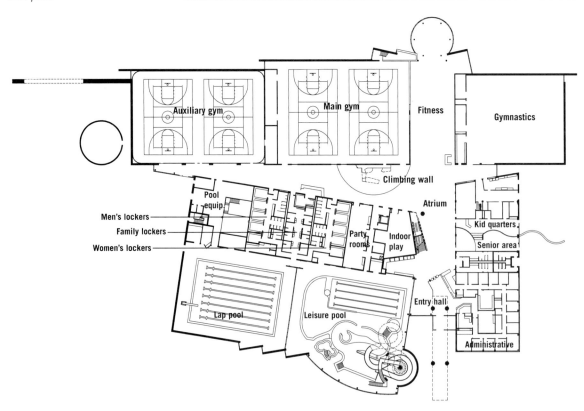

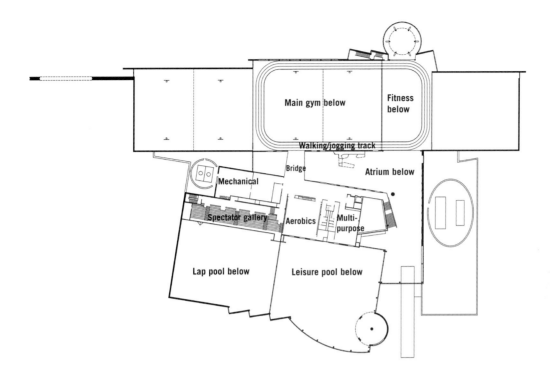

Main gym below

Fitness below

Walking/jogging track

Bridge

Atrium below

Mechanical

Spectator gallery

Aerobics

Multi-purpose

Lap pool below

Leisure pool below

- Senior lounge
- Game room
- Administrative offices, adjoining the entry hall and reception and control desk.

The circulation streets

Beginning in the arrival area, with the exterior and interior glass walls open to the leisure pool, the user is shown the center's activities. Ahead, for the user, is the fitness area, including the mezzanine-level running track that emerges from the gymnasium block. The climbing wall extends as a 42 ft high sculpture along the cross aisle. Portholes and glazed walls open to indoor play, kid quarters, and the gymnastics center. Inviting stairs (and the mezzanine overlook) lead to the multiuse space and the movement studio.

Pool technical points

Combining two major indoor pools of different functions with an array of adjoining spaces is a challenge to the architect and the mechanical engineer. The pools encompass 11,670 sq ft of water surface. Each pool has its own "internal weather" that requires a vapor barrier to prevent transmission of vapor and chlorine to other building areas. The common walls, roof cavities, and the mechanical system must work together to encapsulate the pools. The aquatic center mechanical system generates negative pressure to draw air from adjoining spaces. In addition, an ample supply of fresh air provides a clear window surface without fog or water droplets. The system prevents any chlorine smell from reaching adjoining spaces, including the building arrival area that adjoins the pool.

▲ *Livonia Community Recreation Center, second floor plan.*

Indoor Water Parks

Water-park attractions such as slides and spray features have increasingly become a part of indoor pools. Also becoming common, however, are entire water parks enclosed in large atrium-type spaces. The indoor water entertainment amenity has also become the focus and theme for hotels and regional malls. Significant indoor water parks date back to that at the West Edmonton Mall, in Edmonton, Alberta, which was built in 1986. An indoor water park is being planned for its sister super-regional mall, The Mall of America in Minneapolis, Minnesota.

The Ocean Dome

The Ocean Dome, the world's largest indoor water park, is part of the Sheraton Phoenix Seagaia Resort in Miyazaki, Japan. Its vaulted roof covers a footprint of 390,000 sq ft, with retractable sections that open one half of the roof structure.

The water park includes:

- A water surface area of 94,600 sq ft
- A white sand beach 459 ft long
- A wave-making machine that can produce waves over 8 ft high for surfing and body boarding
- A boardwalk with restaurants and shops that overlook the beach, water, and entertainment such as surfing shows
- Three tube slides and two body slides
- Grottos of storm, light, and mist
- A "lazy river"
- A clubhouse water-play area

▶ Ocean Dome, Phoenix Seagaia Resort, Miyazaki, Japan, aerial view of vaulted roof open. Mitsubishi Dome Structures, architect. Courtesy Phoenix Seagaia Resort.

◀ Ocean Dome, interior view with vaulted roof closed. Courtesy Phoenix Seagaia Resort.

The retractable roof consists of four steel-framed, arched sections that span 328 ft. Roofing is translucent Teflon; thus the water park is bathed in natural light even when the roof is closed.

The white beach is made of marble grains that will not stick to users. A buffer tank is set below the beach to allow the waves to seep through the sand. The system prevents the granular material from being swept back into the water.

AQUATIC SUPPORT FACILITIES

A number of facilities provide aquatic support, in particular the:

- Bathhouse or cabanas
- Pool snack bars
- Beach club clubhouses
- Pool equipment buildings

Bathhouses

Bathhouses primarily contain the restrooms that are required by health codes that pertain to swimming pool facilities. Pools come under state or local health departments jurisdiction rather than building and plumbing codes. The number of fixtures required is usually based on the pool and pool deck surface area. In reviewing the code, note especially the requirement for showers. Positioned so that the user may shower before entering the pool, some of the showers required may be provided by open showers on the exterior deck.

Bathhouses also provide space for towel storage and a counter from which to dispense them. In a private club or resort, this may provide a point of control to limit use of the pool to members or guests.

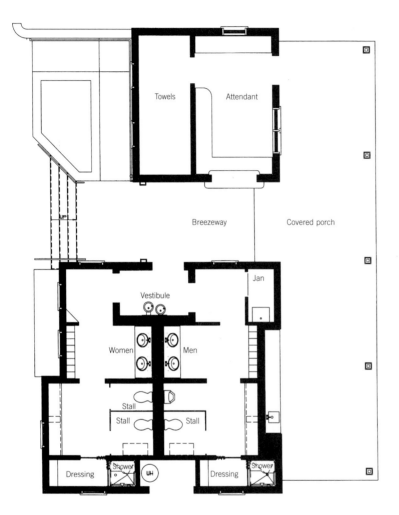

Beach Clubs

Regardless of the beach and natural water feature, most beach clubs feature a fresh water pool and pool deck for those who do not care for sand and saltwater. The essence of the beach club, however, is a vista of the water and the shore and a seat from which to view the scene.

Food and beverage facilities

The beach club is the most casual of the "club" facilities, with the user typically dressed for swimming or sunning. The outdoor bar and lounge, perhaps built into the pool, is an important element. Dining is casual, again, with a strong outdoor component, as good weather prompts a visit to the beach. A location offering the sunset over the water is ideal, and event pavilions at gathering areas support group receptions.

Changing areas and restrooms

Changing areas at beach clubs are required; usually they will need day lockers. Because of sand from the beach and wet floors, restrooms need to be separated into those serving the dining area and those serving the pool and beach areas. Since a pool is typically a part of the scene, local health department codes may well apply to restrooms, showers, and in some cases, eating areas related to the pool.

Indoor Pool and Deck Areas

The essence of indoor pools is moisture and corrosive chlorine and treatment chemicals. Both architectural surfaces and the mechanical system need to address the moisture and chemical issues. Inherent in the hard, nonabsorbent surfaces that solve the moisture problem is an acoustic problem, if not thoughtfully addressed. Another factor that may com-

▲ Prototypical pool building floor plan. Diedrich LLC.

Pool Snack Bar

Pools often have snack bars. See Chapter 12, "Dining," for data on snack bars. Note that some jurisdictions do not allow food to be served on the pool deck. A wall, railing, or level separation is required between the pool deck and dining patio. For safety reasons, pools require a surrounding fence, and that barrier provides the separation from the food area.

◀ Beach Club, Florida, site plan.
Diedrich/Niles Bolton & Associates,
architect; Meyer Bongirno MSI,
landscape architects.

E Guest drop-off at porte cochere
F Shell fountain feature
G Parking
H Service area
I Guest locker facilities
J Breezeway
K Restaurant
L Children's pool
M Dune crossover
N Beach access
O Beach bar
P Feature pool
Q Spa
R Function lawn
S Restored dune landscape
T Outdoor dining terrace

▼ The Beach Club, Kiawah Island,
South Carolina, site plan. Robert
A. M. Stern, architect.

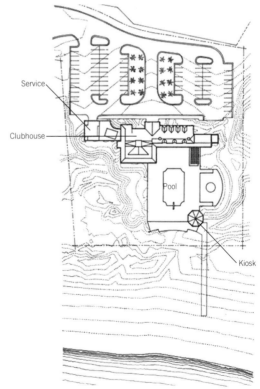

pound the problem is the use of hard-surface skylights, which are used to provide natural lighting for the pool during the day. The indoor pool at Amelia Island Resort in Florida is enclosed with a preengineered skylight roof structure. It features sliding roof panels as well as patio doors, so that the enclosure may be opened in good weather. For noise concerns, use of a moisture-proof acoustical material, beyond the user's reach, on the walls is warranted.

Whirlpools
Even small pools, such as an indoor whirlpool with jets, may cause problems

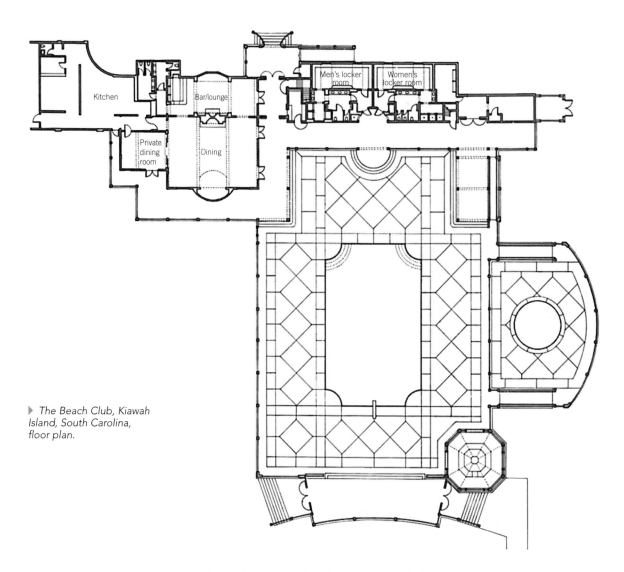

▶ *The Beach Club, Kiawah Island, South Carolina, floor plan.*

not only for the moisture but the moist heat generated. Note that the health code will require access on three sides for safety reasons (to assist a stricken person from the pool). Prominent code-dictated signage and safety railings might render a whirlpool amenity to appear more as an installation for physical therapy rather than leisurely use.

For information on outdoor pools, see *Ramsey/Sleeper Architectural Graphic Standards* (Ramsey et al. 2000).

BOATING

POWER AND SAIL BOATING

Among major recreational activities that require associated building structures, motor boating heads the National Survey on Recreation and the Environment (NSRE) list, adding the most participants between 1982–2002. In that period, those participating in power boating (to use the participants' term) rose in absolute numbers by 17.8 million to total 51.4 million people in 2002 (Green et al. 2003). In 2003 in the United States, 840,000 recreational boats of all types were sold.[1] The popularity of jet skiing, however, which reflects an increase in the popularity of risk and

1. National Marine Manufacturer's Association. http://www.nmma.org/facts/boatingstats/2003.

adventure pursuits that are coupled with technological innovations, saw participants grow from 9.26 million in 1994 to 20.31 million in 2002, or a 119.33 percent increase. Overall, boating, in a variety of forms, is among the fastest growing types of recreation over the past seven years.

Looking to future decades, participation in boating is expected to grow slightly faster than the population. Because of an already significant base number of those actively participating in boating in the United States, by 2050 72.85 million people are expected to be involved in boating. Although tempered by fewer places with access to water and boat-porting facilities, the projected rise in real

▼ Conceptual sketch for a yacht club. Drawing by E. Addison Young.

income will drive growth over time in boating, which is considered an expensive recreation (Bowker et al. 1999, p. 330).

SITE ELEMENTS
In the design of boating facilities, the regional impact on the building structures will need consideration. For evaluation of these concerns, the continental United States may be divided into five regions that have similar marine characteristics: the Eastern Seaboard, the Gulf Coast, the southern Pacific (California), the northern Pacific (Oregon and Washington), and the Great Lakes. The architectural facility considerations for the Great Lakes region are, for the most part, applicable to other freshwater, inland waterways.

Regional differences may include such considerations as tidal range, freshwater versus salt water, and weather protection versus open slips. For instance, a fuel dock and harbormaster facility on fixed pilings within a tidal range of 18–24 in. (e.g., on the southeast coast of Florida) is a significantly different problem than the design of a similar facility, founded on a floating dock that reacts to a tidal range of 5–7 ft (e.g., on the southwest coast of California). Other examples of regional differences stem from the type of boating activity pursued. For example, destination cruising of moderately sized powerboats, traversing the Eastern Seaboard between New England and Florida, may promote a need for fuel, provisions, laundry and shower facilities, and captain and crew quarters. Boating participation is quite different in the Pacific region off California, however. Most boating consists of day cruises that begin and end at the same facility, requiring no transient support facilities. While the Great Lakes

do not experience significant tidal variances, climatic conditions require winter storage for watercraft. Wet storage is not a solution except for very large craft with deicing capabilities. As a result, winter storage facilities may be required.

BOATING SUPPORT FACILITIES
Because this book primarily addresses buildings and architectural facilities, planning and design of marinas, docks, and boat maintenance facilities is not included. (See Ramsey et al. 2000.)

Buildings supporting boating include the following:

- Marina support facilities
    Harbormaster
    Ship's chandlery or ship's store
    Dry-stack storage
    Land-based storage lockers for boating equipment and supplies
    Restrooms and showers for the small boat user
    Self-service laundry facility
- Yacht clubhouses
- Kayak and canoe storage
- Boat houses for rowing boats and equipment

Harbormaster
The harbormaster office is the control center of the marina. Most importantly, it houses the equipment and the operator (the harbormaster staff) who communicates with boaters. The check-in counter for leased slips, whether short- or long-term, is located in the harbormaster's office. Although retail is concentrated in the ship's store, charts and navigational aids may be sold in the harbormaster's office. Including a private office for the

harbormaster, this facility is in the 400–600 sq ft range.

The harbormaster building is best located where there is visual control over the marina operations. To be on the water and in command of daily operations and the coming and going of boats, the location may require a floating foundation in areas of extreme tidal range. The harbormaster building may be joined with the fueling station building, enabling the dock master staff to handle refueling operations, as well, during slow periods of activity.

The Ship's Chandlery or Ship's Store

The ship's store is, essentially, a convenience store that caters to the boater. A ship's chandlery is the more traditional version of the ship's store, with more emphasis on boat hardware and equipment. In the ship's store, marine supplies, equipment, and parts are available, to a varying degree, but more important are reach-in coolers of beer, soft drinks, milk, wine, and other beverages. The other food and household supplies that one would find in a convenience store might also be included, as well as logo-ware and products, tee shirts, and mugs that serve as mementos for short- and long-term transient boaters. With the continuing growth of various water sports, ranging from jet skis to windsurfing rigs, more space must be dedicated to related paraphernalia. Local interest and regional impact will affect merchandise assortment planning and related space needs.

Snacks and beverages, coupled with interesting boats and activity at the marina, warrant a deck outside the retail facility overlooking the marina. The best view of a marina is from an upper level, which prevents the water vistas and views of boat activity from being cut off by the docked boats.

Dry Storage

More boats and boaters, coupled with the additional difficulty and expense in adding wet slips, is an ongoing issue for the boating industry. Storing boats on trailers on valuable land convenient to the water is becoming less viable. These conditions will continue to lead to more dry-stack storage. The lightness and strength of fiberglass-hulled boats makes dry storage more feasible. Dry stacking increases the total number of wet slips, mooring cans, and at-grade storage for larger boats and unique hull boats such as sail- and "cigarette"-type competitive powerboats without creating or requiring more waterfront.

▼ Harbourgate Marina, North Myrtle Beach, South Carolina. View of marina building. Diedrich Architects.

Dry-stack storage buildings are preengineered, warehouselike buildings. The structural steel frame has intermittent beams that may be adjusted to create racks in which boats may be inserted and stacked, typically, four to six boats high. A large marina forklift, called a "marina bull," transfers the boat between the storage rack and the water. Storage of boats as large as 20–24 ft is typical; bigger boats may be handled, depending on the forklift capacity.

Dry storage depends on the marina operator getting the boat in and out of the water. Looked at like a valet service, the boater calls ahead for the boat to be put in the water, and when finished may leave it in the water to be picked up, washed down, and racked. The only disadvantages to this approach to boat storage may be the marina operating hours and the inacessibility of the boats. Boaters cannot board and tinker with the boat any time they wish. The degree of enclosure provided by dry-stack storage, however, may mean much less boat maintenance is required. Enclosed storage protects the boat finish from the harmful ultraviolet rays of the sun. Dry storage, as well, minimizes the bottom fouling caused by prolonged storage in a wet slip.

The challenge for the architect is that these tall warehouselike buildings (starting at a minimum 35 ft eave height) are most effective when forklift travel is minimized by placing them at or near the waterfront. The large barnlike mass, especially if the access aisle is covered, is difficult to handle architecturally. Uncovered access aisles reduce the mass of the structure. Exterior surface materials, handled with sensitivity, may help disguise the building but are rarely successful. A solution may be found if the architectural program for the marina offers other building elements with which to work. The ship's store, other retail, yacht brokerage, the harbormaster, and restaurant buildings may be used to integrate the storage building into the complex and diminish the impact of the large building mass. Because of the storage of gas-engined boats, however, the building code will require a rated wall between the different buildings.

▶ Aerial view of dry-stack storage buildings at Sara Bay Marina, Sarasota, Florida. Photo by Jack Elka.

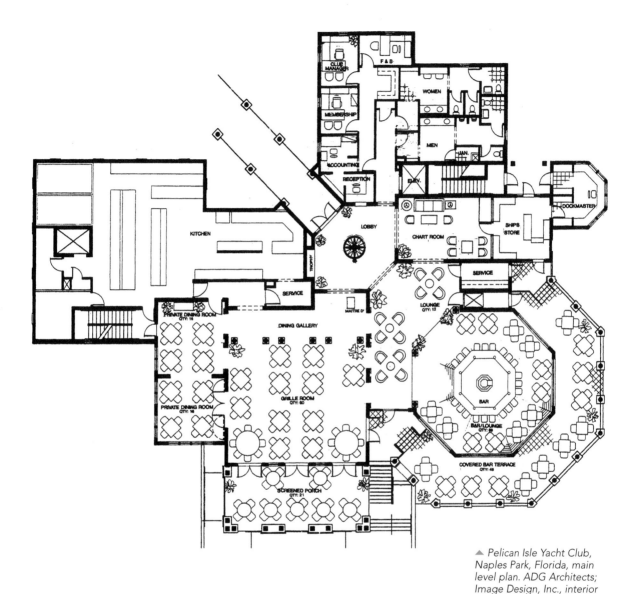

CLUB MANAGER

F&B

WOMEN

MEMBERSHIP

MEN

JAN.

ACCOUNTING

ELEV.

RECEPTION

DOCKMASTER

KITCHEN

LOBBY

SHIPS STORE

CHART ROOM

SERVICE

TROPHY

SERVICE

LOUNGE
QTY: 12

PRIVATE DINING ROOM
QTY: 16

MAITRE D'

DINING GALLERY

PRIVATE DINING ROOM
QTY: 16

GRILLE ROOM
QTY: 60

BAR

BAR/LOUNGE
QTY: 60

COVERED BAR TERRACE
QTY: 48

SCREENED PORCH
QTY: 21

▲ *Pelican Isle Yacht Club, Naples Park, Florida, main level plan. ADG Architects; Image Design, Inc., interior design.*

Yacht Clubs

Yacht clubhouses are often dining clubs in a marina setting. For that reason, the view orientation of such dining rooms comes into play (see Chapter 12, "Dining"). Because marina activity is best viewed from an overlooking vantage point, the case for receiving at grade level and using an island kitchen to serve upper level dining rooms is reinforced. The principles of access and service for view-oriented dining rooms, such as the Commodore's Room, are set forth in Chapter 12.

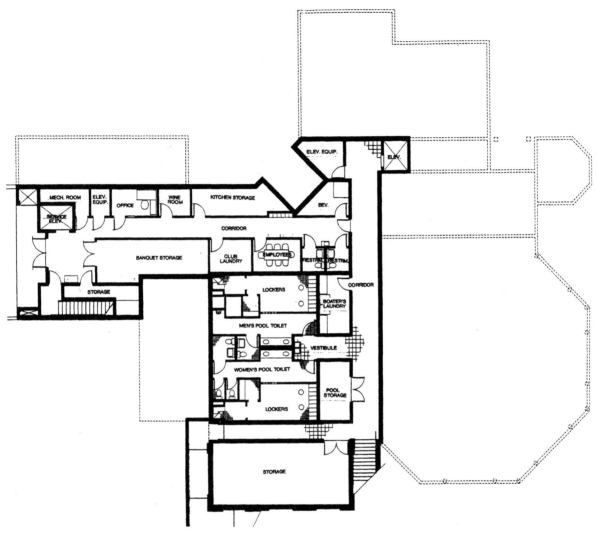

ELEV. EQUIP.

ELEV.

MECH. ROOM

ELEV. EQUIP.

OFFICE

WINE ROOM

KITCHEN STORAGE

BEV.

SERVICE ELEV.

CORRIDOR

BANQUET STORAGE

CLUB LAUNDRY

EMPLOYEES

RESTRM. RESTRM.

CORRIDOR

STORAGE

LOCKERS

BOATER'S LAUNDRY

MEN'S POOL TOILET

VESTIBULE

WOMEN'S POOL TOILET

POOL STORAGE

LOCKERS

STORAGE

▲ Pelican Isle Yacht Club, lower level plan.

▼ Bay Harbor Yacht Club, Bay Harbor, Michigan, yacht basin view. Archiventure Group PC, architect.

▶ Bay Harbor Yacht Club, site plan.

Family-oriented yacht clubs may also have country club–like elements such as an outdoor pool and fitness facilities. Yacht clubs that host a competitive sailing contingent will need meeting space to discuss race strategy and areas to house related memorabilia—for example, trophies, photographs, and sail plans. Additional loft space may be required for sail repair and storage. Elements found in marina support facilities may also be found in a yacht clubhouse.

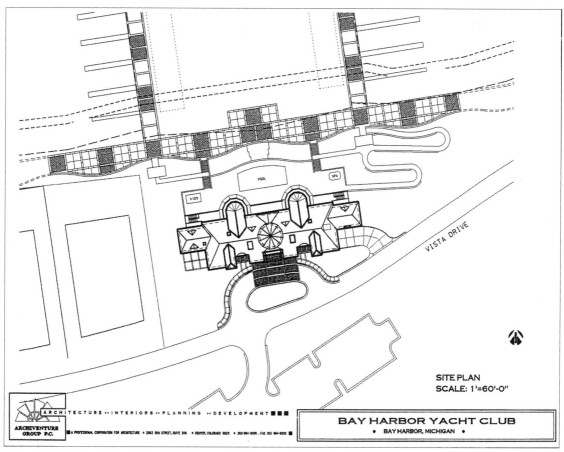

SITE PLAN
SCALE: 1'=60'-0"

BAY HARBOR YACHT CLUB
◆ BAY HARBOR, MICHIGAN ◆

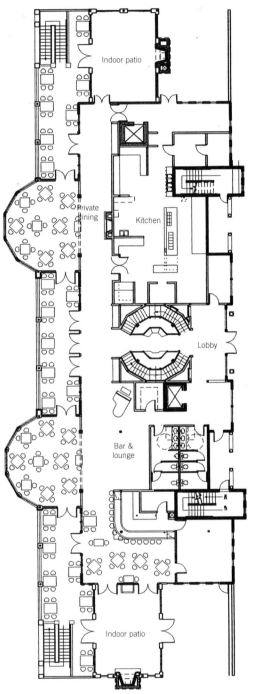

▲ *Bay Harbor Yacht Club, water-side view.*

▶ *Bay Harbor Yacht Club, main level plan.*

▶▶ *Bay Harbor Yacht Club, lower level plan.*

▶▶▶ *Bay Harbor Yacht Club, upper level plan.*

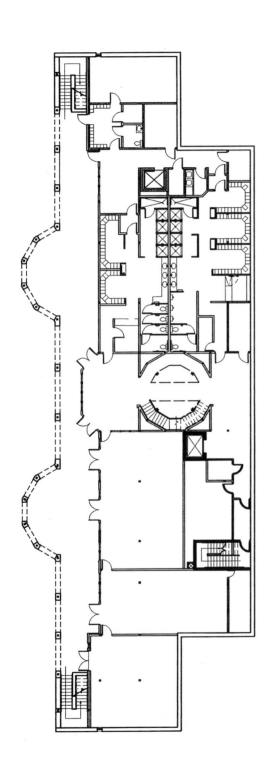

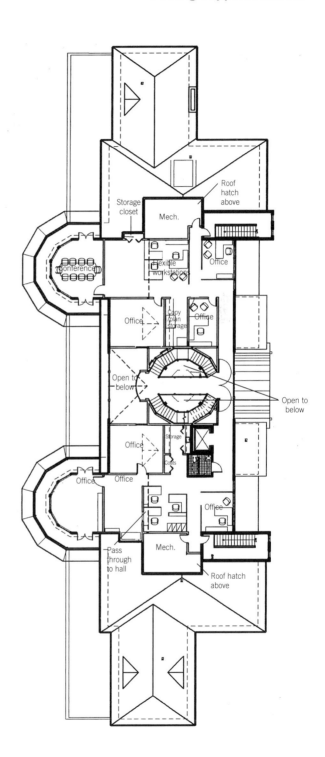

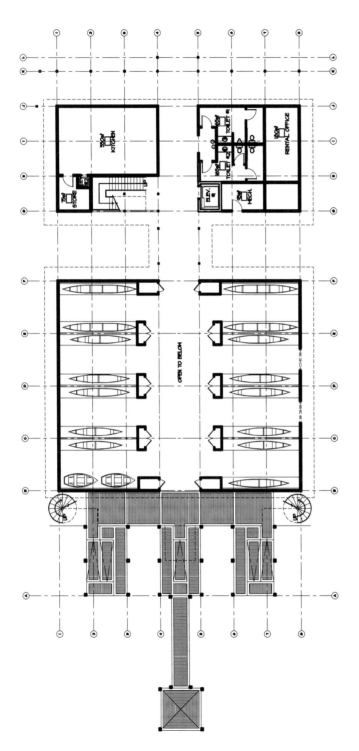

MUSCLE-POWERED BOATS

The participation percentages for motor boating show an increase of 10.2 percent from 1994 to 2002; however, this pales in comparison to the growth of muscle-powered kayaking: from 2.58 million in 1994 to 7.29 million in 2002, which is a recreational activity leading 182.56 percent increase. Participation in canoeing, also echoing trends in fitness and concern with the environment, increased from 13.76 million in 1994 to 20.63 million in 2002, for an increase of 49.93 percent. Kayaking and canoeing are among the fastest growing of all recreational pursuits in the last seven years (Green et al. 2003).

Kayak and Canoe Storage

Muscle-powered light boats like kayaks and canoes are easily stored in small, racklike buildings. The buildings protect the boats from the sun and also efficiently store boats stacked up to four high.

◀ Wilson's Landing, Palmetto Bluff Canoe Club, Bluffton, South Carolina, ground floor plan. Hart Howerton, architect; Crescent Resources LLC, developer.

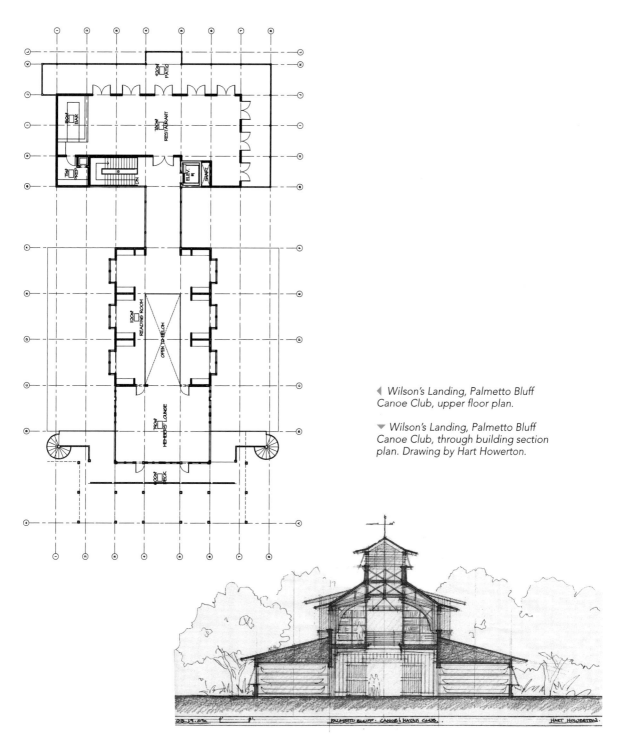

◀ Wilson's Landing, Palmetto Bluff
Canoe Club, upper floor plan.

▼ Wilson's Landing, Palmetto Bluff
Canoe Club, through building section
plan. Drawing by Hart Howerton.

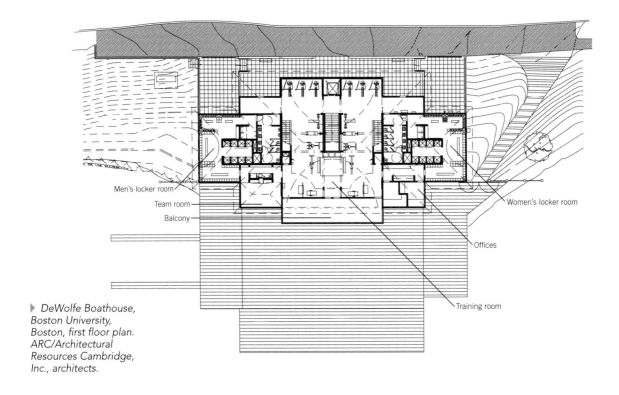

Men's locker room

Team room

Balcony

Women's locker room

Offices

Training room

▶ DeWolfe Boathouse,
Boston University,
Boston, first floor plan.
ARC/Architectural
Resources Cambridge,
Inc., architects.

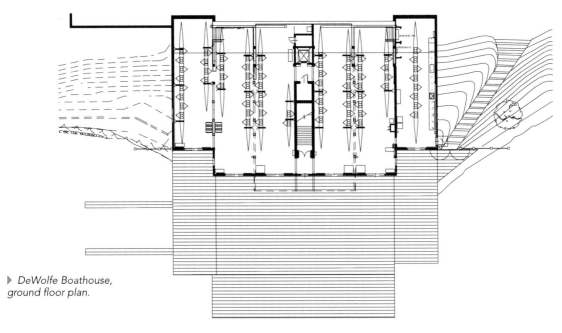

▶ DeWolfe Boathouse,
ground floor plan.

◀ *View across the Charles River, Boston, of DeWolfe Boathouse. Photo by John Horner.*

▼ *DeWolfe Boathouse, shell storage area. Photo by Nick Wheeler.*

Boat Houses for Rowing

The dramatic increase of women in rowing has led to a spate of new boathouses at universities. In addition to balancing the locker rooms, the new facilities have enlarged training workout rooms as well as storage space.

The working configuration puts the storage of shells, predominately eights for university competition, with a shop on the lower level of the boathouse with easy access to the water. The upper level then houses workout areas and locker rooms with showers and restrooms, thereby achieving gender parity. Also upstairs a team room for meetings and administrative offices is provided.

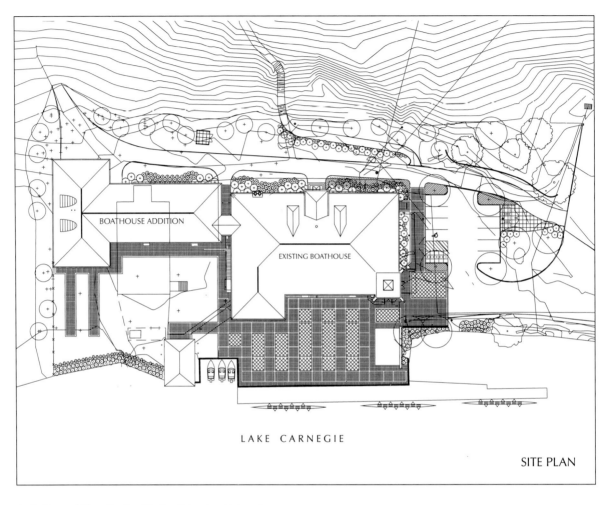

BOATHOUSE ADDITION

EXISTING BOATHOUSE

LAKE CARNEGIE

SITE PLAN

▲ C. Bernard Shea Rowing Center, Princeton University, Princeton, New Jersey, site plan. ARC/Architectural Resources Cambridge, Inc., architect.

Princeton University's C. Bernard Shea Rowing Center addition houses extra boat bays with trailer access from the landside. Also, at grade level there is a room with rowing tanks that allows all-weather practices. Upstairs are workout rooms and, in the renovated clubhouse, locker rooms and a large clubroom.

Minneapolis Rowing Club Boathouse

With this boathouse, architect Vincent James of Minneapolis, Minnesota, achieved a spare but elegant expression consistent with the rowing craft that it houses. The scheme uses the classic arrangement of boat storage on grade

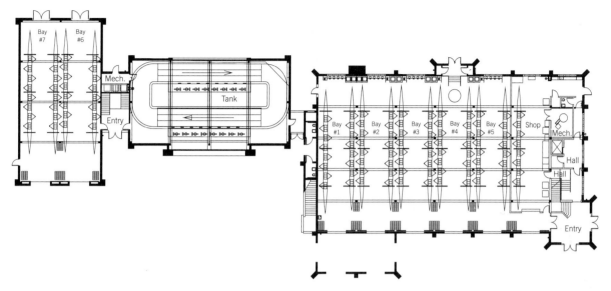

▲ C. Bernard Shea Rowing Center,
first floor plan.

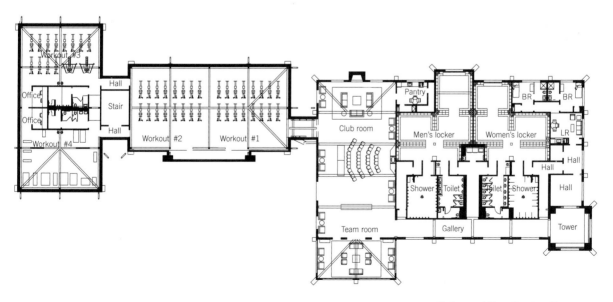

▲ C. Bernard Shea Rowing Center,
second floor plan.

▲ C. Bernard Shea Rowing Center, waterside view of addition. Photo by Nick Wheeler.

◀ C. Bernard Shea Rowing Center, workout room view. Photo by Nick Wheeler.

▼ C. Bernard Shea Rowing Center, through-building section, showing rowing tanks

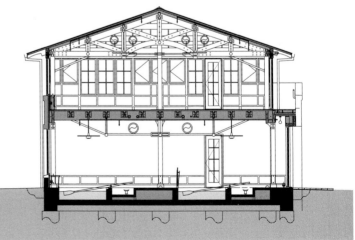

level and workout and club space on the mezzanine level. James used large cutouts in the floor structure to wash the natural light from clerestories throughout the building. The clerestories are achieved by capping the simple, rectilinear form with a gently warped roof. The roof trusses, with wood cords, tension cables, and connecting rings also recall the elegant hardware of the stored sculls. The gentle swooping of the roof depicts the movement of the oar in rowing. In its form and detail, the building expresses the recreational activity that it supports.

▼ *Minneapolis Rowing Club boathouse, Minneapolis, Minnesota, site plan. VJAA.*

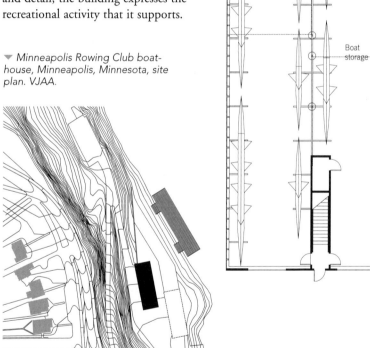

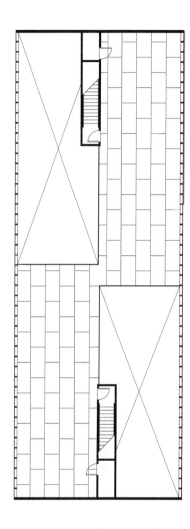

Boat storage

▼ *Minneapolis Rowing Club boathouse, lower level plan.*

▲ *Minneapolis Rowing Club boathouse, mezzanine level plan.*

Regional Concerns

In all of these boat facility programs, regional differences may dictate basic design decisions. For instance, the interface of boat launch facilities with tidal variances must be carefully considered. Also, weather considerations in northern regions may present significantly different housing challenges if all-weather practice is to be considered. Finally, the threat of hurricanes poses yet another set of standards affecting at least two of the regions: the Eastern Seaboard and the Gulf Coast.

CHAPTER 5

HANDBALL, RACQUETBALL, SQUASH, AND INDOOR TENNIS

Handball, racquetball, and squash have a shared genealogy. Although handball exists today in three forms (one-wall, three-wall, and four-wall) and racquetball in two (three-wall and four-wall), squash is squash—there is only one form. Because this book is about building design, the focus will be on the indoor, four-wall games.

In the United States, racquetball is the most popular indoor court game. From its peak in the 1980s, the number of

players has stabilized at just below five million. The game of handball may be found all over the world, but it is most popular in the United States, Ireland, and Australia. The United States Handball Association (USHA) estimates there are about three million players in the U.S., but participation in the game is slowly declining. One of the goals of the USHA is to attract a greater number of young players by promoting the game at schools and universities.

▼ *Conceptual sketch of a tennis center. Drawing by E. Addison Young.*

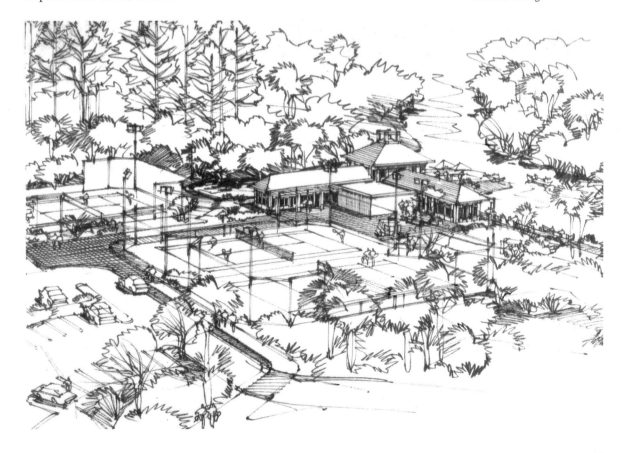

The game of squash has the fewest number of players in the United States, about one million, but the greatest number of players internationally. The number of players in this country is growing, especially where the game is most popular—the Northeast and California.

COURT CONSTRUCTION, EXCEPT SQUASH

The most economical way of providing playing facilities for any of the court games is to build the courts outside, using the exterior wall or walls of a building that contains other functions or activities. Outdoor courts are de rigueur for three-wall handball and racquetball.

They may be masonry or cast concrete construction. The walls should be finished with a hard cement plaster applied

to a good bonding agent. Broom-finished concrete floors should be slightly pitched from front to back for drainage.

Indoor courts may be built using the same materials and methods as outdoor courts, with the addition of a full ceiling and insulation as required for climatic conditions. Regardless of the materials and methods of construction used, the courts should be built for handball. The handball is smaller, weighs more, and is much harder than a racquetball; it will require the stiffest and most durable wall that can be built.

Resin panel construction installed by specialty contractors is the most common and cost-efficient way to build courts. The critical concern is if the panels are too thin or mounted on a backing of steel studs that are spaced too far

▶ Diagram of a prototypical handball and racquetball court. Reprinted from Ramsey et al. 2000.

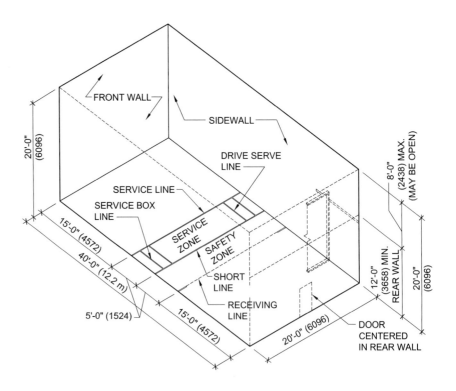

apart. This results in a "dead wall" or an uneven rebound or, in the worst case, both. This problem is especially critical on the front wall of the court.

Any joint in a playing surface will cause the ball to take a bad bounce, or it will produce what is known as a "court hinder." Therefore, joints should be minimized or eliminated. Where required, they should be as small, narrow, and as smooth as possible.

If wood is used for the floor, tongue-and-groove hardwood boards are installed over "sleepers," that is, timber, stone, or steel supports, as for a gymnasium floor. Similar to the court walls, if the hardwood is too thin or the sleepers too far apart, dead spots and an unsatisfactory playing surface will result. There are gymnasium floor products that are made to be applied directly to a concrete subfloor with thin-set adhesive, which may eliminate the dead floor problem. A steel-troweled and painted concrete floor may be an acceptable and cost effective solution.

The ceiling is a playing surface in handball and racquetball (though not for squash); therefore, the design and construction of the ceiling requires the same design considerations as the walls, but with the addition of light fixtures. The better the lighting, the better the court. Good lighting, however, means more light fixtures, which means more joints and uneven surfaces. The junction of light fixture frame, lens, and ceiling is never perfect. The architect should detail the best joint possible and opt for better lighting. One hundred foot-candles (fc) at the floor level (evenly distributed) is the goal. Light fixture lenses need to diffuse the light and provide close to a 180° distribution pattern to light the ceiling

corners. The light fixtures must be shock resistant and the lens not only shatter-proof but rigid enough so that balls striking the lens rebound almost as if they had struck the ceiling. This will eliminate bad bounces and ensure continuous play.

The door to the courts should be centered in the back wall. For the door to provide a playable rebound of the ball, it should swing into the court so that a tight closure against the jamb keeps the door from "giving" from the impact of the ball. The door may be of either glass or wood but should be as heavy and solid as possible. The door hinge is a special hardware item. It must provide a rigid connection for ball rebound and should not protrude into the court. If no glass is provided in the back wall, either a small window (flush with the inside of the door) or a "mail slot" should be provided in the door so that people outside may see if the court is occupied. One may then see when it is safe to open the in-swinging door if play is in progress. Confirm that the local code review and enforcement people understand the special requirements of court construction versus normal ingress amd egress, fire safety, the Americans with Disabilities Act (ADA), and other codes. For instance, to pass plan review in one jurisdiction, a court was required to be constructed with electrical outlets spaced evenly on the interior walls.

SQUASH COURTS

Squash court construction is similar to that for racquetball and handball. The court dimensions are different, of course, and the ceiling is not in play. The major addition in construction is the bottom "board," "tell-tale," or "tin" added to the front wall.

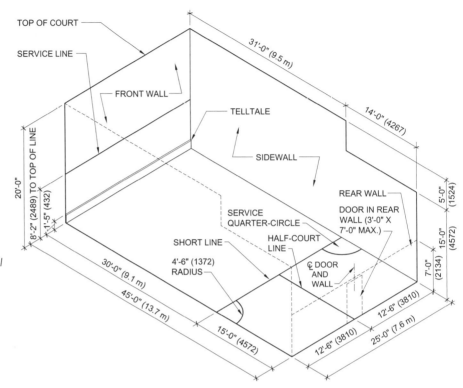

TOP OF COURT

SERVICE LINE

FRONT WALL

31'-0" (9.5 m)

14'-0" (4267)

TELLTALE

SIDEWALL

20'-0"

8'-2" (2489) TO TOP OF LINE

1'-5" (432)

REAR WALL

DOOR IN REAR WALL (3'-0" X 7'-0" MAX.)

5'-0" (1524)

15'-0" (4572)

SERVICE QUARTER-CIRCLE

HALF-COURT LINE

SHORT LINE

4'-6" (1372) RADIUS

℄ DOOR AND WALL

7'-0" (2134)

30'-0" (9.1 m)

45'-0" (13.7 m)

15'-0" (4572)

12'-6" (3810)

12'-6" (3810)

25'-0" (7.6 m)

▶ *Diagram of a prototypical doubles squash court. Reprinted from Ramsey et al. 2000.*

Squash courts are sized for singles or doubles. Glass rear walls are used more and more to allow spectators to watch games.

SPECTATOR AREA

When racquetball became popular, a need for increased spectator viewing capacity had to be met. More people wanted to watch tournament play, but viewing access was also used to promote the social aspect of the clubs. The traditional spectator area was an upper-level gallery, usually little more than a wide hallway. Initially, windows were introduced into the back wall with the glass set flush with the inside of the interior surface using silicone and "frameless" construction. The glass in the back wall

increased in area with the final result being an all-glass back wall. The design and construction of structural glass walls with flush joints and vertical glass stiffeners is done by specialty contractors who have experience in court construction.

On "exhibition" courts the all-glass wall extends around one or both sides. Glass walls present two concerns for the designer. One, the glass wall is by far the most expensive way to enclose a court; and, two, it is hard for the player to follow and play the ball when the rebounding surface is all but invisible. Increased lighting levels inside the court help, but the challenge for the designer is to make it easy for the players not to "lose the ball in the glass" while permitting spectators to see the players. Determining the needed viewing area and spectator capacity is part of project programming and early planning.

HEATING, VENTILATING, AND AIR-CONDITIONING

Heating, ventilating, and air-conditioning (HVAC) of the courts demands special attention. Dehumidification is just as important as heating and cooling and must be addressed by the design engineer. If at all possible, the court should be placed on a separate system. The separation will not only allow for the particular design needs of the courts to be met but may result in operational cost savings by allowing operation on a run-when-needed basis.

There are two problems the building designer and HVAC engineer must solve. First, how will properly treated air be supplied to a 20' x 40' room with a 20' ceiling, where the supply and return must be in the same place? The air supply location needs to be high in the back (entry) wall or in the rear portion of the ceiling. Second, how will the humidity generated by four players engaged in strenuous exercise be exhausted before condensation forms on the walls? If the on-court humidity problem is not solved, player activity on the court will cause the walls to "sweat." They become slick, causing the ball to skid instead of bounce, thus interfering with play.

INDOOR TENNIS COURTS

Housing the game of tennis is such a specialized program that it is typically achieved with a preengineered structure known as "a tennis frame." The basic structure is a rigid steel frame, spanning the length of the court or 120 ft. The spring line, or eave line, of the frame (at

the back of the court) is a minimum of 16 ft and preferably 20 ft high. The roof pitch toward the center of the court is a minimum of 4 in 12. This puts the ridge over the net at 36–40 ft high. Therefore, the building envelope generally fits the flight of the ball, even for a lob shot. The massing of the resulting "tennis barn," however, is an architectural challenge.

Since the tennis frame is a preengineered structure supporting a large building envelope, it is often produced by a metal building supplier. It is up to the architect to use the ancillary elements of the indoor tennis center to create architectural massing.

Surfaces and finishes

The ceiling of an indoor tennis court is typically a colored, vinyl-finished batt insulation. The batts are fitted between the structural bents, which are painted a similar color to provide a passive background

▲ The glass-walled court with spectator overlook at Morrison Athletic Center, Noble & Greenough School, Dedham, Massachusetts. ARC/Architectural Resources Cambridge, Inc., architect. Photo by Nick Wheeler.

for the ball to aid visibility by the players. If skylights are to be installed, a translucent material should be used to reduce glare and contrast with the ceiling surfaces. Wall surfaces are nets, similar to the wind screens typically used on exterior courts.

The court surface is typically a hard court, or cushioned asphalt. A soft court effect on the action of the ball may be achieved with a carpetlike material. Each may be put over a concrete or asphalt slab. If the tennis building is partially buried or set into a hill, however, hydrostatic pressure and uplift on the slab is a concern.

Country Club Clubhouse, Moscow, Russia

At a country club in Moscow, Russia, architects Richard J. Diedrich and Mark A. Diedrich responded to the program set by a former world number one–ranked tennis player. The indoor tennis center is connected by a bridge to the winter gar-

▲ Drake University Tennis Center, Des Moines, Iowa. View of the indoor tennis center, showing the 120 ft span-steel bent structure and indirect lighting.

▼ Country Club, Moscow, Russia. Sketch showing tennis center, winter garden leisure pool, fitness center, and golf clubhouse. Diedrich LLC and Kuo Diedrich, Inc., architects. Drawing by E. Addison Young.

den, a pool and fitness area, which is part of the country club. Entering via the bridge, one overlooks the courts from an indoor pavilionlike structure. Food and beverage service is available to those watching the action on the courts as well as those viewing the green, the landscaped area outside. Below the pavilion are the tennis pro shop and the locker rooms. This two-story building element is set into the hillside, which mitigates the mass of the tennis enclosure.

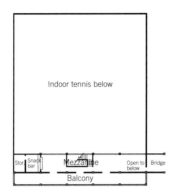
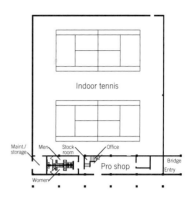

▲ Country Club Tennis Center floor plan.

◀ Country Club Tennis Center, interior sketch showing wood laminated trusses and spectator overlook. Drawing by E. Addison Young.

Tennis Court Heating, Ventilation, and Lighting

Indoor tennis courts are such large-volumed, high spaces that forced-air systems are not an effective means to heat or cool the space. Typically the space is mechanically ventilated with low-speed, court-level fans. Heating is achieved with gas-fired radiant heaters, which warms surfaces and players but not the space itself.

Indirect lighting is one of the most effective ways to light indoor tennis courts. High-intensity discharge (HID) lighting bounced off the ceiling provides

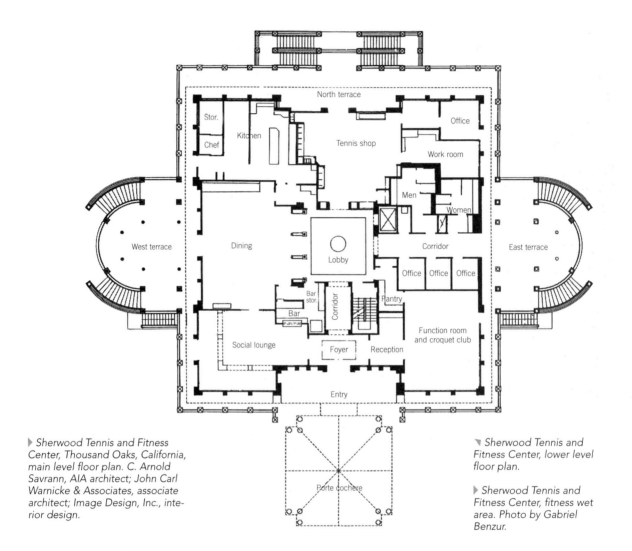

North terrace

Stor.

Kitchen

Chef

Tennis shop

Office

Work room

Men

Women

West terrace

Dining

Lobby

Corridor

East terrace

Office | Office | Office

Bar stor.

Pantry

Corridor

Bar

Function room and croquet club

Social lounge

Foyer

Reception

Entry

Porte cochere

▶ Sherwood Tennis and Fitness Center, Thousand Oaks, California, main level floor plan. C. Arnold Savrann, AIA architect; John Carl Warnicke & Associates, associate architect; Image Design, Inc., interior design.

◥ Sherwood Tennis and Fitness Center, lower level floor plan.

▶ Sherwood Tennis and Fitness Center, fitness wet area. Photo by Gabriel Benzur.

a glare free and neutral backdrop for the tennis ball. The system is economical in initial cost and to operate.

Tennis Shop

The tennis shop is typically smaller than a golf shop. There are exceptions in large, active tennis centers, particularly resorts, where the tennis shop may become a sports boutique. Typically, for up to 12 courts, the sales area of the tennis shop is approximately 500 sq ft. Layout of the shop should follow the principle of retail design, requiring the player to pass through the merchandise display to get to the control counter to check in. A small changing area for trying on clothes is included. The shop area includes offices for the head tennis professional and teaching professionals. Offices are

typically small to encourage the professional to be out interacting with the tennis players in the court area. Stock storage of about 20–25 percent of the sales area should be provided. In addition, an area is needed for racquet restringing equipment.

Locker Rooms

Tennis locker rooms usually contain day lockers. Stacked lockers are adequate but must be sized to contain a tennis racquet. The large head size of today's racquets warrants a locker 24" deep and 36" high. The deeper locker also holds more shoes, which is useful for a tennis player.

Restrooms and showers are not extensive, considering that there is a maximum of only four people per court plus those waiting or finishing at any point in

time. Tennis restroom and shower facilities that are combined with a fitness center are well used because of the active nature of these sports.

Pavilion

The best vantage point for watching tennis is from above. Therefore, a pavilion on an upper level, overlooking the courts, works well. Whether in an indoor tennis barn or outside, a building element with tennis shop, restrooms, and storage on the first level, with a pavilion above, supports the game. Keep in mind that the ADA necessitates handicapped access to the upper level overlook.

Tennis and Swim Building

Outdoor tennis and swimming are often combined at country clubs and recreation centers. A modest building may support both recreational activities. It would include a tennis pro shop of approximately 500 sq ft with an office, stock storage, and a changing room to

▲ Sherwood Tennis and Fitness Center, terrace overlooking the tennis courts. Photo by Gabriel Benzur.

▶ Oldfield Community Tennis Center, Beaufort, South Carolina. Evening view of tennis pavilion. Historical Concepts, architect.

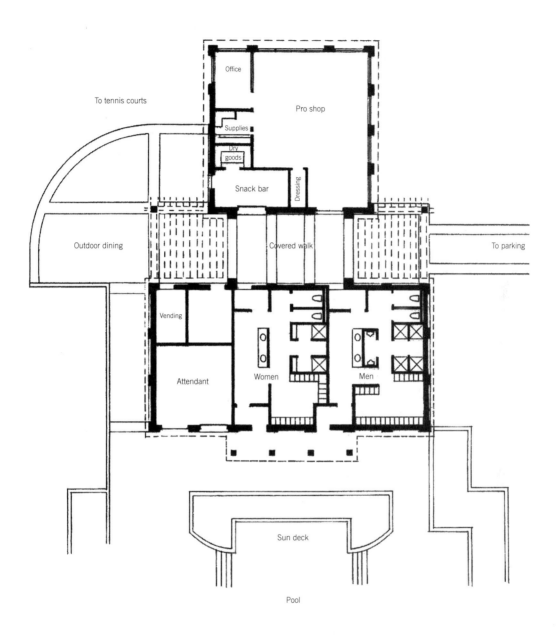

Office

To tennis courts

Pro shop

Supplies

Dry goods

Snack bar

Dressing

Outdoor dining

Covered walk

To parking

Vending

Attendant

Women

Men

Sun deck

Pool

▲ *Prototypical swim and tennis building floor plan. Diedrich Architects.*

try on clothes. A snack bar or vending would work with patio dining.

The other component would have restrooms, showers, and day lockers accessible from both the swim and tennis venues. Note that the health department jurisdiction will determine the restroom fixture count based on the pool size. An attendant's area might provide towels and serve as the base of operation for lifeguards and pool control.

Equipment and Material Storage

Soft tennis courts, in particular, need a storage area for equipment and materials. An area of 200 sq ft is usually adequate for storage of the utility vehicle and drag for dragging the courts. Bags of the court material are also kept in this structure, often a freestanding outbuilding centrally located among the courts.

CHAPTER 6
SKIING AND WINTER SPORTS

Although downhill skiing is among the slowest growing sports in recreational participation in the United States, other winter sports are among the fastest. According to the National Survey on Recreation and the Environment (NSRE) 2000, snowboarding is second only to kayaking in percentage of change. From 1994 to 2002 snowboarding went from 4.43 to 10.53 million participants, for a jump of 138 percent. Reflecting an increase based on new equipment technology, including subzero sports clothing, snowmobiling is also seeing sizable increases, rising from 6.95 in 1994 to 11.81 million participants in 2002, up 70 percent (Green, Cordell, and Stephens 2003).

Over the decades to come, downhill skiing is projected to be one of the fastest growing activities, at 93 percent growth by 2050. A major factor accounting for this expansion appears to be the strong link between skier and income and the large expected rise in real personal income over that same period (Bowker et al. 1999, pp. 323–351).

◀ Ski village. Drawing by E. Addison Young.

DOWNHILL SKIING: SITE ELEMENTS AND BASE AREA

Planning the ski base area involves organizing the arrival of the skier, whether by automobile, shuttle, or on foot. Because of the personal ski gear and equipment involved, most skiers arrive by car to a day-ski facility, therefore, parking is a major issue. With the concentration of mountain base facilities and the resulting high real estate value, structured parking, although much more expensive than surface parking, is the solution. A parking space close to the mountain is a valuable feature of a private membership ski club. A ski resort can make the mountain convenient to the guest by providing parking underground or remotely, storage for ski equipment at the base of the mountain, and shuttle transport for skiers. Ski-in and ski-out lodging of any sort is highly valued.

The essence of the ski facility is that the skier is dressed to ski and outdoor circulation is expected. Also inherent is the beautiful natural setting of the snow-covered mountains. Solar orientation comes into play when designing such facilities. Most ski slopes in the Northern Hemisphere are oriented to the North, to some degree. Therefore, base facilities looking toward the mountain have a southern orientation, receiving the sun; this orientation provides the opportunity for popular après ski sundecks.

Warm clothing and the difficulty of walking in ski boots dictate that facilities allow for quick in-and-out access for restrooms and equipment rental. Consequently, a base lodge is best planned with exterior circulation and multiple entrances to provide immediate access to needed facilities.

Skiers' Service Building

The prime location at the base of a ski mountain is assigned to the skiers' service building. In some cases it may be underground, below the skiing landing area. This building serves the immediate needs of the skier who is heading to the slopes or taking a break at the end of a run.

The skier, in general, has to buy lift tickets, possibly rent or buy gear, use restrooms, and purchase a beverage before going to the lift. The Skier Services' Building at The Village at Copper, Copper Mountain, Colorado, by OZ Architects, addresses the skier's needs. Lift ticket windows are in an open but covered area, opposite and between two lifts. Taking advantage of the sloping terrain, there is easy access to the building on two levels. One approach is past a large après ski deck and bar and lounge to lockers and rest rooms. The other approach—to a lower level but also at grade—is into a large ski shop surrounding a coffee shop. The rental equipment area flanks one wall, including ample benches for trying on gear. Lost and found and a skiers' service desk backs up to the lift ticket windows. Open stairs in the interior connect to the upper level circulation and entrance. Sidewalk cafe seating oriented to the mountain spills out from the coffee shop onto the skiers' plaza. Skiers have additional choices for food and beverage on levels above. Restaurants require a service area, and locating and screening this area is a challenge in this high-density pedestrian environment.

Other elements of the design respond to skiers' need to deal with the cumbersome gear when they want to take a break. At Copper, ski-check kiosks are

◀ Copper Station Skiers' Services Building, Copper Mountain, Colorado. Outside view of skier services building with après ski deck. OZ Architects; Intrawest Corporation, developer. Photo by Bob Bloch.

▼ Copper Station Skiers' Services Building, viewed from the skiers' plaza. Photo by Bob Bloch.

handy, but they might have been better integrated into the facility.

The Base Village

Given that some ski areas host over 20,000 skiers per day and that the average skier spends only four hours a day on the slopes, other activities may be offered. Developers, planners, and architects have recognized the opportunity and are creating mixed-use villages that cater to the skier and, incidentally, to family members who do not ski. The village is also part of many winter resort operators' efforts to become year-round destinations to level out the labor, facility, and financial aspects of their operations.

Radiating from the base of the mountain and lift stations, the village pedestrian streets are lined with bars, restaurants, retail, and offices and services such as real estate. Shopping is certainly recreation. All pedestrian area surfaces have a snow melting system, to ease walking. Other activity nodes may be created or developed such as ponds and waterways,

providing ice skating in the winter and kayaking in the summer. A rock-climbing tower creates excitement in the summer and serves as architectural sculpture in the winter. Generally, throughout the village, mid-rise housing is aboveground, and parking and services are underground.

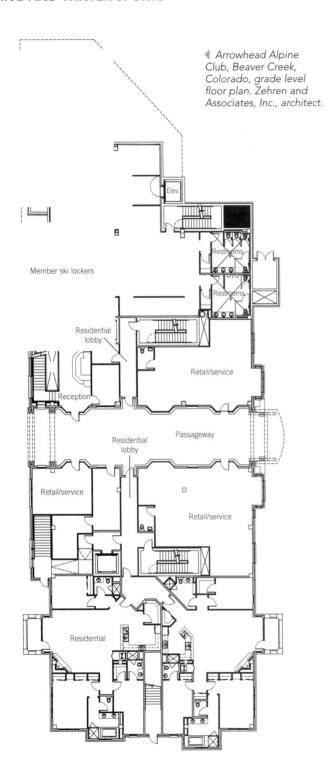

◀ *Arrowhead Alpine Club, Beaver Creek, Colorado, grade level floor plan. Zehren and Associates, Inc., architect.*

A planned village like Beaver Creek, near Vail, Colorado, caters to the resort guest as opposed to the day skier. Underground parking is provided, but it primarily serves the mid-rise residential housing and hotel. Shuttles drop off skiers, and the street path to the ski mountain is lined with the skier service elements addressed earlier. Significant changes in grade (as this is a mountain village) are addressed with exterior, covered escalators. These overcome the difficulty of stairs for people in ski boots. The discomfort of walking in ski boots shows up in other ways. At Beaver Creek, ski bridges through the village facilitate ski-in and ski-out to lodging. Ski resort planners recognize the difficulty and how far a skier will walk in boots (1,000 ft). Upscale restaurants and clubs have fleece-lined slippers available and a place to change as skiers enter. The main après ski deck at Beaver Creek has a wall lined with coin-operated boot lockers, convenient but obviously an afterthought.

The Alpine Club

The value of an Alpine Club is enhancement of the skiers' experience. Catering to the affluent skiing family, the club provides services and facilities convenient to the mountain. At Arrowhead, a ski area that is part of Beaver Creek, the alpine club is immediately adjacent to the base of the mountain and the main lift. Designed by Zehren Architects of Avon, Colorado, the building serves as a gateway to the ski area. A public passage goes through the building at grade and some skier service elements are along the covered pathway.

The club, however, is private. Members enter with a key card, and the reception

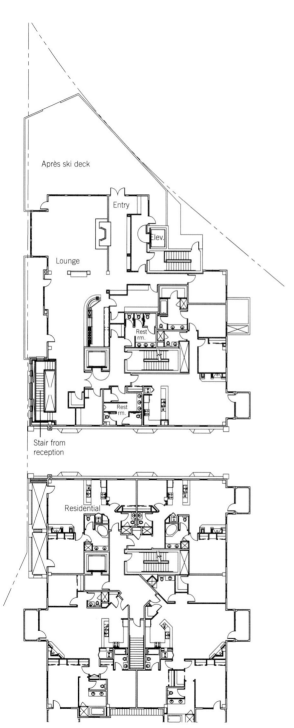

Après ski deck

Entry

Elev.

Lounge

Rest rm.

Rest rm.

Stair from reception

Residential

▲ *Arrowhead Alpine Club, view from slopeside. Photo by Zehren and Associates, Inc.*

◀ *Arrowhead Alpine Club, second level floor plan.*

area includes a concierge or receptionist. At slope side, a bar-lounge overlooks the ski area. Members who ski may also enter from the slope side and change from boots to slippers. Condominiums occupy the upper levels of the club. The lower level includes a coed locker room for ski gear. The upscale wood lockers are full height, 72 in. high and 15 in. wide.

The spa and fitness area of the club is also on the lower level. The fitness area includes cardiovascular and strength training equipment. The spa area is more secluded and provides treatment areas and men's and women's relaxation lounges, whirlpool, steamroom, and sauna. The club also includes underground parking and lockers for skis and snowboards that are convenient to the ski area.

Gondola Ski Lift Stations

Gondola ski lifts are important for two reasons. One, they have stations, or building structures, at the base and top of the lift. Two, gondolas greatly expand

▲ *Aspen Mountain gondola, Aspen, Colorado. Gondola base station exterior. Cottle, Graybeal, Yaw Architects. Photo by J. Curtis.*

▶ *Aspen Mountain gondola base station, interior view. Photo by J. Curtis.*

the use of top of the mountain and mid-mountain lodges. These facilities, equipped with gondolas, may be accessed throughout the four seasons of the year and in the evening by nonskiers.

The gondola stations themselves, like all mass transit stations, are pavilions in which a high volume of people change from a pedestrian to gondola transport mode or vice versa. Since the primary purpose is to transport the downhill skier in the winter, enclosure and screening of prevailing winds is important. Keep in mind, however, that expeditious movement of a high volume of people encumbered with ski gear is the number one priority.

As architecture, the building not only houses active people but the mechanism and movement of the equipment that powers and handles the cable. The structure is, appropriately, a focus of the base of the ski mountain; with transparency, it may provide an aesthetic view of people and machinery, a kinetic sculpture.

Mountaintop and Midmountain Lodges

Once the exclusive province of the downhill skier or snowboarder, on-mountain lodges are now able to offer their awe-inspiring vistas to the nonskier in the off-season as well. Gondola lifts direct from base to lodge have enabled these facilities to be used for special events and private parties. The on-mountain lodges still provide a midday break and lunch for the all-day skier, with inside space and sun decks with food and beverage service as well. High-speed lifts, however, have enabled the skier to do more skiing in a shorter amount of time. Coupled with the aging of the skiing population, a day of skiing today may mean a half-day on

the slopes. Après ski may begin at lunchtime at the midmountain or mountaintop lodge. The skier ultimately may decide that it is more judicious to ride the gondola down rather than ski to the base. At Aspen Mountain, Colorado, this use has led to expansion of the mountaintop facility by one-third after just a few years.

Après ski on the mountain rather than at the base means a large sun deck, but other uses impact the programming of the facility. Because the gondola is usable in virtually all weather, it may be used in the evening by those more dressed to party than to ski. The biggest use in the summer of the mountaintop restaurant at Keystone, Colorado, is for weddings

▲ *Aspen Mountain Sun Deck lounge, Aspen, Colorado, a mountainside lodge. Cottle, Graybeal, Yaw Architects. Photo by David Marlow.*

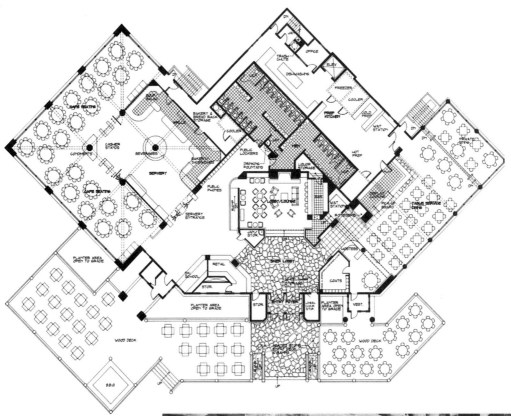

▲ Sunspot Restaurant, Winter Park Resort, Colorado, main level floor plan. Zehren and Associates, Inc., architect.

▶ Sunspot Restaurant interior, showing view orientation, scramble service area, and large table seating. Photo courtesy Winter Park Resorts.

and receptions. The indoor space of the lodge thus becomes more important, and the architect must plan views that are spectacular from the inside as well as the outside. See Chapter 12 for the principles of view-oriented dining.

The restaurant is serviced by snowcats and, to a minor degree, the gondola. The receiving area will need screening, and one cannot count on adequate landscaping. Normal concern with snow cascading from pitched roofs is compounded by the numbers of people taking part in activities around the building.

Schaffer's Camp mountaintop lodge, as part of Tahoe Mountain, is accessible only to skiers. It is, however, one of the many structures of sustainable design in East-West Partner's redevelopment of the Tahoe Mountain ski facilities.

Après Ski
Fulfilling the tradition of camaraderie and refreshment after a challenging sport, après ski is a big attraction for skiers and snowboarders. Meeting this need takes

▼ Schaffer's Camp, Tahoe Mountain Resort, Truckee, California, main level floor plan. Faulkner Architects.

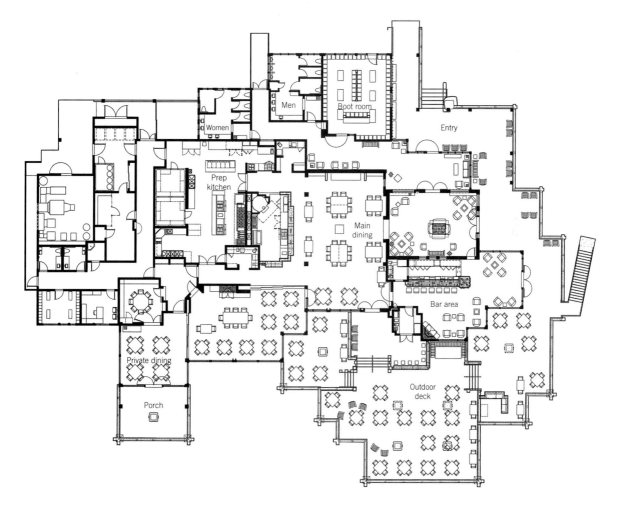

▶ Schaffer's Camp perspective sketch of mountaintop lodge, showing skiers' deck. Rendering by Faulkner Architects.

some planning and the commitment of valuable real estate. Since the ski trails on the mountain demand northern exposure, a structure at the base looking at the mountain orients to the south, or in the Northern Hemisphere, to the sun. Assuming that après ski starts in the afternoon and continues into early evening, the ideal après ski setting is a large deck that allows many participants to gather, a sun pocket with winter sun angles throughout the afternoon, a view of skiers and snowboarders finishing their run, and an easy walk in snow boots. Also essential is beverage and light food service.

Consider also the competition for this space. At one time at Aspen Mountain in Colorado, a huge, highly active, après ski deck occupied the area right at the base of the ski slopes. Currently this site is the location of the highly successful Little Nell Hotel, positioned for ski-in and ski-out for its affluent guests at this prime mountain in this highly recognized com-

munity. The locals and the repeat skiers realize that the ski experience has suffered; there is now no great après ski deck at the base of Aspen Mountain. Recognizing the shortcoming, after many years, an area has been targeted east of the existing base of the slopes to re-create such an amenity.

CROSS-COUNTRY SKIING

Nationally, participation in cross-country skiing is expected to increase by 95 percent by the year 2050. This is one of the faster-growing outdoor recreational activities, well exceeding projected population growth. The Rocky Mountain region will have the largest rise in participation, at some 144 percent. Growth in cross-country skiing may be attributed to technology; clothing and equipment designed for the sport; fitness consciousness, as it provides a demanding and complete body workout; and projected growth in personal income (Bowker et al. 1999, p. 327).

Nordic centers

Nordic centers serve as base of operations for the cross-country skier. As access to trails becomes more difficult, joint use of venues may be the answer. In Aspen, Colorado, the Aspen Golf Club is a golf clubhouse in the late spring, summer, and early fall. From November through April, however, the clubhouse becomes a Nordic center. The use is transformed; the golf shop becomes a ski shop, with a total transformation of merchandise to skis, boots, and appropriate clothing. Ski trails are created on the golf course. In use of the clubhouse, the skier with skis replicates much of the circulation pattern of the golfer with a golf bag. Upon arrival skis are stacked in what was the bag drop and cart staging area. The skier

checks in at the ski shop and goes to grade-level, where day lockers are available. An area is provided with easy access to the trails to prepare ski gear.

Following skiing, après ski may function much as the 19th hole for golf. The bar-lounge and grill adjoin a deck overlooking the open space and mountains.

An additional feature of this municipal facility is the junior clubhouse, which serves those under 16 for cross-country skiing and golf. It was adapted from the original interim clubhouse.

One vestige of golf in the clubhouse in the winter is the area planned for indoor golf hitting stations, used for practice and learning. The golfer will hit into nets, but adequate height, 12 ft of clear space, was built into the lower level.

▼ Aspen Golf/Tennis and Nordic Facility, Aspen, Colorado, site plan. Charles Cunniffe Architects.

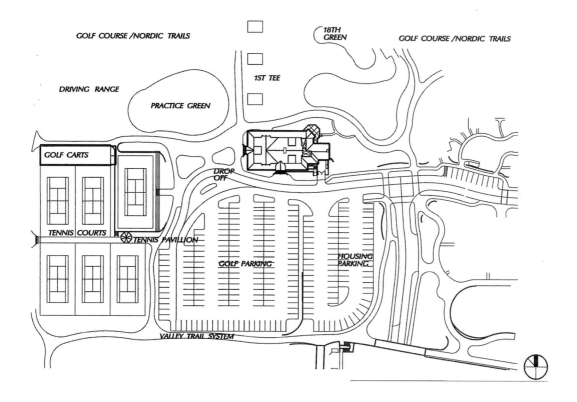

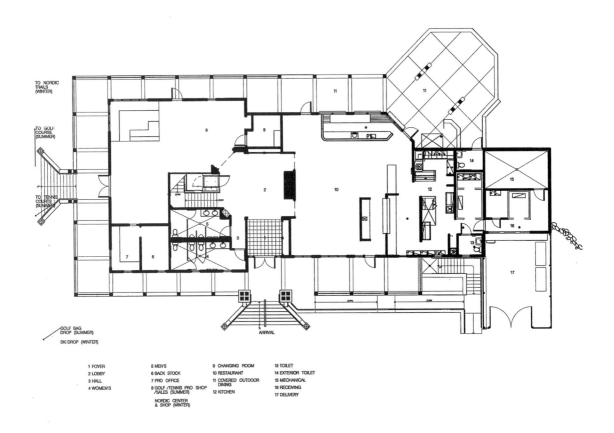

TO NORDIC
TRAILS
(WINTER)

TO GOLF
COURSE
(SUMMER)

TO TENNIS
COURTS
(SUMMER)

GOLF BAG
DROP (SUMMER)

SKI DROP (WINTER)

ARRIVAL

1 FOYER	5 MEN'S	9 CHANGING ROOM	13 TOILET
2 LOBBY	6 BACK STOCK	10 RESTAURANT	14 EXTERIOR TOILET
3 HALL	7 PRO OFFICE	11 COVERED OUTDOOR DINING	15 MECHANICAL
4 WOMEN'S	8 GOLF /TENNIS PRO SHOP /SALES (SUMMER)	12 KITCHEN	16 RECEIVING
	NORDIC CENTER & SHOP (WINTER)		17 DELIVERY

⌃ Aspen Golf/Tennis and Nordic
Facility, main level floor plan.

⌄ Aspen Golf/Tennis and Nordic
Facility, lower level floor plan.

▶ Aspen Golf/Tennis and Nordic
Facility, winter view from the approach
side of building. Photo by Steve
Mundinger.

▶▶ Aspen Golf/Tennis and Nordic
Facility, summer view of the golf side.
Photo by Steve Mundinger.

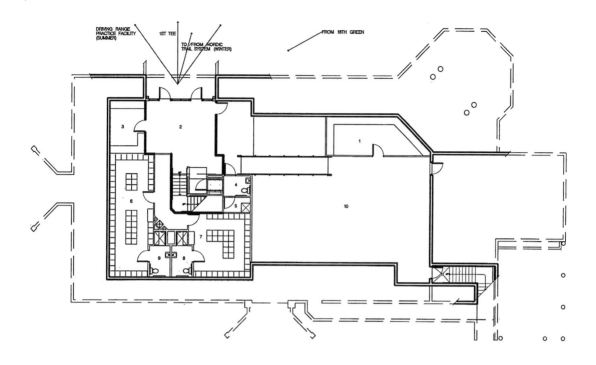

DRIVING RANGE
PRACTICE FACILITY
(SUMMER)

1ST TEE

TO /FROM NORDIC
TRAIL SYSTEM (WINTER)

FROM 18TH GREEN

1 RESTAURANT STORAGE
2 WORK AREA
3 CLUB REPAIR ROOM
4 WATERCLOSET
5 JANITOR ROOM

6 MEN'S LOCKERS
7 WOMEN'S LOCKERS
8 TOILET /SHOWERS
9 TOILET /SHOWERS
10 GOLF INDOOR PRACTICE FACILITY

GOLF /SUMMER
NORDIC /WINTER

HELI-SKI LODGE

Reflective of the search for the unique experience by the avid and affluent sportsman, heli-ski lodges are being created in remote areas. The lodge serves as a base for the skier who will be dropped from a helicopter into pristine areas of ideal snow for skiing. The adventurer then skis back to the lodge.

The LaBlond Partnership Architects & Planners in Calgary, Alberta, designed the Monashee Lodge in Mica Creek, British Columbia. The lodge serves as a heli-lodge in ski season; but it is one of the few of its kind accessible by road. This accessibility allows the lodge to support year-round activities. The structure consists of three levels plus a roof-top spa with sauna, steam, outdoor pool, and fireplace. Guests may relax in a spalike environ-

ment in a snow setting that provides vistas of the peaks surrounding the lodge.

The entry level of the building reaches the main social areas, such as the great hall, dining room, and kitchen areas. With the flat roof, large overhangs, and double-height spaces in the dining room, the dressed, heavy timber structure defines spaces with a vision and scale in sympathy with the grandeur of its surroundings. The roof structure is designed to support the year's entire snow load of 200 lbs per sq ft or 8 ft of snow pack. The lodge has a total of 72 suites, 48 guest suites, and 24 staff accommodations. The lower level includes a multipurpose meeting room, a business center, and a fitness area. For an additional example of a heli-ski lodge, see Chapter 8.

▼ Monashee Lodge, Monashees, British Columbia, a heli-ski lodge. LeBlond Partnership, architect.

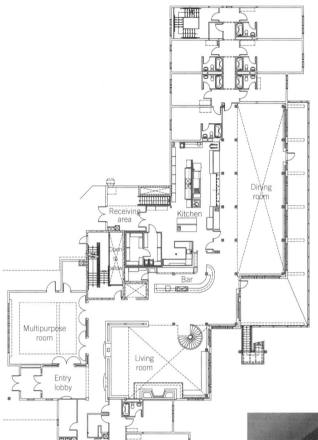

◀ Monashee Lodge, main level floor plan. LeBlond Partnership, architect.

▼ Interior of Monashee Lodge, showing view orientation and the timber structure that supports the flat roof snow load. LeBlond Partnership, architect.

▲ Northstar Village, Tahoe Mountain Resort, Truckee, California. Ice rink with retractable roof at skiers' plaza. OZ Architects.

ICE RINKS

Ice rinks are a natural supplement to snow skiing. Indoor rink surfaces are easier to maintain in any weather, but they do not offer the enchantment of an outdoor rink. At the planned, new Northstar Village at Tahoe Mountain, California, the ice rink is a focus of the village. It uses a retractable fabric roof to cover or uncover the rink.

The structure, designed by OZ Architects of Boulder, Colorado, is part of the new ski village, which was planned and designed by the same architects. The ice rink is wrapped on one side by the skiers' service building, which is under the land-

ing area at the base of the ski slopes. The rink's remaining perimeter is surrounded by retail. Lodging overlooks the rink.

The rink is roofed by a vaulted structure. The low, arched metal skeleton remains fixed at all times. Fabric roof panels within the frame roll up or down depending on the degree of cover desired. Even closed, the fabric is translucent to natural light.

The skiers' service building floor plans show the value of tucking this building under the landing area. All services address the skier as one approaches, and then escalators take him or her to the lift when ready. Lift

▲ Northstar Village ice rink, with fabric roof open.

▶ Northstar Village ice rink, with fabric roof closed.

▼ Northstar Village, site plan.

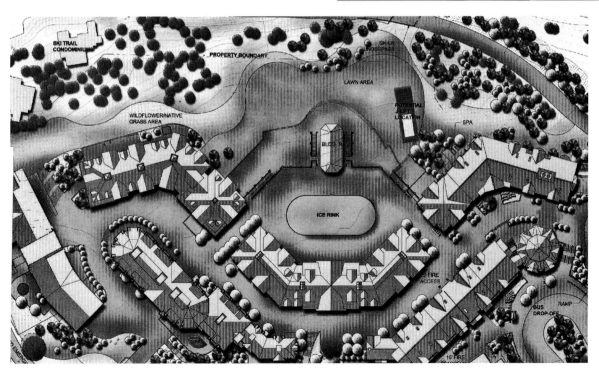

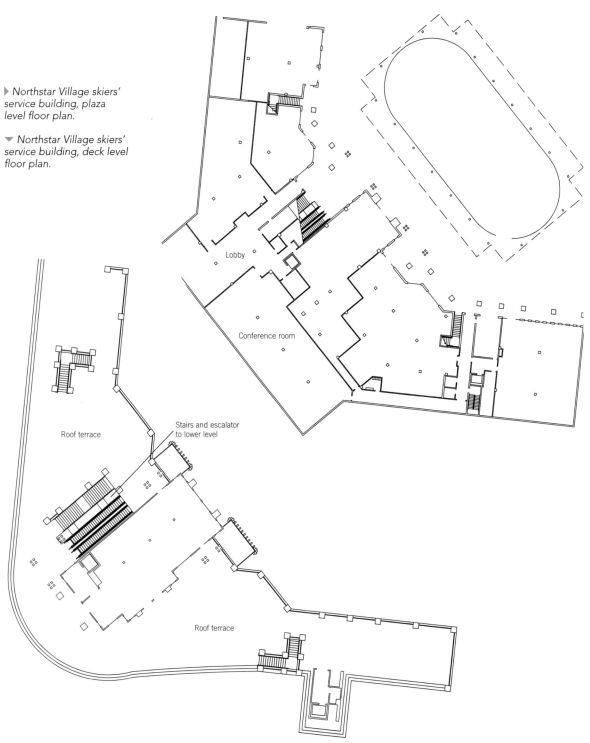

▶ *Northstar Village skiers'
service building, plaza
level floor plan.*

▼ *Northstar Village skiers'
service building, deck level
floor plan.*

Lobby

Conference room

Roof terrace

Stairs and escalator
to lower level

Roof terrace

tickets, day care, and ski clothing and gear—for sale or rent—are handy, as well as lockers and restrooms. A restaurant is below, but beverages are available at the ski pub where the action is, at the top of the escalator and overlooking the ski area.

The Alpine Club is located in the adjacent building complex.

All buildings at the Northstar Village reconstruction are based in sustainable design. The developer, East-West Partners, is dedicated to all buildings qualifying for Leadership in Energy and

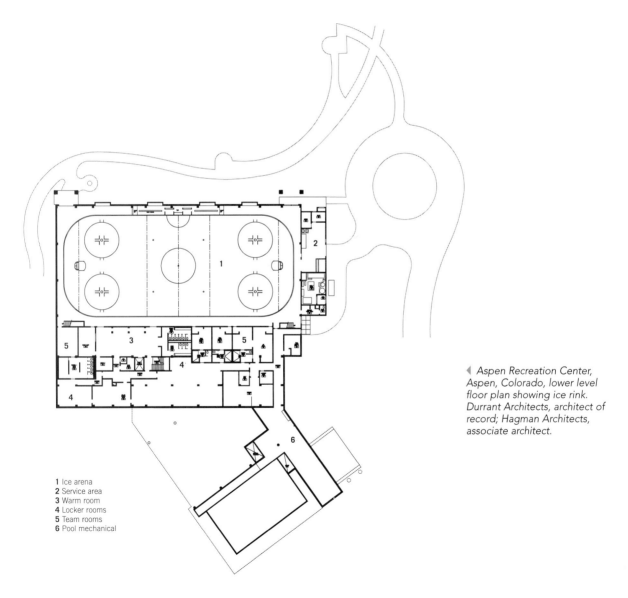

◀ Aspen Recreation Center, Aspen, Colorado, lower level floor plan showing ice rink. Durrant Architects, architect of record; Hagman Architects, associate architect.

1 Ice arena
2 Service area
3 Warm room
4 Locker rooms
5 Team rooms
6 Pool mechanical

▶ *Aspen Recreation Center, Aspen, Colorado, interior view of ice rink. Photo by Timothy Hursley.*

Environmental Design (LEED) certification. See Chapter 14. East-West Partners has found that the premium in capital cost for sustainable design is less than 5 percent. It is felt that additional costs will be more than offset by lower operating costs and the advantage of demonstrating environmental sensitivity in the marketplace.

Aspen Recreation Center

Another indoor sport venue at the Aspen Recreation Center is a regulation hockey–sized ice rink. Used for competitive and casual recreational skating, the rink is supported by team rooms and locker rooms. A warm room serves all skaters.

CHAPTER 7
EQUESTRIAN FACILITIES

Although horse riding groups claim that trails for riding are becoming scarce, activity days in horseback riding are projected to grow significantly faster than the population by 2050 (Bowker et al. 1999, p. 339). The projected gains are based on a substantial rise in real income and the means for enthusiasts to support equestrian activities.

Facilities addressed in this book are those basic structures needed by the recreational riding segment of the industry and does not include the professional segments, which include racing, showing, polo, farm work, rodeos, and police work.

Equestrian facilities are about housing horses. The many breeds of horses have different appeal and are trained to do different things. This chapter, however, will focus on the basic elements needed to house and care for the animal.

SITE ELEMENTS
Planning for equestrian facilities involves consideration of both natural ventilation and fire protection.

Ventilation
Effective ventilation, preferably natural, is essential in a stable. Consider that the average 1,000 lb horse passes 2.4 gal of

◄ Conceptual sketch of stable and paddock. Drawing by E. Addison Young.

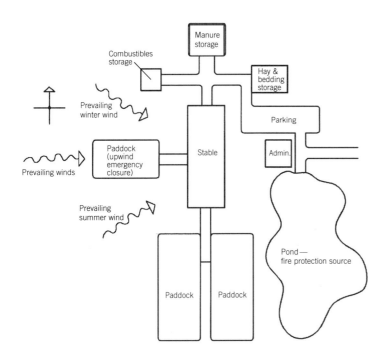

Combustibles storage

Manure storage

Hay & bedding storage

Prevailing winter wind

Parking

Prevailing winds

Paddock (upwind emergency closure)

Stable

Admin.

Prevailing summer wind

Pond— fire protection source

Paddock

Paddock

▲ *Prototypical stable site plan. Diedrich, LLC.*

urine and 31 lbs of feces daily. In addition, the horse naturally hangs its head to feed, and head down is its normal posture. Therefore, hygiene demands that the stable and stall itself be well ventilated and easily cleaned (Wheeler 2003).

In considering ventilation, recognize that the comfort level of the horse is a much broader range than that of humans. A temperature range of 45–75° is most comfortable for housing horses. During winter, however, horse stables should be kept no more than 5–10° warmer than the outside temperature (Wheeler 2003). The most direct approach for ventilating of a stable is a combination of eave vents and an open volume underroof area exhausted by a ridge vent. Ridge vents may be continuous prefabricated, clerestory, or cupolas. Other design approaches may be even

more effective in generating ventilation within the stall. Barred gates open the stall to the aisle. Barred areas within the partitions separating stalls are effective for ventilation, interest, and contentment of the naturally sociable horse.

The stable exterior wall is an opportunity for direct and indirect ventilation at the stall level. A shuttered window may be open in comfortable or warm weather and closed in extreme temperatures. The wall itself may also sustain ventilation. Wood board sheathing, whether horizontal or vertical, inherently has spaces between the boards that provide natural ventilation.

Fire Protection

Fire is a major hazard in equestrian buildings. Hay used for bedding and forage is an easily ignited fuel. Of additional concern, baled or piled hay may support internal combustion. Also, buildings housing horses most commonly are of wood, although heavy timber has a degree of fire resistance. Stables need to be naturally well ventilated; however, such ventilation supports the rapid spread of flames (Zajaczkowski and Wheeler 2001a).

Planning considerations

A direct means of fire protection is to store hay and flammable materials in a separate building from the stable. Although straw may be used for bedding in a stall, the concern for internal combustion in stored quantities is limited to the storage building itself.

Other aspects of fire protection in planning include access for fire trucks and a water source for hydrants or a pond for a pumper truck or sprinkler system. Stable gates should swing out or easily slide, allowing the horse to be led quickly to the outside or an aisle with two exits. Ideally, exits should lead directly to a paddock upwind from the stable where the horse may be contained but distanced from a fire.

In an extensive facility, a fire protection engineer should be on the design team.

Fire protections systems

Smoke and flame detectors as early warning devices are an essential part of fire protection in an equestrian facility. Keep in mind that the spaces, however, are unconditioned and especially subject to dust, which may hamper the operation of most generic smoke detectors. Thermal detectors identify heat or flame, and may be more effective in the harsh barn environment.

Automatic sprinkler systems are an option, but unconditioned buildings necessitate a dry pipe system in most regions. An additional concern is adequate water pressure, which may require a fire pump in rural areas.

Lightning protection

All barns, recognizing the often open rural setting, should have a professionally installed and properly grounded lightning protection system.

Materials

Fire retardant or resistive materials, such as masonry, heavy timber, or fire-retardant treated wood, contribute to a fire-resistive structure. Because of their durable but somewhat resilient characteristics, wood partitions are a preferred choice in the typical horse stall. Treated wood products will also withstand humid or moisture-laden conditions. Fire retardant materials, however, may not be safe for horses that nibble or for extended contact with foals. Cap all wood edges with metal. Use fire retardant wood impregnated with chemicals that bond directly with the wood and will not leach out (Zajaczkowski and Wheeler 2001a).

Check local codes for agricultural buildings. Wiring is best housed in polyvinyl chloride (PVC) piping for protection from humidity and rodent proofing. Lighting fixtures and fans should be selected for agricultural use. ABC type fire extinguishers should be located every 50 ft in a stable (Zajaczkowski and Wheeler 2001a).

The Stall

Since the stall is the basic unit housing a horse, it is essential that it be sized correctly and provide a healthy environment. A 12' x 12' stall is recommended for an average 1,000 lb horse. The stall wall should be 1½ times the horse's length but not less than 10'. The separating partition should be 8' high, but a

▼ *Lady Jean Ranch, Jupiter, Florida. Stable interior from above. Photo by Darryl Larson.*

horses. Wood shavings also reduce the amount of bedding that needs to be disposed of. The challenge in the flooring is to find a surface that is durable but comfortable for the standing horse and easily cleaned.

Washing and grooming stalls

The horse is accompanied and restrained in the wash stall so the aisle wall may be open. All surfaces should be masonry or concrete and finished as for a high-moisture area. The concrete floor should be a non-slip surface and sloped toward a cleanable sediment drain. The typical horse wash stall is in the same module as the stall itself.

Tack room

Equipment, like saddles and blankets, needed for horseback riding is stored in the tack room. The basic fixture is a large bracket—3 ft on center—to support a saddle. If boarding of horses is a primary business, however, secure, private lockers are required for tack even in an upscale facility. Lockers need to be 36" wide, 48" deep, and full height.

The Grand Cypress Resort Equestrian Center

The Grand Cypress Resort Equestrian Center, Lake Buena Vista, Florida, provides recreational horseback riding for resort guests and local area residents. The guest arrives at a clubhouse building that houses a pro-shoplike reception area, with a tack and gift shop. Locker rooms, administration, and light fare and beverages are available in this facility.

The 44-stall barn is the center of the facility. It is coupled with a lighted and covered 20,000 sq ft arena. The equestrian setting of the arena and stables is used for themed receptions and dinners.

barred opening may be used for the upper 3–4' for ventilation.

The bars need to be of 1" diameter pipe that is not more than 3" apart. Partitions are commonly 2" thick tongue-and-grove plank, or ¾" minimum plywood. Prefabricated stall doors on the interior aisles are typically about 7' high with a 42–45" width.

Hardware should be heavy duty and free of sharp edges and projections. Open attic space is preferable for ventilation, and the lowest structural member overhead should not be less than 10' (Zajaczkowski and Wheeler 2001b).

Opinions vary on the best floor, material preferences range from compacted clay or road base with hay bedding to concrete with rubber mats. Wood shavings are another often used surface material, which is equivalent to "kitty litter" for

St. Mary of the Woods College Equestrian Facility

St. Mary of the Woods College, near Terre Haute, Indiana, has three degree programs in equine studies. The equine facility is expanded from an existing barn to form a courtyard as a teaching and exercise area.

The new stable has 31 stalls and a central area with wash and grooming stalls, a tack area, and tack-ready staging area.

▼ St. Mary of the Woods College, Terre Haute, Indiana, equestrian facility exterior. MMS A/E, Inc., architect.

▶ St. Mary of the Woods College stable, through-building section.

▼ St Mary of the Woods College equestrian facility floor plan.

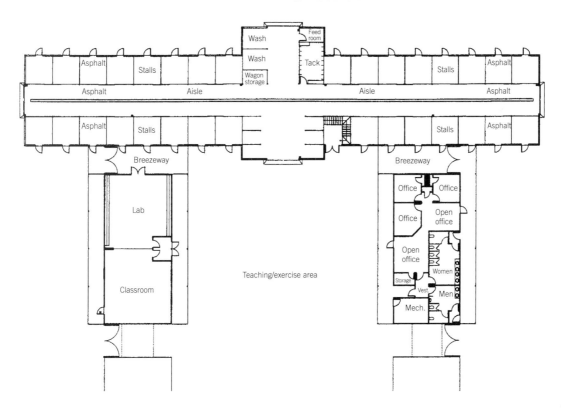

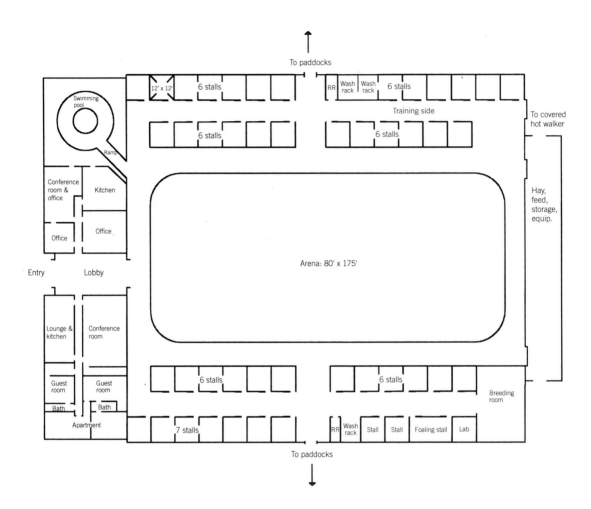

To paddocks

12' x 12' 6 stalls   RR Wash rack Wash rack 6 stalls

Training side

To covered hot walker

Swimming pool

Ramp

6 stalls   6 stalls

Conference room & office   Kitchen

Office   Office

Entry   Lobby

Arena: 80' x 175'

Hay, feed, storage, equip.

Lounge & kitchen   Conference room

Guest room   Guest room

Bath   Bath

Apartment

6 stalls   6 stalls

Breeding room

7 stalls   RR Wash rack Stall Stall Foaling stall Lab

To paddocks

▲ Talaria Farms, Newnan, Georgia, stable and indoor arena floor plan.

One wing houses the Equine Department administrative offices and restrooms for the complex. The other wing includes a classroom and laboratory for equine studies.

Talaria Farms

At Talaria Farms, Newnan, Georgia, an indoor ring is the heart of the equine recreational facility. Because the ring is on axis with the main lobby, equine activity in the ring may be seen upon entering the facility. A private dining room with catering kitchen and the general manager's office flank the lobby and overlook the ring. The emphasis at Talaria is on Arabian horses, recognized among the horse set for their naturally smooth gait and beauty. As with other breeds, the horses are the focus of social activity for devotees of the breed. The central enclosed ring supports that interaction with events held for showing of horses. A tented bar is set up with dancing in the arena and tables in the surrounding aisles to seat up to 500.

The concept also recognizes the sociable nature of horses. A double row of stalls is on either side of the arena. The entire upper side of the stalls is made from open, barred partitions. The horses are alert to the activity in the arena as well as that of their neighbors.

The main barn is a preengineered metal building, and the rows of 12 ft x 12 ft stalls set up a module on either side of the clear spanned arena. Interspersed within the module are the support areas, such as wash stalls, tack rooms, and storage. Main aisles and cross aisles end in large openings typically open for ventilation but sealable with overhead doors. Stalls have easily opening sliding doors, leading to aisles and cross aisles for two exits in case of fire.

Stall partitions are pine planks below the barred area. The openness of the barred area also facilitates ventilation. Floors are compacted clay with pine shavings as bedding. Concrete floors with mats are not used because of the chance of the horse scraping its hocks, which is unacceptable for a show horse like an Arabian. Wash stalls are cast-in-place concrete, with hot and cold water provided. Storage of wash and grooming supplies is required.

One corner has an equine conditioning pool. The horse enters via a ramp into a circular ring of water. The resistance of the still water in the pool provides exercise and therapy.

Another corner houses the breeding facility. At Talaria Farms, breeding is normally by artificial insemination. The sire and the mare participate in every way short of natural cover. A laboratory for the veterinarian is adjacent.

Bay Harbor Equestrian Club

The Equestrian Club is an amenity for the Bay Harbor recreational community

▼ *Bay Harbor Equestrian Club, Bay Harbor, Michigan, exterior view. David V. Johnson Development, developer. Photo by Bay Harbor Company.*

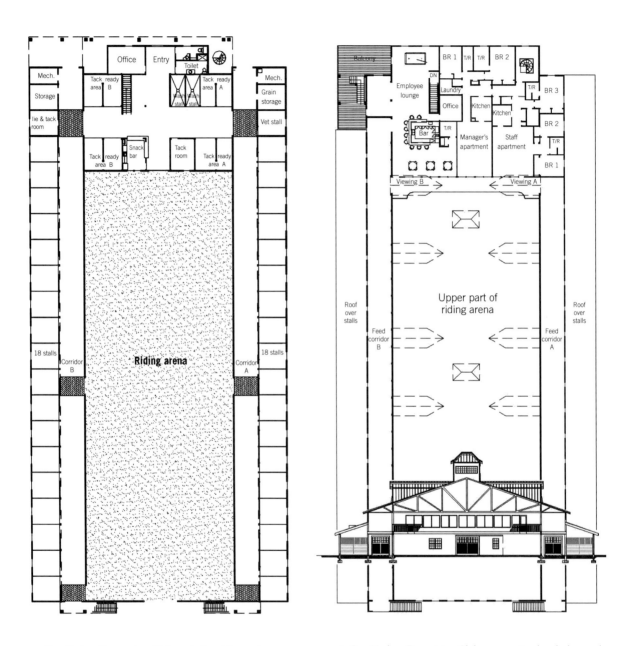

▲ Bay Harbor Equestrian Club, main level floor plan of stables and enclosed riding arena.

▲ Bay Harbor Equestrian Club, mezzanine level plan and through-building section.

on Lake Michigan in Michigan. Developed by the Victor International Corporation, the community won an Award for Excellence in 2003 from the Urban Land Institute. The concept for the 42,000 sq ft structure wraps 36 stalls with matted floors on two sides of a large heated arena. The stalls are one story with a sloping roof, and the arena is two stories with a mezzanine wrapping around three sides. The complex is anchored at one end with two stories of support spaces. Administration, restrooms, a snack bar, wash and grooming stalls, and tack spaces are on the main level. Upstairs are staff housing and a members' bar and lounge, which has balconies overlooking the arena and outside. The mezzanines flanking the arena act as feed corridors to the stalls from above but also provide spectator space for the arena.

CHAPTER 8
EXTREME SPORTS

For the younger generation, recreation may be on the edge. What are now called extreme sports—skateboarding, BMX bikes, in-line skating, and snowboarding—are coupled with rock climbing and white-water kayaking to challenge the more adventuresome.

To date, there is little expression of these sports through architecture. As these activities become more mainstream and see increases in the number of participants, the entertainment value of these sports will lead to construction of buildings designed to house them. Currently, most skateboard parks are outside or, if indoors, are in unfinished retail or warehouse space. The focus of extreme sport site design is on the course and the activity itself. Initial concepts using different approaches, however, are coming to light.

EXTREME SPORTS PARTICIPATION*	
Activity	Participants (thousands)
In-line skating	29,024
Mountain biking	16,988
Skateboarding	11,649
Snowboarding	7,151
Paintball	7,121
Artificial wall climbing	6,117
Train running	5,232
BMX biking	3,977
Wakeboarding	3,581
Roller hockey	3,287
Street hockey	2,448
Mountain/rock climbing	1,947

*Figures from Fitness News Service, Inc., 2002.

◀ Conceptual sketch of a skate park. Drawing by E. Addison Young.

INDOOR EXTREME SPORTS

Of the extreme sports, those that are already housed in buildings include:

- *Skate parks:* Although supporting skateboarders, BMX bikers, and in-line skaters, the impetus behind generation of these venues is the skateboarder.
- *Climbing walls:* A feature in new municipal recreation centers, YMCAs, and commercial sports and outdoor equipment stores, these elements bring the outdoor sport of rock climbing indoors.
- *Multiuse adventure parks:* These buildings house recreational "streets" or skateparks, climbing walls, and indoor streams for kayaking; they are intended to be interesting to the casual spectator as well as the participant. The facility may also house more traditional but complementary elements, such as an ice rink and a health and fitness club.

The Louisville X-treme Park

Recognizing that their citizens active in these sports are as deserving of facilities as residents playing tennis, golfing, or swimming, Louisville, Kentucky, developed a municipal skateboard park. The cast-in-place concrete "street" has become a bas-relief architectural sculpture in a city block. Designed by landscape architect Zach Wormhoudt of Santa Cruz, California, who specializes in planning and design of skateboard parks, the course is 40,000 sq ft of skating surface, with seven bowls, a 24 ft full pipe, and a

▼ Louisville X-treme Park, Louisville, Kentucky, aerial perspective. Jack Wormhoudt, landscape architect and skate-park designer; Stanley Saitowicz, phase II building (concept only; unbuilt), architect. Rendering by Jeff Moneypenny.

112

◀ Louisville X-treme Park interior perspective. Rendering by Jeff Moneypenny.

▼ Aspen Recreation Center, Aspen, Colorado, view of climbing wall. Durrant Architects, architect of record; Hagman Architects, associate architect. Photo by Timothy Hursley.

vertical (vert) ramp. In addition, as part of the master plan, architect Stanley Saitowitz of San Francisco has designed a building that flows from the course and completes the venue. The course continues on the roof of the building, connected to the rest of the "street" at grade by a long ramp. Spectator space, concessions, and restrooms would be housed in the building. The City uses warning signs and the absence of site staff to avoid liability for the risk of the sport.

Climbing Walls

Climbing walls are a universal challenge. For the architect, they often are a multistory architectural sculpture acting as a focus in a recreational setting. At the Aspen Recreational Center in Aspen, Colorado, the climbing wall anchors the public space of the facility, linking the two main levels within the spiral stair

▲ Livonia Community Recreation Center, Livonia, Michigan, view of climbing wall. Neumann/ Smith Architects & Associates; Barker, Rinker, Seacat Architecture. Photo by Justin Maconochie.

common to ski resort communities, such as how to become a year-round destination so that the facilities and service industries that support the thousands of skiers are needed to serve visitors in the spring, summer, and fall. Another issue is how to entertain that skier who, on average, only spends four hours on the slopes. Family members who may not ski need also be accommodated in program planning.

As envisioned by Zehren Architects of Avon, Colorado, and the Denver office of EDAW, Planners, the concept creates the Vail "X-stream" Adventure Park as part of a 50,000 sq ft mixed-use space. The center would feature the action sport space aligned along the street, in front of the existing parking structure. The Vail X-stream would be a three-story transparent indoor adventure center that would include a flexible BMX, skateboard, and in-line skate street course, and a pair of hydraulics for kayak playboating. Climbing walls would be integrated into the action sport venue. The street would be glazed along its length, with vistas of the mountains from the inside. Equally exciting would be the view into the adventure park, especially at night. The mixed-use center would incorporate a hockey-size sheet of ice and a fitness gymnasium. Also included would be a large banquet function space and meeting rooms.

The adventure space would introduce winter visitors to the activities that Vail offers in other seasons, for example, white-water kayaking, mountain biking, and rock climbing. It would be a center of activity in all seasons and serve as an alternative sporting venue for skiers, snowboarders, and their families in the winter.

well. The climbing wall at the Livonia Community Recreation Center, Livonia, Michigan, lines the indoor pedestrian street.

Vail X-Stream Adventure Park

In Vail, Colorado, the town sponsored a planning and design charette to consider ideas to activate the part of town adjacent to a parking deck that was primarily used by skiers. The concept, although not yet built, addresses issues that are

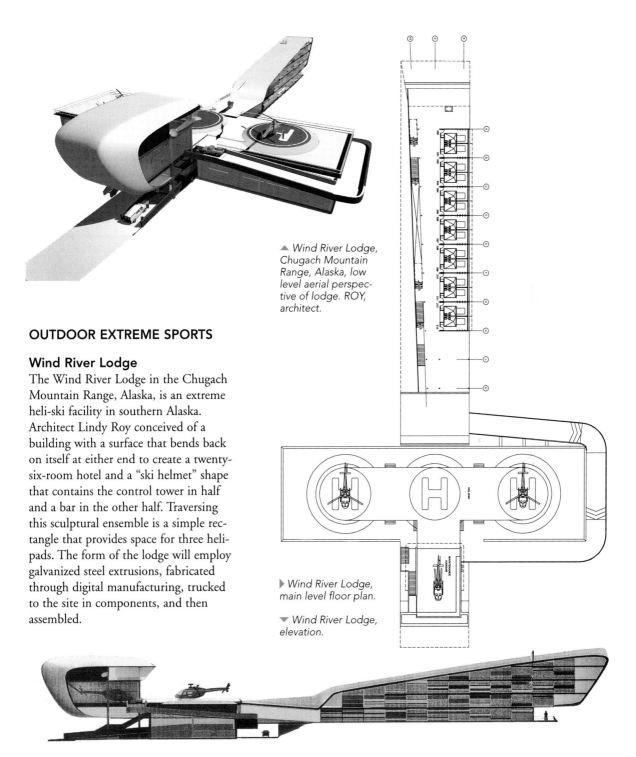

▲ *Wind River Lodge, Chugach Mountain Range, Alaska, low level aerial perspective of lodge. ROY, architect.*

OUTDOOR EXTREME SPORTS

Wind River Lodge

The Wind River Lodge in the Chugach Mountain Range, Alaska, is an extreme heli-ski facility in southern Alaska. Architect Lindy Roy conceived of a building with a surface that bends back on itself at either end to create a twenty-six-room hotel and a "ski helmet" shape that contains the control tower in half and a bar in the other half. Traversing this sculptural ensemble is a simple rectangle that provides space for three helipads. The form of the lodge will employ galvanized steel extrusions, fabricated through digital manufacturing, trucked to the site in components, and then assembled.

▶ *Wind River Lodge, main level floor plan.*

▼ *Wind River Lodge, elevation.*

TRENDS IN INDOOR RECREATIONAL SPORTS

Beyond the state of the art and cutting edge concepts in this book, one may look to New Zealand or Anaheim, California, for the direction of future indoor recreation facilities.

In New Zealand, Action Sports Indoor Stadiums runs thirteen multisport arenas, housing "social sports." Amateur teams are created and compete in indoor soccer, cricket, sandball (beach volleyball), and netball (volleyball). Sporting events take place concurrently in the arena to generate an atmosphere of activity and excitement.

The Anaheim city council, in late 1998, approved the first indoor snowboard and surf park in the United States. The 435,000 sq ft facility would house two snowboard pipelines, a snowboard terrain park, a beginner ski and snowboard learning area, and a free-skating rink. The surf park would have six stationary wave pools. Also included would be retail, food and beverage concessions, a fitness center, birthday suites, and a children's snow-play area. A planned indoor and outdoor skate park was replaced by a 42,000 sq ft surfing park when an indoor skate park was built nearby.

The largest indoor rock-climbing surface in the U.S. would be 75 ft high with 18,000 sq ft of climbing surface. Although approved by the city of Anaheim, the project, as of this writing, is stalled. Just as water parks have gone indoors, however, other recreational activities will not be limited by their geography or climate in the future.

FITNESS AND SPA FACILITIES

CHAPTER 9
FITNESS AND WELLNESS

Fitness is the most popular indoor physical activity today.[1] In response to a recent survey, 47.2 percent, or 97.8 million, Americans report regularly visiting a fitness club or exercising at least three times a week (NSRE 2002). Based on the increasing numbers of baby boomers facing the infirmities of aging, the trend is projected to accelerate until 2010.

[1]Community Preferences Study, America LIVES in cooperation with InterCommunications Inc., Carmel Valley, Calif., 1999.

Fitness facilities take on different configurations based on their position in the marketplace. Also called sports clubs or wellness centers, the physical training facility may be a:

- Commercial venture
- Private club (part of a country club, city club, or yacht club)
- Resort amenity (often connected to a spa)
- Hotel guest facility (a necessity)
- Hospital and extended care therapeutic center

▼ *Sun City Hilton Head Fitness Center, Beaufort, South Carolina. Diedrich Architects. Drawing by E. Addison Young.*

University of Massachusetts, Lowell, Campus Recreation Center, approach view. Architectural Resources Cambridge, Inc., architect. Photo by Warren Patterson.

University of Massachusetts, Lowell, Campus Recreation Center, first floor plan.

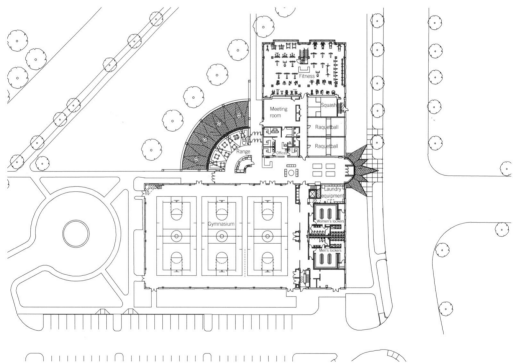

- Recreational community amenity
- Retirement and active adult community amenity
- Destination spa
- University campus recreation facility
- Church family center

In fact, second-home communities that position themselves as gathering places for multigenerational families look at fitness facilities as an amenity for the range of generations. Westin Hotels has determined through a study by Lieberman Research Worldwide that "69% of trav-

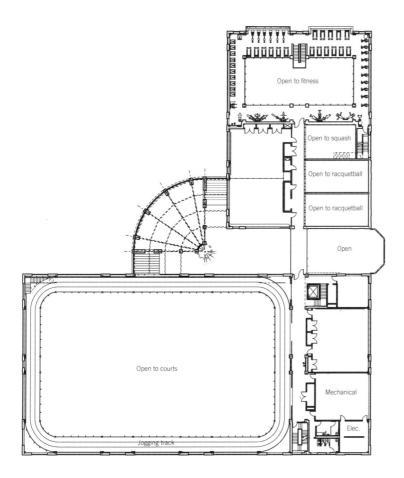

Within the floor plan:

Open to fitness

Open to squash

Open to racquetball

Open to racquetball

Open

Open to courts

Jogging track

Mechanical

Elec.

◀ *University of Massachusetts, Lowell, Campus Recreation Center, second floor plan.*

elers would favor a hotel with a good gym in considering where to stay" (Binkley 2003b).

The essence of a fitness facility is human energy. Communicating that energy for youth, or "hard bodies," suggests a transparency to the exercise floor of the facility. Openness is achieved by using a glass wall on the approach side whether that approach is from the exterior or from a circulation area to an interior space.

Other clientele getting in shape may prefer a more private facility.

ARRIVAL AND RECEPTION

As the emphasis of the facility is on physical activity, the reception area is often open to exercise areas, whether the weight and strength area or a cardio-theater. Although an aerobics area may also thrive with activity, the acoustic separation is a concern because of the rhythmic music accompanying most classes. Aerobics also demands wall space for mirrors and equipment storage.

The arrival area of a fitness facility focuses on a control desk. For members or transient guests, it is the place to check in

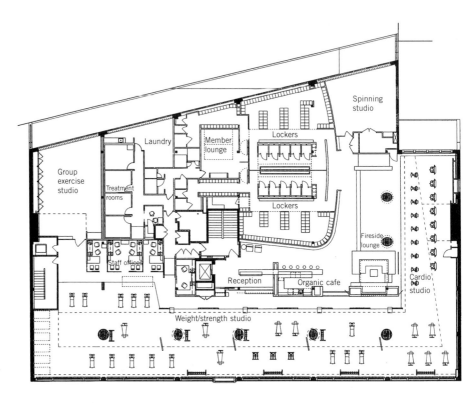

▶ *Clay Fitness Center,
New York City, floor plan.
Studios Architecture.*

and, if a day locker is needed, the place to get the key. The size of the reception area is a function of the volume of users of the fitness center. Desk functions include making appointments by phone or in person for personal trainers or physical exams, checking credentials, and dispensing and collecting keys. An important function may be dealing with towels. Every participant in the fitness center needs a sweat towel. The towel may be supplied by the facility. In that case, towels would not only be passed out at the check-in but used towels would be returned as the user leaves. If there are retail sales in the facility, the desk may serve as a point of sale and cash/wrap. Merchandise may include equipment and workout togs. The latter is especially true

in a resort, where logo-ware soft goods are in demand to commemorate the visit.

The reception area also includes the juice bar or health food and drink outlet. Food and beverages may range from vending or a reach-in cooler to a full-service health food restaurant. A restaurant would be directly accessible for diners as well as given a physical connection to the fitness center. This reception lounge also serves as the lounge and break area, meeting the need for socializing and camaraderie among those in serious training. The Clay Fitness Center in Lower Manhattan by Studios Architecture provides an upscale minimalist setting for its lounge and juice bar. A child-sitting area is also an essential amenity to enable parents to work out.

EXERCISE FLOOR, "THE GYM"

The floor of exercise equipment is the heart of the fitness facility and is called the gym. The floor houses the equipment that meets the needs of most individual workouts. Most often it is one room with areas assigned to equipment with differing purposes.

A small counter area must be set aside for the members' files. This should be easily accessible to members so that goals may be set and daily fitness activity toward those goals recorded. In this digital age, this station may be a kiosk in which a member inserts a card upon arrival at any machine used. The day's effort is automatically recorded to one's total body of work. A report may be printed out at any time. This record of goals, effort, and achievement is a great motivator in reaching a sound fitness regimen.

For commercial fitness clubs the architect has to plan for peak times. Peak times for fitness are typically early morning (before work), mid- to late-morning through lunch, and early evening (after work). A regular member will have a regimen that fits his or her schedule and meets his or her commitment to fitness. The personal schedule does not allow for waiting for cardiovascular machines, for instance; each user ties up the machine for 30–45 minutes. Strength (or weight) equipment is more adaptable, with each set at a machine lasting only a few minutes. Those with limited time may start the weight training circuit with an available machine.

Therefore, programming the facility requires taking a snapshot of the projected facility at its peak use, usually Monday evening for young adults or Saturday for a family-oriented facility. Peak use also determines parking needs.

Cardiovascular Equipment Area

Often called a cardio (cardiovascular) theater, this space houses treadmills, step machines, stationary bikes, and elliptical machines. Exercise on this equipment raises the heart rate to achieve a cardiovascular training effect. While new equipment may create trends, treadmills still outnumber other types of cardio equipment 4 to 1.

Because the user is standing or sitting on one piece of equipment for 30 minutes or more, providing TV or video monitors to enhance the time during the workout is common; hence the name cardio-theater. Controls for the monitor are attached to the exercise equipment,

▼ *University of Massachusetts, Lowell, Campus Recreation Center, strength studio with cardio-theater on mezzanine. Photo by Warren Patterson.*

▲ *Livonia Community Recreation Center, Livonia, Michigan, cardio studio, with running track above. Neumann/Smith & Associates, architect; Barker Rinker, Seacat, architect. Photo by Justin Maconochie.*

▼ *Desert Highlands, Scottsdale, Arizona, clubhouse fitness center, floor plan. Studio ATI, architect; Image Design, Inc., interior design.*

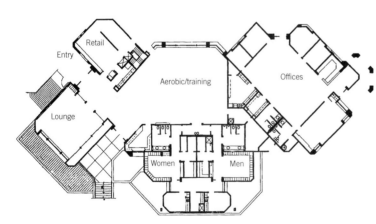

and speaker systems are individualized with earphones. For space planning purposes, use an average of 60 sq ft per machine.

WEIGHT AND STRENGTH STUDIO

The weight and strength studio houses the strength training equipment, which is sometimes divided into two areas by type of equipment: circuit weight machines and free weights.

Circuit weight and resistance machines

Each piece of resistance equipment varies in that its focus is on a particular muscle group. The machines may be organized to provide a circuit or series of exercises aimed at developing or toning all the muscle groups of the body for those users wanting overall fitness. One full circuit of equipment is 12–15 pieces and requires 800–900 sq ft, if properly spaced. Users of all types of strength training equipment benefit from a mirrored wall area.

In a facility focused on bodybuilding, the equipment may be grouped by focus on a muscle type. In either case the equipment producer or supplier is the source of the specific layout of equipment.

Free Weights

Within the weight and strength studio there is an area for free weights. In planning for the average user, however, circuit weights should have priority over free weights in a limited space. As proper form is essential for safety and effectiveness in the use of free weights, the wall opposite the equipment should be mirrored.

Some facilities also mirror the ceiling in this area.

Free weights may or may not be part of the main exercise floor. If one facet of a family-oriented fitness center is focused on power-lifting or bodybuilding, that aspect may be emphasized by separating that area from the other. Acoustical separation may be warranted in a family facility because of the language often generated by the exertion of the body builder. Lighting for bodybuilding is unusual for a fitness facility in that ambient lighting should be supplemented with directional lighting to model the body. The participant wants to see clearly how muscles are responding under the stress of a particular activity. Some clubs may have a focus on power-lifting to the exclusion of general fitness.

▲ Celebration Health Fitness Center, Celebration, Florida, weight circuit area, with mirrored wall. Robert A. M. Stern, architect; NBBJ, architect.

◀ Clay Fitness Center, strength and weight studio. Studios Architecture. Photo by Warren Patterson.

GROUP EXERCISE, MOVEMENT, AND AEROBIC STUDIO

A big step in an operator's commitment as a fitness facility is the inclusion of group programs. Whereas cardiovascular equipment requires no staff and strength and weight equipment requires very little staff assistance, group programs require a staff facilitator and an enclosed space. In fact, the success of these programs relies mainly on the facilitator. Effective utilization of this group space is a challenge. For instance, a facility sponsoring aerobics four to five times a day is exceptional. Therefore, utilization of the space demands commitment to a variety of programs and more flexibility in the space. For example, a sizable family-oriented fitness facility may develop a large range of group activities for women and children. That also may impact the selection of floor material; for instance, carpet is more flexible than a wood floor. The range of use also demands convenient storage, as the paraphernalia that supports the range of activities needs an accessible storage room to itself.

The group exercise studio is best seen as a multiuse room housing a variety of activities oriented to group training. In addition to aerobic classes, the room often provides a venue for yoga, karate, tai chi, a range of dance activities, and individual stretching and floor exercises. In a facility generating only 2–3 group classes per day, an 800–1000 sq ft facility is adequate for a class of 15–20 people.

To cushion the impact of step movements, the finished floor material and installation is of great importance. The traditional floor is made of wood set on sleepers and a cushioning material to provide resiliency. There are also various cushioned or suspension floor systems that may serve multiuse room needs, especially if the room is used for a range of fitness activities. The traditional wood floor works well for aerobics with a sliding motion, but perspiration may cause slippery spots.

Another possible use of the aerobics space is for classes that use stationary bikes for studio cycling, often called "spinning." The bikes are the most complex equipment used for group aerobics. Ideally, the space dedicated to studio cycling should not require relocation of the bikes. In any case, the need for storage related to the group exercise studio must be addressed. The range of activities in a "movement" space requires floor mats, steps, hand weights, stretch ropes, medicine balls, studio cycles, clothes hooks, audio equipment and a water source. Storage should be broad and shallow for easy access by the class.

The studio itself is programmed for 50 sq ft per person plus 10–20 percent

▼ *Celebration Health Fitness Center aerobic and movement studio.*

of the room's total area for storage of equipment. Again, because proper form is essential to getting the most benefit from the exercise, at least two walls should be mirrored.

A source for music is needed in a movement studio. With mirrored walls and a possible wood floor, other surfaces should be acoustically treated. Acoustical separation from adjoining spaces should be provided with a sound transmission class (STC) rate of 40 or better.

GYMNASIUM

The gymnasium is another multiuse sports area. It is a high-bay, clear-spanned space. A cushioned wood floor is ideal. Since a high school basketball court is 84 ft long and 50 ft wide, plus a surrounding 10 ft overrun, the minimum floor size for a full court is 104 ft x 70 ft. There is normally no need for spectator bleacher space in a fitness center gymnasium, although some seating is needed for waiting players.

▲ Celebration Health Fitness Center gymnasium showing openings to surrounding spaces.

▼ Celebration Health Fitness Center, third floor plan.

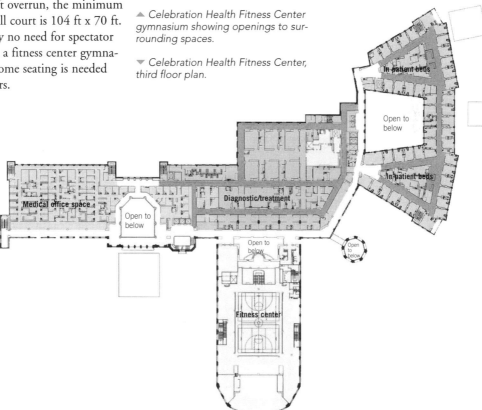

Floor markings for basketball, volley-ball, and location of equipment may be found in *Architectural Graphic Standards* (Ramsey et al. 2000). Acoustics is an issue in a gymnasium. Although the dribbled ball and screech of sneakers is noisy, a more important concern is the language generated by the intense com-petition.

INDOOR POOLS

Pools are increasingly a part of fitness routines, especially with seniors. Swimming laps offers an effective all-around body workout. Group water aer-obics, however, has grown sharply in popularity as the population ages because such aerobics are less hard on the body. The water is effective in giving overall resistance but without joint-irritating impact; pool exercise is welcome to mature users.

Celebration Health Aquatic Center

The indoor pools at Celebration Health in Celebration, Florida, are oriented to fitness and therapy. The lap pool is five 25-meter-long lanes plus a free swim area. Swimming lessons for children and adults are offered. A huge therapy pool, 25 ft x 40 ft and a constant 4 ft 6 in. deep, has perimeter jets. Classes in the pool include aqua aerobics, water tai chi, pre- and postnatal water exercise, and water arthritis exercise. Underwater treadmills are even available. Handicapped access is by a poolside lift, although zero-entry access is preferred. The relatively high temperature of the pool (92–94°F versus normal 82–84°F) requires the chlorine content to be close-ly monitored. Variation beyond accept-able limits is electronically reported to permanently monitored areas.

▶ *Celebration Health Fitness Center pool.*

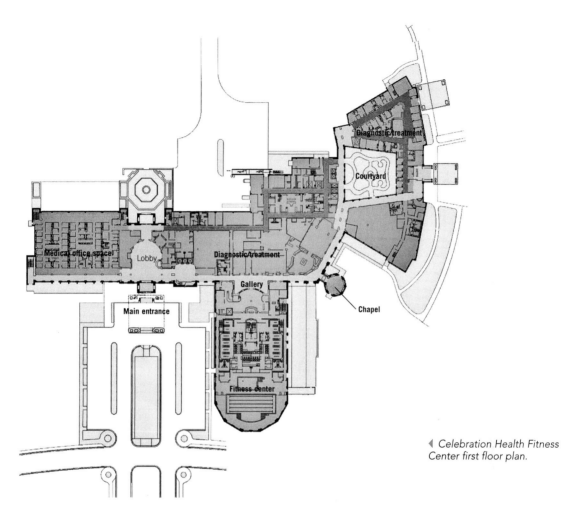

◀ *Celebration Health Fitness Center first floor plan.*

Lightning nearby is a primary concern even with indoor pool use. Detectors identify lightning strikes in an 8–3 mile range. If lightning is detected within a predetermined distance—three miles, or in the case of visible bolts—an alarm is activated in both the pool office and the reception area, which is always staffed. The pool is immediately shut down.

The pool equipment room for the two pools at Celebration Health is approximately 700 sq ft for 4,800 sq ft of pool area. In each locker room, swimsuit water extractors are a user-oriented piece of equipment.

The Oakridge Fitness Center

One of the clubhouses serving The Landings, an active adult community near Savannah, Georgia, is the Oakridge Fitness Center. The Center, designed by Diedrich Architects, includes a workout equipment room with both cardiovascular and weight and strength machines. The Center has already doubled in size since the initial building. The facility also

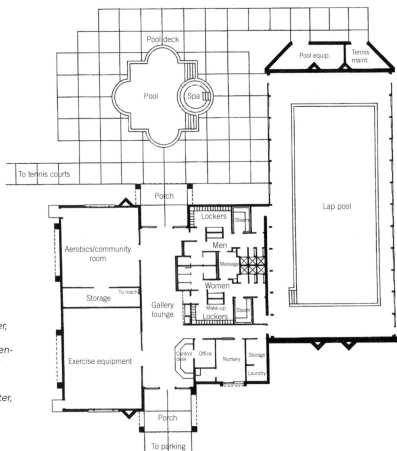

▶ *Oakridge Fitness Center, The Landings, Skidaway Island, Georgia, fitness center and indoor pool floor plan. Diedrich Architects.*

▼ *Oakridge Fitness Center, indoor pool interior. The Landings Club, Inc.*

includes a movement studio, locker rooms, and a reception lounge area. The building features an indoor pool for swimming laps and water aerobics. The pool is enclosed with a preengineered glass and steel enclosure. Roof and side walls open during pleasant weather.

Indoor Tracks

Indoors tracks are best located in a mezzanine space, often above a multicourt gymnasium or gym area, to prevent interfering with access to what would be the infield area, bounded by the track. A track in a fitness complex is typically three lanes, each 4 ft wide. The running surface is a cushioned, composite material. The acoustics of a gymnasium court is an additional concern with the incorporation of a track in the same space.

LOCKER ROOMS

Locker rooms in a commercial facility are typically off to the side or in the back, beyond the exercise floor. It is important that the locker rooms do not block the view of the activity. In addition, many people come dressed ready to exercise so accessing the locker room is not part of the initial arrival sequence. An exception to this is the corporate or commercial facility, where a member will arrive from work, change, work out, and then go home. See Chapter 10, "Spas and Salons," for a discussion about the layout of spas in which the member or guest may have a spa treatment after a workout and needs to shower and change.

Locker rooms house day lockers and changing areas; and wet areas, including toilet facilities, showers, and amenities

◀ *Morrison Athletic Center, Noble & Greenough School, Dedham, Massachusetts, running track with gymnasium below. Architectural Resources Cambridge, Inc., architect. Photo by Nick Wheeler.*

like steam, sauna, and whirlpool tubs. Whirlpool baths and steam rooms, in particular, are a concern for project planners because of the moist heat they generate. The steam room should open to a wet area like the hallway to the showers because of steam condensation when the door is opened. Moisture-proof light fixtures should be used in the ceiling inside and outside the steam room entrance.

There is a need for towel racks and hooks in the wet areas, hampers for used towels in the locker room, and hooks for robes at the steam, sauna, and whirlpool. Water as a beverage is a necessity, and juice or fruit on a buffet are the hallmark of an upscale facility.

The locker room attendant's area includes supply storage as well as a convenient washer and dryer to keep up with the laundering of towels. In an upscale facility the attendant may have a counter and a customer-service orientation for assisting the user.

Lockers are typically a combination of stacked and full height. Stacked are 12" wide, 20" deep, and 12–36" high. Full height is 72" high. A "Z" configured locker offers higher hanging space in a stacked locker. Usually lockers in fitness facilities are day lockers, that is, occupied only when the user is at the facility. Member clubs, however, typically have permanently assigned lockers available as well.

STAFF AREA

An all-inclusive staff area for a fitness facility includes space for the following:

- General manager
- Program directors
- Membership secretary and user orientation
- Administrative assistant
- Financial
- Counseling
- Examining room: user orientation, diagnostic, and condition analysis
- Personal trainer base area
- Break room
- Staff lockers and changing area

The type of facility impacts the program for the staff area. A stand-alone commercial fitness facility would need personnel to address all of the above, although some individuals may handle multiple responsibilities. In an institutional facility, however, the financial office, staff break room, and staff lockers and changing areas may be part of the larger facility. A membership secretary may not be needed, but user or potential user orientation is always necessary.

CHAPTER 10
SPAS AND SALONS

Several consumer trends identified in the last decade indicate a strong market for fitness and health-oriented recreation that is expected to continue to grow.

- *Shifting consumer values:* American consumers have shifted from acquiring things to acquiring experiences.

    Pollack and Williams note in their health tourism study that "facilities like spas and wellness centers uniquely provide the space and place that allow guests to seek harmony, balance and permanent lifestyle changes" (Pollack and Willams 2000, p. 91).
- *Increased stress:* The working week has grown, and leisure time has been reduced.
- *Aging boomers:* Pursuit of healthier lifestyles and self-fulfillment is a trend linked to the graying baby boom generation. The trend may be most pronounced among women, reacting to years of the heavy responsibilities that come with having children, a family, and professional careers.
- *Retirees:* Healthier and more affluent than their predecessors, retirees consider themselves younger and more active than their age and demand a greater range of recreational and learning activities.
- *Personal health care:* Spas are positioned to provide the facilities and staff to sustain guests' search for healthy living programs.
- *Mind and spirit attention:* Once considered "new age" or unusual, yoga and meditation are now common activities at spas and fitness facilities.

▲ *Banff Springs Fairmont Hotel Spa Pool. LeBlond Partnership, architect. Drawing by E. Addison Young*

- *Environmentalism:* Pollack and Williams (2000) noted the interest in combining environmental concerns with health-focused recreation and travel. They explained that "a growing number of health tourism destinations (spas) have been incorporating activities which focus on achieving health through integrating the mind, body, and spirit, with experiencing healthy natural environments."

The list above summarizes the societal trends that are causing the development of spas at all levels of service and making them a necessity in the hospitality and recreational industry. In 2002, Americans visited spas nearly 156 million times.

A SPA DEFINED

Although spa facilities may include or be associated with spaces dedicated to fitness, a spa is more generally focused on nonmedical physical, spiritual, and therapeutic treatment. Therapies range from the traditional massage, albeit in numerous variations, to facials, wraps, pedicures, manicures, and a variety of other pampering treatments.

Spas may be day spas, resort spas, or destination spas. Day spas offer a menu of treatments oriented to the person coming from home. Resort spas are a part of or affiliated with a hotel or resort, but they are not normally dedicated to an exercise or nutritional regimen. A destination spa caters to at least a weekly commitment by the guest to a program of physical exercise, a nutritional menu, spiritually uplifting programs, and pampering treatments.

Reception and Retail

A guest at the spa first arrives at the reception desk. The desk consists of, at least, two workstations for staff to handle check-in, phone reservations, and spa appointments. Some situations use the main desk as a cash/wrap for handling retail transactions or payment for treatments. Service orientation of some spas

demands a staff person to personally escort the guest to the next step in the process.

Retail in the spa derives from the relationship between the guest and the staff member generated by the one-on-one treatment. For instance, the staff member giving a facial—cleansing and enhancing the tone of the skin—is looked upon as an expert in the latest cosmetics beneficial to the skin. Basking in the glow of the treatment, the guest tends to purchase cleansing products or cosmetics recommended by the technician. In a resort or destination spa, there is also the market for robes and other logo-ware commemorating the visits.

Locker Room and Wet Areas

Following check-in, the guest is directed or escorted to the women's or men's reception area and waiting lounge. At this point, the user is assigned a keyed locker and oriented to the locker room and rest rooms. Amenities like steam or sauna may be part of the guest's regimen prior to a treatment. Nearing the appointment time, the user retires to the waiting lounge to be met by the therapist.

Lockers are day lockers; usually they are 12" wide, 24" deep, and 36" high and stacked. A fresh robe is placed in every locker, which is keyed to protect the user's clothes and valuables. The locker room attendant provides slippers in the guest's size. Locker rooms also include a hamper to collect used robes, towels, and slippers. Wet areas are opportunities to project the spa facility's degree of luxury. Stone-surfaced vanities and tile surfaces are enhanced with shelves for a variety of amenities and hand towels. Good lighting, extensive mirrors, and hairdryers are located along the vanity bays. In addition to restroom facilities, spa wet areas include individual showers with ample drying area, steam rooms, saunas, and whirlpools.

The person providing the treatment calls upon the spa user at a central lounge. Since both the therapist and the guest may be male or female, the staff area is located between the men's and women's locker rooms and wet areas, which are entered from behind the main reception desk. The lounge area is a quiet place with consoles for water, tea, and fresh fruit.

Treatment Areas

Treatment areas may be as generic as a massage room or as highly specialized as a hydrotherapy facility.

- *Massage space:* A massage space may range from a 10' x 12' interior room with a small counter and base and wall cabinets to a natural setting with a tent or screen for privacy. More attention is being given to a view of nature or other naturally relaxing elements such as music, water features, or aromatherapies. Consequently, elements that add to the experience, like hot stones for a specialty massage, might be featured as an accessory in the massage room.

- *Hydrotherapy rooms:* Luxurious individual tubs in a relaxing setting are enhanced with lighting, music, scents, and sometimes flowers. Use of tubs may set the mood for other treatments or serve as a relaxing experience after a day of exercise.

- *Wrap treatments:* The menu for wraps may be diverse, ranging from seaweed to therapeutic mud. Of prime con-

cern in the facility is preparation and disposal of the wraps themselves. Large bins on rollers with hot linens and rubberized blankets are easily accessible to the therapist. It may be necessary to provide a Vichy, or horizontal, shower (above a massage or other treatment table) for cleansing the guest after treatment, in which case rubber floor mats are used over tile floors with drains.

- *Relaxation lounge:* Following a treatment, the guest ideally may enjoy some quiet time to savor the previous experience prior to returning to the real world. A relaxation lounge ideally offers a focus on a natural setting or, in a mild climate, within nature itself. For instance, a lounge may be a screened pool deck for sunning "au naturel." Lounges typically provide chaises, music, reading material, water, and juice.

- *Couples' facilities:* A romantic approach provides treatment rooms for couples. The setting becomes doubly important and might inclue paired chaises for waiting and relaxation. A landscaped courtyard with an immersion tub for two is an ideal setting for pretreatment in a mild climate. Some spa suites are designed to be flexible, maximizing use of the space. If couples reserve the suite for a "couples massage," the experience is shared by opening well-designed partitions between adjoining massage rooms.

- *Fitness facilities:* A fitness equipment area and a movement studio are part of the typical facility in a resort spa and to a greater degree in a destination spa.

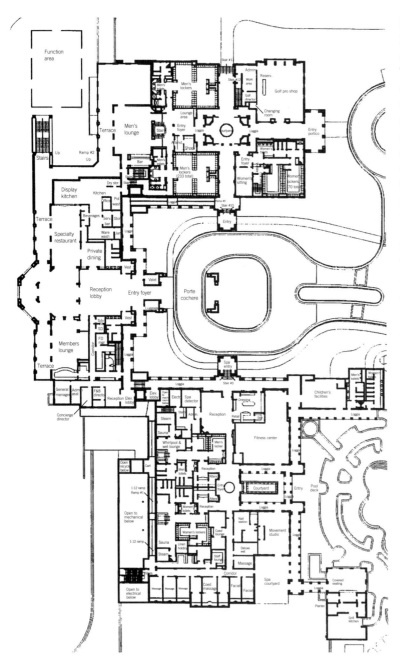

▲ *South Florida club and spa floor plan, showing golf club, social and dining club, and spa. Peacock & Lewis, architect; Image Design, Inc., interior designers.*

DAY SPAS

Day spas serve users in their urban area and do not have overnight guest lodging. They may be commercial ventures or amenities in planned recreational communities. Often they are associated with salons, which provide hair care, manicures, and pedicures. The day spa may also be part of a fitness facility. The day spa is differentiated from the fitness facility, however, by treatment rooms for massages, facials, hydrotherapies, and therapeutic wraps.

South Florida Spa

The spa portion of this South Florida club is a prime example of an upscale day spa serving a second-home community. The spa is one element in a compound formed by a golf club, social and dining club, and the spa itself. The architectural concept recalls what has become the vernacular in South Florida, the Mediterranean architecture of Addison Mizener. Characteristic of the architecture are courtyards and fountains; and, in these elements, the architect and the interior designer, Image Design of Atlanta, found a way to make the spa reflective of South Florida.

The essence of a spa is tranquility, a separation from the everyday world, and a release from stress. At this spa, the entry porch sets the tone with fountains of slowly moving water. This is reinforced upon entering by the natural stone materials—backlit alabaster framing fresh flowers—and the reception desk.

The guest is escorted from the reception area to the attendant, who sees the guest to a locker, where a robe and slippers await. The guest may elect to use the whirlpool, sauna, steam room, shower, or otherwise prepare for treatment.

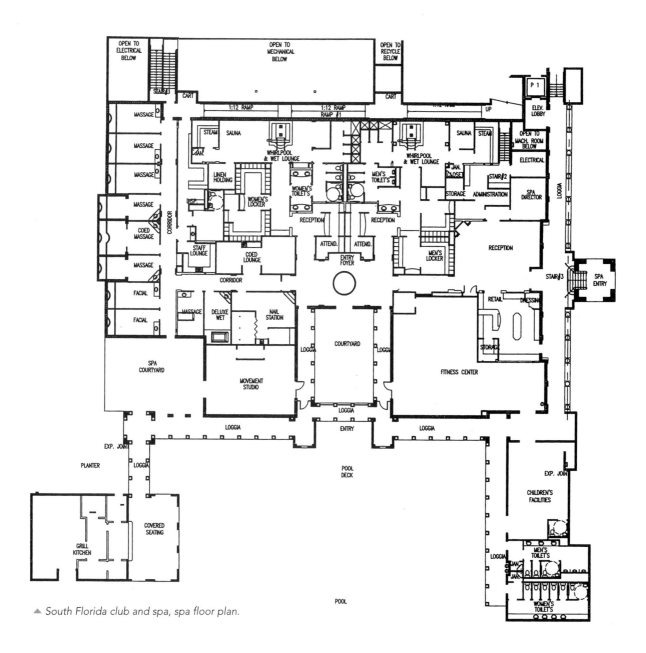

▲ *South Florida club and spa, spa floor plan.*

When ready, the guest waits for the therapist in a coed relaxation lounge.

Circulating from the reception area to the locker room and then to the lounge, the guest passes through the loggia, a stone-finished skylit space with a fountain as a focal point. Next to it is a courtyard with a lineal pool and fountains forming an axis to a water feature in the landscaped outside pool. The sense of

▲ South Florida club and spa massage treatment room, which opens to a private courtyard. Photo by Gabriel Benzur.

two treatment rooms are for facials.

All ceilings in the massage rooms are designed to preclude disturbing elements and may be painted for a trompe l'oeil effect to offer the reclining guest a serene image.

Another treatment room is a deluxe wet area containing a large individual whirlpool tub, an exfoliation table, and a Vichy shower. As the whole room becomes wet, it requires floor-to-ceiling tile and marine-grade cabinetry.

There is a fitness equipment area in the spa; but, in keeping with the goal of tranquility, it is out of sight from the main circulation pattern. The "movement studio," as the aerobics room is called, will mostly support yoga, although storage for studio cycles is provided. Staff areas are convenient to the treatment rooms. Unique to a spa is the dispensary, necessary because of the increasingly exotic menu of oils and scents offered even in this day spa. Additional "back of the house" areas are on a lower level.

Upon returning to the wet area after a treatment, the guest has a choice of whirlpool, steam, or sauna, planned around an area of chaise lounges, as well as the option of adjourning to the sculptural outdoor pool that includes a whirlpool and lap area.

Meanwhile, children may enjoy the convenient child-care area with playroom and kids' pool. The child-care area is brightly colored with a variety of play areas, art stations, and computer terminals.

HOTEL AND RESORT SPAS

Spas used to be a special feature, distinguishing three-plus-star luxury hotels. Now a spa is an almost required feature for hotels (Warwick 2003). The only issue now is what size spa facility the

tranquility is created as this pleasing passage uses light, water, and soothing sounds to separate the guest from the real world.

As a day spa, it offers all basic features and treatments:

- Manicure stations (three)
- Pedicure "thrones" (three)
- Makeup area
- Treatment rooms: seven for massage with private courtyards and fountains that may be turned off if silence or music is preferred; a double room that serves as a coed massage space; and

▲ *Ritz-Carlton Hotel Chicago spa, Chicago, reception lobby. The Gettys Group, interior design. Photo by Hedrich Blessing.*

▶ *Ritz-Carlton Hotel Chicago spa floor plan.*

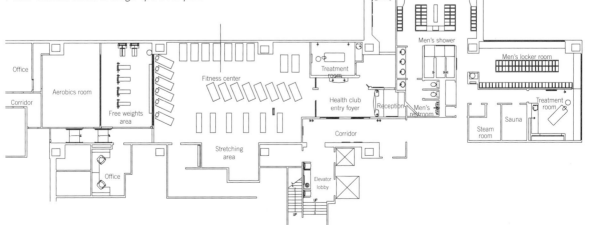

▶ *Four Seasons Hotel Chicago spa, women's vanity area. The Gettys Group, interor design. Photo by David Clifton.*

▲ *Four Seasons Hotel Chicago spa, facial treatment room. Photo by David Clifton.*

▼ *Fours Seasons Hotel Chicago spa, wrap-treatment room with Vichy horizontal shower. Photo by David Clifton*

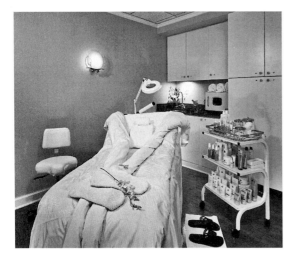

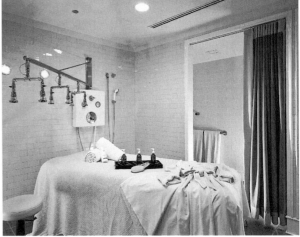

hotel or resort will create. At the Four Seasons, Chicago, and the Ritz-Carlton, Chicago, the spas had to be carved out of existing urban hotel structures. The Gettys Group, the designer, remodeled and added space that had to be luxurious and also communicate the mystique of a spa. In these spaces, it was particularly important that the user feel the serenity of the spa to escape from the intensity of the city.

At the Ritz-Carlton, the owners and The Gettys Group wanted to break from the hotel's traditional interiors to create a more contemporary setting for a luxurious and gracious spa environment. Using clear and etched glass, the designer created the desired elegance. A textured glass mural transformed a dowdy pool into a focal element symbolizing the tranquility of the spa.

Responding to the demands of its clientele, the Four Seasons, Chicago, expanded its conditioned space at roof level to relocate the fitness areas and free up space for a spa. The designer's charge was to develop a spa and workout facility equal to the hotel in quality, functionality, and service level but which went beyond the hotel's traditional interiors.

Spaces include a retail foyer with the spa concierge and the relaxation lounge as an oasis of calm for guests waiting for services. A spa menu is served in the relaxation lounge. In addition to a remodeled women's locker room, the spa connects to the new fitness area and to a lounge overlooking the rooftop pool.

The Spa at Fairmont Banff Springs Hotel

Through a sensitive addition and remodeling, the LeBlond Partnership has created a spa as a special place in an expansion of the baronial castle architecture of the historic Banff Springs Hotel in Alberta. The spa and fitness facility is on three levels with the spa pools on the lower level, allowing for vistas of the valley and the surrounding mountains. The elegant plan neatly dovetails the spa addition with the remodeled indoor pool. Cascading fountains and pools lit by skylights create the mystical space that is the essence of the spa.

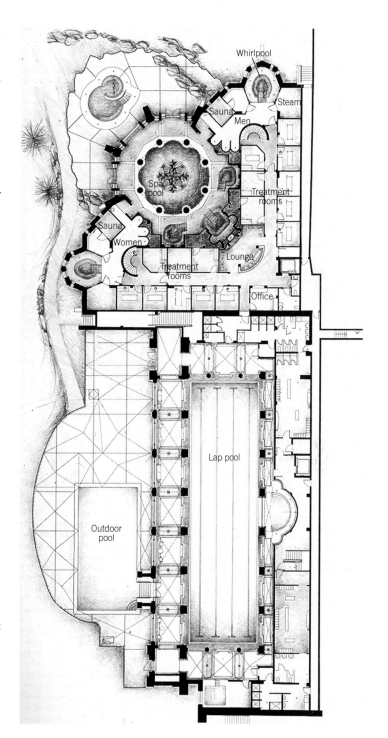

▶ *The Fairmont Banff Springs Hotel spa, Banff, Alberta, main level floor plan. The LeBlond Partnership, architect.*

▶ *The Fairmont Banff Springs Hotel spa, pool interior.*

Facilities include a reception and retail area, a waiting and relaxation lounge that accommodates twenty people, a beauty salon with four stylist stations, and four manicure and pedicure areas. There are twenty treatment rooms, six of which are for wet therapy and one for couples.

The fitness space on a separate level includes an equipment area with 20 workout stations and a movement studio for classes of 20. Locker rooms adjoin and connect with circular stairs to the spa and the separate sauna, steam, and whirlpool amenities for men and women.

DESTINATION SPAS

Rancho La Puerta

Rancho La Puerta, in Tecate, Mexico, is a destination spa that has evolved into the model for this genre of spa. One of the first destination spas in North America, it was founded in the 1940s

as a health camp retreat by Edmond and Deborah Szekely. It has, however, grown by understanding and catering to its primary clientele, women. A growing segment of those visiting destination spas, however, are couples and men who have discovered the benefits of a spa retreat. This market is burgeoning, based on the maturation of the baby boomer market. The spa houses 160 guests and employs 350, a staff-to-guest ratio greater than 2 to 1, which makes the visitor's stay rewarding.

Destination spas have gone far beyond the "fat farms" of the sixties. Targeting "body, mind, and spirit," Rancho La Puerta lives up to its name by opening a door to a life-changing experience. Beginning with a fitness regimen anchored in hiking, the Ranch offers an assortment of sophisticated fitness programs like yoga and dance. The exercise programs are a satisfying accomplish-

▶ *Rancho La Puerta dining hall, showing landscaping and surrounding terrain. Photo by John Durant*

▼ *Rancho La Puerta, Tecate, Mexico, campus site plan.*

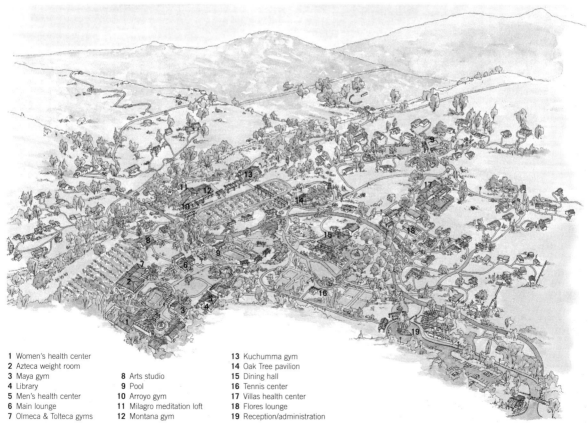

1 Women's health center	13 Kuchumma gym
2 Azteca weight room	14 Oak Tree pavilion
3 Maya gym	15 Dining hall
4 Library	16 Tennis center
5 Men's health center	17 Villas health center
6 Main lounge	18 Flores lounge
7 Olmeca & Tolteca gyms	19 Reception/administration
8 Arts studio	
9 Pool	
10 Arroyo gym	
11 Milagro meditation loft	
12 Montana gym	

ment to the participants. The destination spa, however, also rewards the guest with treatments like a variety of massages that not only pamper but also contribute to the user's understanding of his or her own body. The treatments also ease the soreness that might be generated by the intense physical activity.

The campus

Rancho La Puerta is situated on a 300-acre campus that is almost refreshingly overgrown in its informal landscape. Settled into a valley of the Mexican chaparral, the campus presents a challenge in wayfinding to the newcomer, but it provides a natural setting for each of its buildings. The only relatively formal open space is a vineyard framed by a gravel track. The space is becoming more defined, however, as the newer buildings frame it.

The facilities

The facilities at the Ranch have grown from a small home and tiny chapel to an array of buildings meeting program needs.

- *The Lounge:* A central building that serves for the briefing and starting point for all hikes each morning. It also is the place for posting of announcements and lists for programs requiring sign-up. The facility offers a concierge who answers individual questions and the needs of guests.
- *Seven gyms:* The fitness facilities of Rancho La Puerta have evolved from one open-air pavilion through a series of generic gymnasiums serving multiple uses to seven gymnasiums adapted to or designed for a dedicated use. Gym spaces—in general, beamed and wood decked—feature ceilings that

follow the line of the hipped roofs. Skylights are used to lighten the space. At least one wall is mirrored and one wall may be solid, abutting storage or restroom elements. All other walls are open to the natural environment. The biggest differences in the spaces are the floor surface and built-in storage.

- *Azteca gym:* This gym houses resistance machines and free weights (for strength training) and aerobic equipment. It is used by individuals or for group circuit training, rotating between aerobic and resistance machines. Its floor is painted concrete.
- *Olmeca and Tolteca gyms:* These gyms support basic fitness programs like stretching and low-impact aerobics. The stretch space is carpeted, and the movement studio has a hardwood floor. The carpeted space is also used as a meeting and lecture hall.
- *Arroyo and Montana gyms:* Yoga and mind-body activities are focused in the Arroyo and Montana gyms. Montana, created by experienced fitness instructor Phyllis Pilgram, is recognized as the ideal gym for yoga. It is a clear spanned space with a cushioned wood floor. Shoes are not allowed on the floor; this means that space in the lobby is required for taking off and storing shoes. Adequate restrooms need to be immediately available prior to a class. Storage for the mats, blankets, and bolsters used in yoga are required. One wall is a rope wall, used in a specific type of yoga. The use of doors that open to the outside, allowing the flow of natural breezes, are highly utilized during classes.

▶ *Rancho La Puerta Arroyo gym, Milagro meditation loft, and Montana gym floor plan. Chris Drayer, designer. Photo by John Durant.*

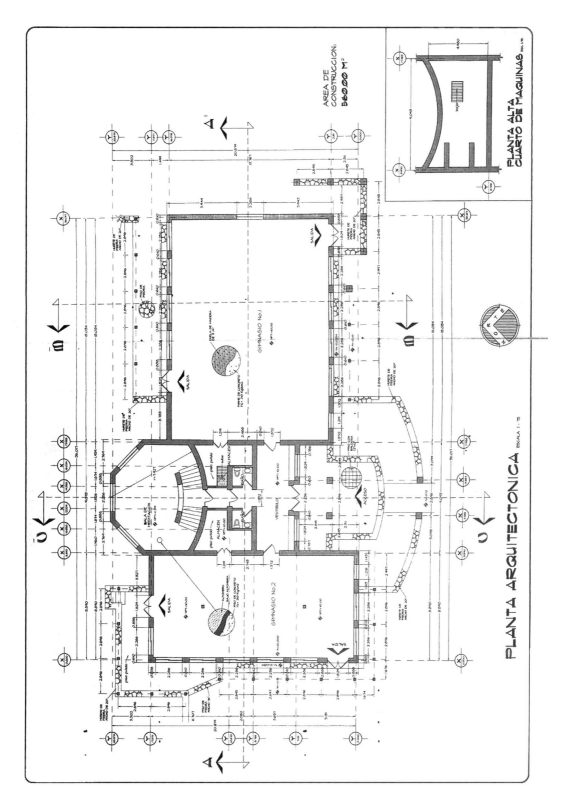

PLANTA ARQUITECTONICA ESCALA 1:75

PLANTA ALTA
CUARTO DE MAQUINAS ESC. 1:75

AREA DE
CONSTRUCCION:
560.00 M²

145

To facilitate the natural flow of heating and cooling in the big, open space, heat is supplied through the floor and cooling is from above. The central air-conditioning duct is combined with the large ridge beam used to minimize the lateral thrust of the gabled ceiling.

- *Kuchumaa gym* is Rancho La Puerta's dance studio. It is a large space, free of columns, and has a mirrored wall that runs the length of the room. Two walls are mostly large windows opening to the surrounding natural landscape. Black metal chandeliers and a sculptural fireplace take the space beyond pure function. Contemporary stained glass and wood doors mark this as a special building. In addition to guest classes and activities, Kuchumaa is the site of special dance presentations by professionals, including workouts by the Metropolitan Ballet.

- *Oaktree pavilion* is the site of the mind and spirit programs. Once an open pavilion, its stone and glass enclosure and surrounding natural environment embody Rancho La Puerta. New programs that encourage self-awareness and well-being are conducted in group settings at the pavilion. Cleverly designed seats, with

▲ *Rancho La Puerta, Oak Tree Pavilion, interior. Photo by John Durant.*

▼ *Rancho La Puerta, Kuchumaa, interior view of exercise room. Photo by John Durant.*

storage below, are movable, facilitating the group sessions and seating for presentations by guest speakers.

Health centers

Rancho La Puerta has three health centers—a women's and a men's health center at one end of the campus and a coed center at the opposite end. The health centers are the location of all spa treatments. The ranch offers three types of full body massages, four varieties of wraps, three kinds of facials, and six other more specialized treatments. Massages, wraps, and facials are done in a typical massage room unless the wrap calls for cleansing with a horizontal shower. At Rancho La Puerta, the typical treatment rooms are somewhat more spacious than a typical massage room and are equipped with a built-in base cabinet, sink, and robe hooks.

Specialized rooms include a wet room with a horizontal spray (a Vichy shower) for a full-body shower on the massage table. The space for the hydrotherapy massage houses a large tub with multiple water jets.

- *The Villas Health Center:* One checks in at reception and receives a robe and locker key. After changing to a robe, the guest returns to a coed lounge where beverages are available. The guest is joined by the therapist and escorted to the treatment room. After the treatment, some women may retire to the upper level relaxation area where steam, sauna, whirlpool, and clothing-optional sunning are available on the terrace or to a relaxation lounge on the first floor. Support areas include those for staff, storage, and preparation for special-ized treatments. Adjacent to the reception and exit is approximately 300 sq ft of retail area.

- *Pools:* Two outdoor pools support water aerobic programs, which are increasingly popular at the facility. As the core clientele ages, exercise using water resistance, as it is easier on the joints than other aerobic exercises, becomes more prevalent. Rancho La Puerta is planning a new aqua center with the main pool designed for water aerobics. A gradual change in depth will accommodate a range in the height of users.

- *The dining hall:* Unique to a destination spa, there is only one location for dining. Most dining is done at six- or eight-seat tables, encouraging guests to meet and share spa experiences. Los Olivos is a private dining room and meeting room upstairs that is used for smaller group dinners, cooking orientation, and demonstrations for first-time spa visitors. A tour of the kitchen is a learning event.

- *Art studio and Flores lounge:* The art studio is dedicated to limited crafts; the Flores lounge, a space filled with natural light, is used for painting classes. Emphasis on art, with resident artists and studios, is anticipated at Rancho La Puerta, reflecting the guest's desire for enrichment and life-long learning.

- *Library and library lounge:* Used for a variety of small group lectures and discussions concerning pertinent topics like nutrition and skin care, the library and lounge seat 25 people in comfortable chairs. It also hosts evening movies.

Other design features

The buildings are a contemporary interpretation of traditional Mexican colonial architecture, linked by paths of oversized clay brick. Even with approximately one hundred residential and program buildings set into the landscape, the structures themselves do not provide orientation to those on the campus. Campus maps are posted intermittently and signage is indispensable, but sculptures are the most unique visual icons in the environment. Their style and feminine quality represent Rancho La Puerta. More than thirty pieces are positioned across the campus.

Art is integrated in the buildings as well, and it carries the architecture beyond its basic vernacular. Artist James Hubbell has been retained to produce several fireplaces and sculptures, in brick and stone masonry. He also designed contemporary stained glass windows, organic metal pulls, and wood doors in the administration building, Pai Pai gym, and the Kuchumaa gym.

Giving Back to the Community

Over its fifty plus years, Rancho La Puerta has become a significant institution on the edge of the town of Tecate, Mexico. In partnering with the community, the Ranch has created the Las Piedras Ecological Center as a place to teach the local school children about the native environment of the chaparral.

Approaching the Las Piedras Ecological Center from town, the visitor travels through Parque del Professor, a large recreational park and stone-paved plaza stepped into the hillside. Stone terraces overlook a soccer field in an inverted pyramid, recalling Mexico's earliest structures. These significant civic structures in Tecate were created through the Fundacion La Puerta, founded by the Szekely family and their lifelong partner, José Manuel Jasso, general manager of Rancho La Puerta and former mayor of Tecate.

The New Royal Bath Spa

The city of Bath, England, a UNESCO World Heritage Site, resolved to restore the buildings of the eighteenth-century spa resort as part of an endeavor to revive the city as a spa destination.

▼ *The New Royal Bath, Bath, England, exterior at night, Nicholas Grimshaw & Partners, architect; Donald Insall Associates, conservation architect. Photo by Edmund Sumner.*

1 Main spa pool
2 Hot bath
3 Treatment rooms
4 Staff area
5 Service tower
6 Entrance/reception
7 Gift shop
8 Changing rooms
9 Restaurant
10 Gymnasium
11 Massage rooms
12 New glazed roof
13 Offices
14 Steam rooms

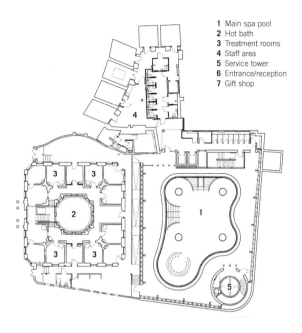

▲ The New Royal Bath, lower ground floor plan.

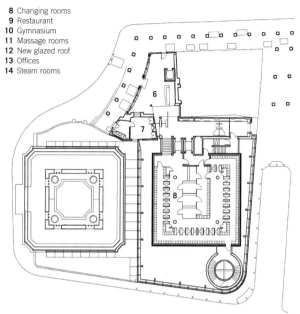

▲ The New Royal Bath, upper ground floor plan.

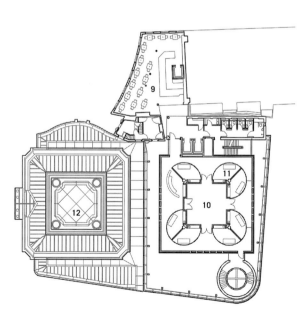

▲ The New Royal Bath, first floor plan.

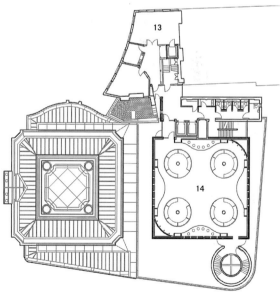

▲ The New Royal Bath, second floor plan.

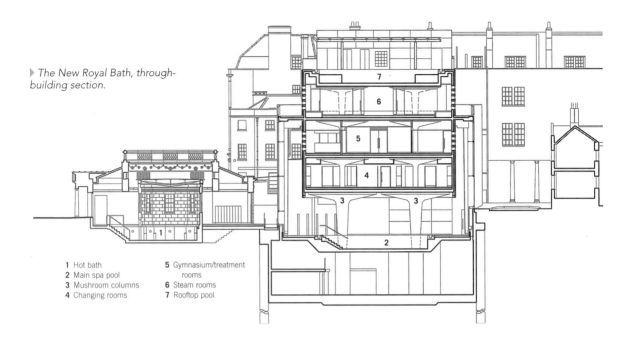

▶ *The New Royal Bath, through-building section.*

1 Hot bath
2 Main spa pool
3 Mushroom columns
4 Changing rooms
5 Gymnasium/treatment rooms
6 Steam rooms
7 Rooftop pool

◀ *The New Royal Bath, interior of main spa pool. Photo by Edmund Sumner.*

▼ *The New Royal Bath, interior of steam rooms. Photo by Edmund Sumner.*

Sir Nicholas Grimshaw won the subsequent competition to restore the 1775 Hot Bath by Wood the Younger and the 1790 Cross Bath by Thomas Baldwin. Adjacent to the historic baths and drawing from the same hot mineral springs, a new building was programmed to provide a state-of-the-art spa based on aqua therapy. The concept paired the new building with the classic square of the historic Hot Bath building. Rising out of the new main spa pool, at the same level as the Hot Bath, is a three-story cube supported by four tapered columns. The stone-clad block contains three levels of locker and changing, workout and treatment, and steam rooms on the top floor. The golden

▶ *The New Royal Bath, view of new skylight over the eighteenth-century Hot Bath building. Photo by Edmund Sumner.*

▼ *The New Royal Bath rooftop spa pool overlooking historic Bath. Photo by Edmund Sumner.*

limestone cube is wrapped in point-supported glass, following the line of Bath Street, and thus bathing the lower ground-floor pool in natural light.

An elegant skylight extends the Grimshaw architecture into the Georgian Hot Bath building, restored by conservation architect Donald Insall Associates.

In like manner a glazed entrance links another historic colonnade to the complex. Also, in the restored spa building, therapy rooms surround the Hot Bath.

Crowning the new five-story building is a roof-top spa pool that provides vistas of the surrounding roofscape and church towers.

PART III

ENRICHMENT AND DINING

Previous page: *Country club of the North, Beavercreek, Ohio, stair to grill room from lobby. Diedrich Architects; Image Design, Inc., interior design. Photo by Gabriel Benzur.*

LIFELONG LEARNING AND ENRICHMENT

Cultural enrichment and learning are increasingly a part of leisure activities. Reflecting a thirst for knowledge and concern with the environment, 143.4 million people participated in viewing and learning activities, according to the National Survey on Recreation and the Environment (NSRE 2002). Facilities for learning and enrichment range from multiuse, classroomlike spaces or generic studios to areas fitted out for specific activities:

- Multiuse studios
- Dedicated studios
    Ceramics
    Computer laboratory
    Painting
    Sculpture
    Woodworking
    Photography
- Nature and interpretive centers
- Teen centers
- Child-sitting and kids' clubs

MULTIUSE STUDIOS
Studios serving a variety of arts and crafts activities have the following features and characteristics. The facilities should encourage, not limit, creativity. This is the place to get messy!

▼ *Conceptual sketch of arts and nature center. Drawing by E. Addison Young.*

- Surfaces: durable, easily cleanable
- Floor: hard tile, sealed concrete, or poured composite material
- Storage: for raw materials and works in progress
- Cabinetry:

  base cabinet
  durable counter/work surface
  full-height wall cabinet

- Sinks: oversize, laundry type
- Drains: sediment type, easily cleanable

Both natural and artificial lighting is important. Doors with a large amount of glass in an exterior wall provide natural light as well as egress to an exterior patio used for craft work and other activities. Artificial lighting should be color corrected to approximate natural light for true color retention in painting and sewing.

DEDICATED STUDIOS

If the number of users warrants it, studios dedicated to a particular activity may be provided. Specific studios and their characteristics follow.

Ceramic Studio

Studios for ceramics need a separate space for the kilns with individual power and exhaust systems. Separate storage for the raw clay and glaze materials is required. Good ventilation is required in the glazing and drying area. A durable and easily cleanable floor is an absolute necessity, but floor drains should not be used because of sediment issues. Floor outlets are required for electric turning wheels. Cubicle lockers or deep shelving best fit ceramic and pottery works-in-progress. Sinks should be laundry sized and have easily cleanable sediment traps.

Computer Laboratory

Computer learning centers are particularly popular as an amenity in active adult communities where seniors are eager to learn how to e-mail their children or to receive digitally transmitted pictures of their grandchildren.

Benches or seating should be ergonomic for use at computer keyboards and workstations. Lighting should be designed to avoid glare or reflections on computer monitors. A screen is needed, as well, at the front of the classroom for

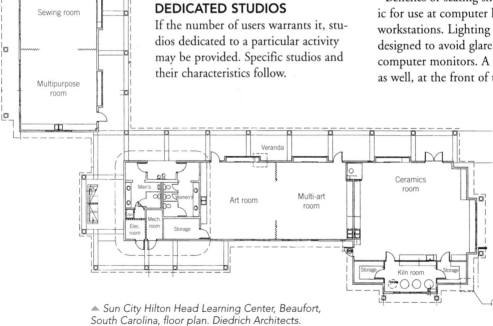

▲ Sun City Hilton Head Learning Center, Beaufort, South Carolina, floor plan. Diedrich Architects.

a projected computer monitor. Power should be uninterrupted and protected from surges.

Painting Studio

Painting settings are about the quality of light and color. Ideally, natural light would have a north orientation and come from above via clerestory windows. Ambient artificial lighting is color corrected to reproduce the color characteristics of natural light. Flexible directional lighting is provided in the area where a model stand would be located. The floor is durable and easily cleaned so as not to inhibit the painter. Sinks are of the laundry type with easily cleanable sediment traps. Walls have an abundance of tack surfaces for pinning up studies and works on paper. Storage is deep, slotlike racks for storage of stretched canvases.

The Viking Culinary Arts Center

The Viking Culinary Arts Center is a unique concept introduced by Viking Range Corporation. Each culinary arts center is a combination state-of-the-art teaching kitchen, theater-style demonstration kitchen, and retail store. The culinary staff offers hands-on classes for students with a range of cooking skills. Multiple cooking stations allow 12–19 students to learn anything from basic baking techniques to preparation of a fine restaurant-quality meal.

Anderson Ranch Arts Center

Located in Snowmass Village, Colorado, near Aspen, the Anderson Ranch Arts Center epitomizes facilities supporting the trend toward lifelong learning in the fine arts and crafts. Beginning with remodeled ranch and homestead buildings, done in 1966, Anderson Ranch has

grown into a casual campus housing 130 workshops with 180 faculty members and 1,300 students every year. One-half of the summer programs capacity is enrolled on the first day of registration, every January. As of 2003, there were 25 full-time members of the administrative staff.

From its beginning, Anderson Ranch has endorsed the blurring of the line between fine arts and crafts. Supporting links among the varied artistic disciplines is one of the planning principles.

Fine arts and crafts disciplines housed at Anderson Ranch Arts Center include:

- Art history and critical studies
- Ceramics
- Photography and digital photography
- Furniture and woodworking
- Painting and drawing
- Printmaking
- Sculpture
- Children's workshops

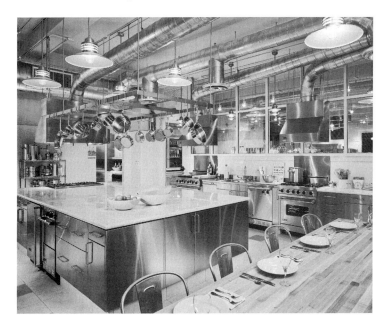

▼ Viking Culinary Kitchens, interior view.

The studios for the various disciplines are grouped around an informal green space that serves as a setting for communication among the artists. Many of the studios open onto patios or porches so that the art can move outdoors, celebrating the usually fine weather for summer workshops. Interaction among the disciplines occurs naturally as the artistic activity rings the same open space that supports circulation to many points of the campus.

Eschewing a uniformity of materials, the campus is nevertheless unified by scale and the additive, casual architecture of the buildings. Literally combining restored log cabins and barns with contemporary vernacular buildings sheathed in corrugated metal, translucent fiberglass, and every sort of wood siding,

architect Harry Teague has designed a compound that easily grows and supports the artistic endeavor. A simple but effective architectural element is the use of wood-and-glass overhead garage doors that open the studios to outdoor working space. The doors are more typically open than closed.

A common characteristic in planning of many of the studios is the combination of an individual master studio with a group studio. The artist and director of artistic discipline or teacher and mentor is housed in an individual studio allowing artists to pursue their vision yet facilitating contact with the group workshops. Other individual studios house active visiting artists. As an example, a leading Japanese potter, Takashi

▼ Anderson Ranch Arts Center, Snowmass Village, Colorado, master plan. Harry Teague, architect.

1 Dows Barn (office and galleries)
2 Powers Ranch House (Finger Library)
3 Fischer Photography Center
4 Wyly Painting Building / Patton Print Shop
5 Gates Barn (Nakazzato Visiting Artist Studio)
6 Lyeth/Lyon Kiln Building
7 Long Ceramics Studio
8 Soldner Center and Sculpture Building / Sorensen Seminar Room
9 Wyly House (student residence)
10 Ranch Café
11 Schermer Meeting Hall
12 Siegel Children's Building
13 Maloof Wood Barn
14 Tool shed
15 Staff residence
16 Staff residence
17 Staff residence
18 Staff residence

Nakazato, comes every summer to test
new directions in his craft.

Photography center

Photography classes at Anderson Ranch
Arts Center include both traditional
black-and-white film photography and
digital imaging and photography.

The photography studio includes:

- Large sinks
- Individual clocks, easily readable
- Layout tables
- Drying screen racks
- Flat-drawer storage, expandable

Adjacent to this naturally lit lab area is
the darkroom, where eight carrels with
enlargers determine the maximum size of
a class. Good exhaust systems are necessary in this area. Although the photography studio is inherently a more enclosed
area, an inviting porch with tack spaces
encourages communication with other
artists in the common area.

The digital photography and imaging
area is a computer lab. Nine Apple com-
puters define the maximum size of a
class. Macs are used because of their wide
acceptance in the graphics industry. One
of the features of the Anderson Ranch is
an annual meeting with Apple designers
and software programmers who seek creative feedback from users.

The photography studio at the
Anderson Ranch is three floors. The art
of digital photography and imaging is
increasingly popular. Reflective of the
trend, in 2004 the space allocation will
reverse, with two of the three floors dedicated to digital endeavors.

Painting studio

As in all the studios, the artists should
not be inhibited by the architecture. It is

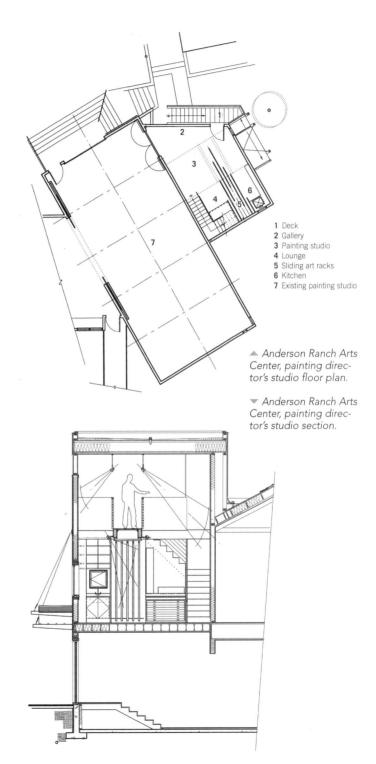

1 Deck
2 Gallery
3 Painting studio
4 Lounge
5 Sliding art racks
6 Kitchen
7 Existing painting studio

▲ Anderson Ranch Arts
Center, painting direc-
tor's studio floor plan.

▼ Anderson Ranch Arts
Center, painting direc-
tor's studio section.

important that this painting and drawing studio not have a high degree of finish. The painter must feel loose and free to splatter paint. Flexibility in the space is achieved through 8 ft x 8 ft caster-mounted partitions. The number of double cubicles that may be created again defines class size. The movable panels are wall height, for mounting large work. The studio space is a two-story volume, freeing up the space and allowing indirect natural light. Flexible track lighting is also provided. The group studio opens out to the patio.

Adjacent is the painting director's studio. The director's area is a two-story space open to (or separated from) the group studio with the movable panels. Sliding screen racks facilitate storage of large canvases. A mezzanine area provides for an office space.

Print shop

The print shop houses an etching press, a lithography press, and print work tables. A graphic arts darkroom adjoins the main space. Because of the way the press equipment is used, there is less opportunity to open the doors to the campus green to integrate with the other disciplines. A crucial mechanical consideration is the exhaust systems, for both the press area and individual workstations.

Ceramics studio

The ceramics studio of over 10,000 sq ft is made up of several spaces. The studio consists of the director's studio and the group teaching areas, which are set up for both hand-building and electric and kick wheel work. Horizontal surfaces everywhere and a "mug wall" are filled with ceramic vestiges of former artists and students.

There is a separate glaze storage and application lab, which is highly ventilated because some of the glazes are toxic. A storage area on the lower level is provided for bagged raw clay and a mixing machine. Delivery of raw clay to this room by semitrailer is required.

Kiln building

The kiln building is an entirely separate structure. Currently it consists of six masonry kilns, exhausted via two chimneys. One of the kilns is wood fired, which is a demanding process requiring several days of hand-stoking. The other five kilns are gas fired. There are also electrically fired kilns, which are much more compact. The kiln room was originally open, but use and adaptation has led to a utilitarian factorylike space with a metal roof and translucent fiberglass walls. In planning a new facility, a fire separation from other buildings may be required. At Anderson Ranch, an exception to the normal twenty-foot separation was allowed because of the historic aspect of parts of the studio building.

Sculpture studio

Necessarily on at-grade level because of the possible weight of the sculpture, this studio also needs a high, clear space.

Metal work is common at Anderson Ranch, so welding equipment is required. A foundry is also provided. A critical concern is the noise generated by cutting and shaping the materials. Locating a metal shop adjacent to group spaces, such as dining or meeting areas and dormitories, may result in a limitation of open hours for this studio. Other spaces are open 24 hours a day.

▶ *Anderson Ranch Arts Center ceramics and sculpture studio, lower level plan. Harry Teague, architect.*

1 Ceramics material storage
2 Sculpture studio
3 Loading room
4 Tank storage
5 Machine room
6 Office
7 Lockup room
8 Lockup room
9 Mechanical
10 Lift

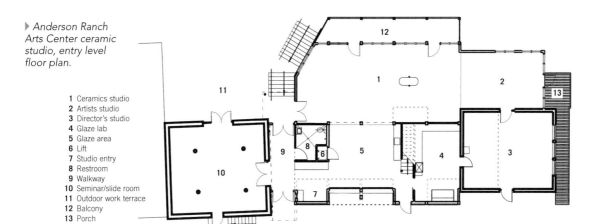

▶ *Anderson Ranch Arts Center ceramic studio, entry level floor plan.*

1 Ceramics studio
2 Artists studio
3 Director's studio
4 Glaze lab
5 Glaze area
6 Lift
7 Studio entry
8 Restroom
9 Walkway
10 Seminar/slide room
11 Outdoor work terrace
12 Balcony
13 Porch

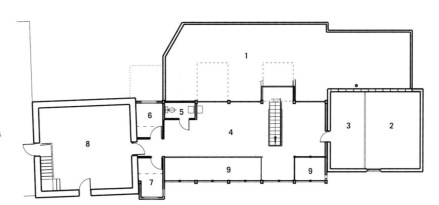

▶ *Anderson Ranch Arts Center ceramic studio, loft level floor plan.*

1 Open to below
2 Open to below
3 Office
4 Residence studios
5 Restroom
6 Slide room
7 Office
8 Community room
9 Open to below

▲ *Anderson Ranch Arts Center ceramic studio, interior view.*

▼ *Anderson Ranch Arts Center ceramic studio exterior, showing new building combined with historic log structure.*

Wood barn

The furniture-making and woodworking studio is extensive. It consists of two bench-shop areas for work with hand tools. With several workbench stations, it is separate from but adjacent and easily accessible to a woodworking machine area. Each machine is served by a dust collection system piped to a collector that is easily accessible for cleaning outside the building. Flanking the machine room is a studio for wood turning, another craft growing in popularity.

Above the woodworking area is a multiuse space for drafting and highly detailed finish work. It is equipped with drawing boards for planning and design for any discipline within the Arts Center.

Children's building

This studio is a multiuse open space, with sliding barn doors and adjacent patio for a full range of children's arts and crafts. It has two electric kilns for ceramics. The building is most convenient to parking for drop-off and pick-up of day students for half-day classes. Because it is close to the art gallery, shop, and administrative building, the building patio is a major activity node on the campus. Watching children creating art appeals to everyone.

The children's studio is not heated or cooled; in the off-season it is used for storage of equipment. Resident artists chosen on artistic merit use all other studios in the off-season.

Arts Center group support areas

The Barn is an original horse barn converted and expanded to gallery and administrative space. The gallery shows the work of artistic discipline directors, visiting artist instructors, and resident

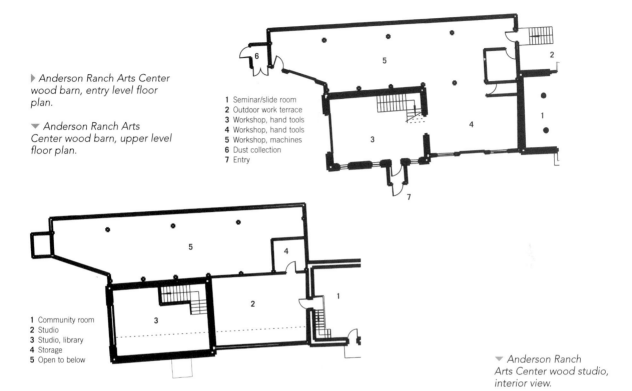

▶ *Anderson Ranch Arts Center wood barn, entry level floor plan.*

▼ *Anderson Ranch Arts Center wood barn, upper level floor plan.*

1 Seminar/slide room
2 Outdoor work terrace
3 Workshop, hand tools
4 Workshop, hand tools
5 Workshop, machines
6 Dust collection
7 Entry

1 Community room
2 Studio
3 Studio, library
4 Storage
5 Open to below

▼ *Anderson Ranch Arts Center wood studio, interior view.*

artists. There is also a small shop for artists' supplies and logo-ware goods.

The Ranch Café serves breakfast, lunch, and dinner to all on campus. With a full campus of up to 200 people, the Café may serve almost everyone for lunch. Most seating is outside, under awning or umbrella picnic tables. The room itself seats about 75 people and has overhead door–walls to open the space.

The meeting hall houses a series of slide lectures by faculty, occasional concerts, and an annual art auction of work contributed by faculty and resident artists for fund-raising. Again, the overhead door–walls open to expand the capacity of the space.

An eighteen-room dormitory—with basic twin bed guest rooms and two

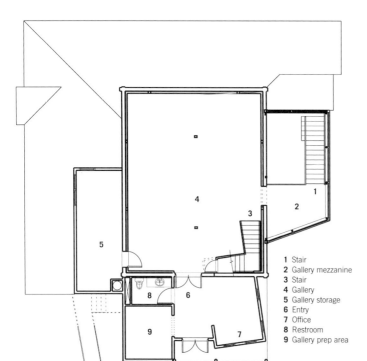

other rooms that share a bath—adjoins the campus. There are also four residential buildings of staff housing nearby. Three of the buildings are adapted from historic cabins.

Also incorporated in the variety of the campus structures are studio and resident space for visiting artists as well as a visual arts library.

Over thirty years, architect Harry Teague has created a complex of over 50,000 sq ft of buildings consistent in scale and relationship of individual structures. The eclectic studio buildings show a casual face to those taking a workshop. Many buildings have had elements such as decorative doorjambs added by artists. The architecture easily accepts the art, effectively supporting the intended integration and links among the varied artistic disciplines.

1 Stair
2 Gallery mezzanine
3 Stair
4 Gallery
5 Gallery storage
6 Entry
7 Office
8 Restroom
9 Gallery prep area

▲ Anderson Ranch Arts Center Dow's Barn gallery, upper level floor plan.

▶ Anderson Ranch Arts Center Dow's Barn gallery and administration, entry level floor plan.

1 Reception area
2 Stair
3 Gallery foyer
4 Restroom
5 Fire closet
6 Gallery
7 Gallery store
8 Work space
9 Kitchen
10 Storage
11 Mechanical
12 Office
13 Office
14 Vestibule
15 Office
16 Office
17 Office
18 Receptionist
19 Porch

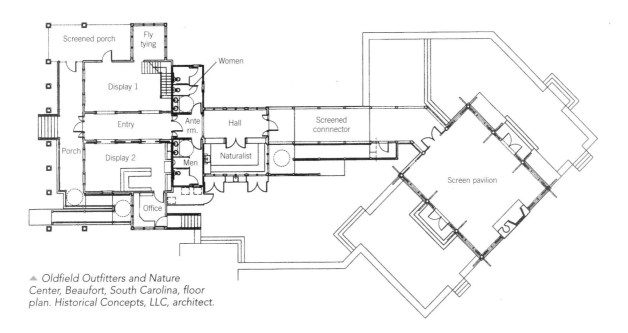

▲ Oldfield Outfitters and Nature Center, Beaufort, South Carolina, floor plan. Historical Concepts, LLC, architect.

NATURE AND INTERPRETIVE CENTERS

With people more sensitive to the environment, nature and interpretive centers are a growing destination for those with leisure time. According to the 1999–2002 National Survey on Recreation and the Environment, 122 million people visited nature centers; that is a significant 34.5 percent rise since the comparable survey in 1994–1995.

Nature Centers

A nature center is a small demonstration lab for teaching about local flora and fauna. It includes a central, island bench for demonstrations and presentation of samples and exhibits. The laboratory perimeter is made up of banks of cages, aquaria, and exhibits of indigenous material. Tack surfaces are for posters and presentation materials. Flexible lighting is well situated over the central bench area. Office space for the environmentalist is required. The nature center logically expands onto a surrounding deck or patio for lessons in the environment. The center also serves as the base for field study trips.

▲ Oldfield Outfitters and Nature Center, exterior from Okatie River.

At Oldfield, a recreational community in Beaufort, South Carolina, the Outfitters and Nature Center introduces residents to the surrounding low-country environment of marshes and waterways. Canoes and kayaks are provided to explore the area.

The Promontory Outfitter's Cabin

The Ranch Club outfitter's cabin is the base for recreational activities in the natural environment at Promontory, a planned recreational community in Park City, Utah. The 5,700 sq ft building houses the resident outfitter with equipment to serve four seasons of recreational activities. Summer includes a range of fishing, mountain biking, and river rafting. In the winter, the cabin is a Nordic center supporting 50 miles of cross-country skiing trails. Snowshoeing is also an option.

The cabin itself offers comfortable lounge space and a large view-oriented deck and dining terrace. There is also a state-of-the-art instructional kitchen for culinary classes and cooking workshops.

Las Piedras Kuchumaa Ecological Center

Las Piedras, created by Fundacion La Puerta (see "Rancho La Puerta," Chapter 10), is planned as a place to teach the children of Tecate, Mexico, about their native chaparral environment.

Geologist Enrique Cevallos, artist James Hubbell, and architect Drew Hubbell, teamed to create a building that is a piece of sculpture in itself, integrated into the granite boulders of Kuchumaa mountain, striking in its mystery, and fascinating to children as a special place of learning.

▶ *Promontory–The Ranch Club, Park City, Utah, outfitter's cabin.*

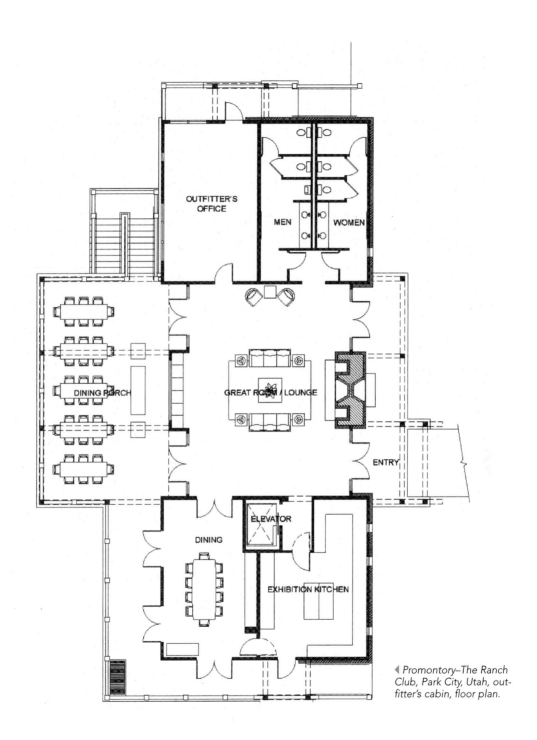

OUTFITTER'S OFFICE

MEN

WOMEN

DINING PORCH

GREAT ROOM / LOUNGE

ENTRY

ELEVATOR

DINING

EXHIBITION KITCHEN

◀ *Promontory–The Ranch Club, Park City, Utah, outfitter's cabin, floor plan.*

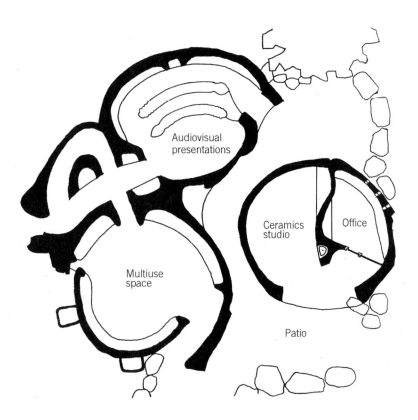

▶ *Las Piedras Nature Center, Tecate, Mexico, floor plan. Enrique Cevallos and James Hubbell, designers; Drew Hubbbell, architect.*

The sculptural form houses three spaces, an audiovisual theatre connected by a cavelike passage to a classroom, and a lab and office. The magic inside is not only the natural cavelike forms but also clefts and holes in rock filled with stained glass windows and prisms. Benches in the form of a rattlesnake provide seating for the classes.

Interpretive Centers
An interpretive center is a smaller-scaled science museum focused on the indigenous material of the immediate local environment. It also might be a small museum of anthropology, conveying the essence of the local culture. Photographic exhibits prevail, as they are able to present the local flora and fauna at different scales, different times, under different lighting, and in different contexts. A group lecture and demonstration room is appropriate, seating about thirty. Provide for the latest audiovisual (AV) equipment, including projection from an overhead view of the demonstration bench.

A retail shop selling written and pictorial material in support of the museum focus is appropriate. Center staff offices and storage for both the exhibit area and the retail are needed.

A natural extension of the interpretive center is decks or patios in the environment. These may provide additional space for gathering, lectures, and briefing or staging for field trips.

◀ Head Smashed-In Buffalo Jump Interpretive Center, Fort MacLeod, Alberta, exterior view, The LeBlond Partnership, architect. Courtesy Alberta Community Development.

▼ Head Smashed-In Buffalo Jump Interpretive Center, interior view showing buffalo and cliff diorama.

Buffalo Jump Interpretive Center

The Head Smashed-In Buffalo Jump Interpretive Center in the Porcupine Hills, Fort MacLeod, Alberta, conveys the significance of the buffalo jump, which was once a means of survival for First Nations people of southern Alberta. The Center commemorates the cliff site where natives herded buffalo over a precipice as a means to gather food.

The building is recognized for being one with the land and demonstrating an understanding of World Heritage sites by blending with the terrain in form and color. Architect Robert LeBlond of Calgary, Alberta, created a series of open-level galleries from the top to the bottom of the cliff. Visitors approach the main entrance doors at the bottom of the cliff and understand the scale of the buffalo jump. The interior space is organized around and focuses on the sculptural depiction of the buffalo jump itself. The Spirit of the Buffalo, its relationship to the land, and its importance to the native people dominate the confines of the complex.

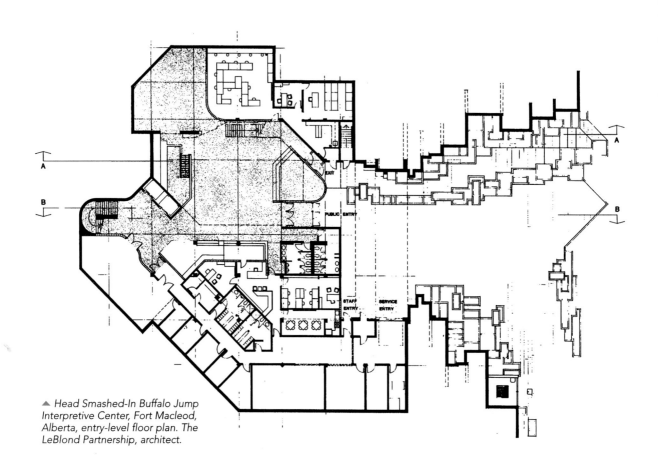

▲ Head Smashed-In Buffalo Jump Interpretive Center, Fort Macleod, Alberta, entry-level floor plan. The LeBlond Partnership, architect.

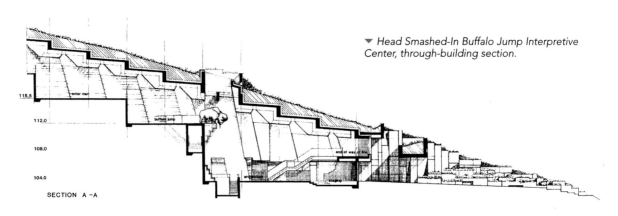

▼ Head Smashed-In Buffalo Jump Interpretive Center, through-building section.

SECTION A-A

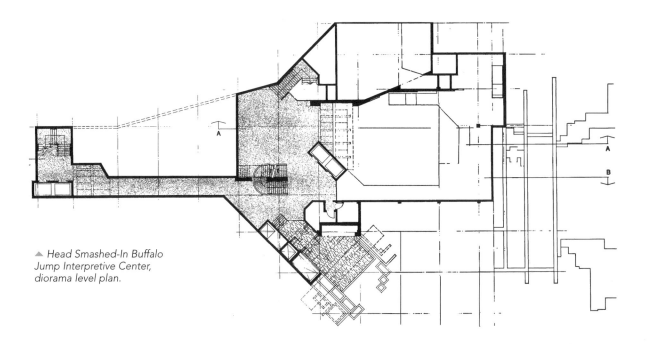

▲ Head Smashed-In Buffalo Jump Interpretive Center, diorama level plan.

Four Seasons Hualalai Cultural Center

This resort on the Kona Coast on the big island of Hawaii devotes an area on the lower level of the main lobby to an interpretive center. Presenting the historic culture of Hawaii, graphics and exhibits of artifacts focus on local events in the history of Hawaii's largest island. Paintings by a native Hawaiian artist depict the inhabitants performing the life-sustaining activities of a typical coastal Hawaiian village. A library offers books and videos on the region for reference and sale. An adjoining pavilion shelters artists and craftspeople invited to demonstrate their craft.

The Robert Tyre Jones, Jr., room

At the Atlanta Athletic Club clubhouse in Atlanta, Georgia, the great golfer Bobby Jones is commemorated as a founder of the club. In another variation of an interpretive center, trophies, memorabilia, and photographs are exhibited to communi-

▲ Four Seasons Hualalai Resort Cultural Center, Kona Coast, Hawaii, interior view. Photo by Kyle Rothenborg.

▲ *Atlanta Athletic Club Robert Tyre Jones Room, Norcross, Georgia, interior view. Image Design, Inc., interior design. Photo by Gabriel Benzur.*

cate the history and tradition, which are considered the club's unique culture.

TEEN CENTER

In planning a center for youth from 13–19 years of age, recognize that what teens want is a space to hang out with peers. Music, games, and videos are as acceptable to teens as structured, programmed activities.

Locating the teen space near the outdoor swimming pool plays off the energy of these users on the pool deck in the summer. A teen center effectively splits into two areas. One is a game room with video games and structured table games such as air hockey, bumper pool, and table tennis. The other space is an entertainment space, or miniature cinema, with a large screen for videos and movies.

Spaces should have a fresh, contemporary, edgy decor, albeit relatively indestructible and easily maintainable.

Aspen Recreation Center Youth Center

The sign on the door clearly states that no adults are allowed at this center in Aspen, Colorado. The design of the facilities used input from teen users. A TV lounge and media and game rooms are not surprising. The computer lab for study and homework and the culinary teaching kitchen, however, reveal the creative thinking in the programming. A large multiuse room accommodates dances, miscellaneous events, and a range of classes. An arts and crafts work area supports "Cool, Crazy Crafts," to appeal to ages 8–18.

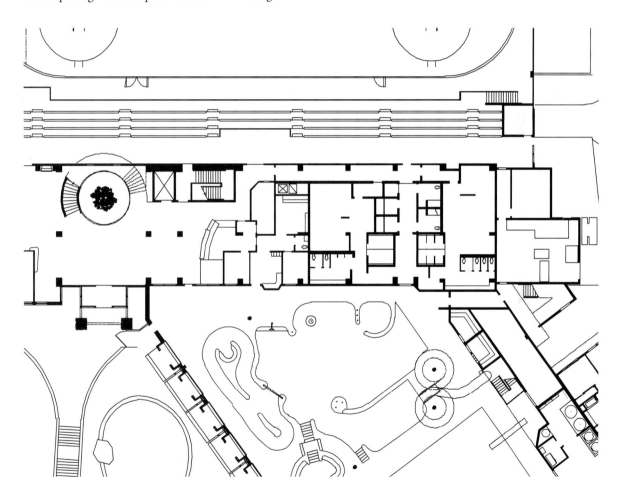

▲ Aspen Recreation Center Youth Center, Aspen, Colorado, floor plan. Hagman Architects; Durrant Architects.

CHILD-SITTING AND KIDS' CLUB

Child-sitting is an important amenity for a family-oriented recreational facility. This is not day care but child care for parents while they are on-property par- ticipating in fitness or sports activities. This amenity is attractive to young parents, allowing them to break their child-care routine to join in a recreational activity.

▼ Kinnikinnick Cabin, Promontory, Park City, Utah, floor plan.

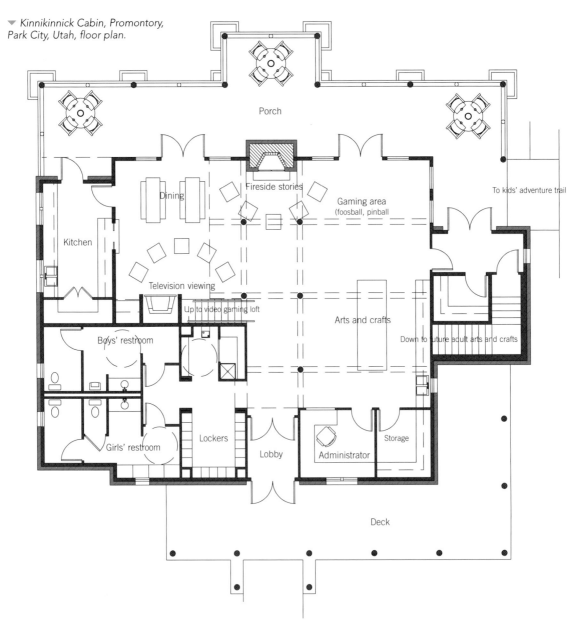

Porch

Fireside stories

Dining

Gaming area
(foosball, pinball)

To kids' adventure trail

Kitchen

Television viewing

Up to video gaming loft

Arts and crafts

Boys' restroom

Down to future adult arts and crafts

Girls' restroom

Lockers

Lobby

Administrator

Storage

Deck

◀ Livonia Community Recreation Center, Kid Quarters, Livonia, Michigan, entrance to Kid Quarters. Neumann/Smith & Associates, architect; Barker Rinker Seacat Architecture, architect. Photo by Justin Maconochie.

The main space is not large, usually 250–300 sq ft; but it is walled with storage cabinets and cubicles as well as tackable surfaces. Storage includes each child's kit, mats for naps, toys, and arts and crafts supplies. Tables and chairs for activities and snacks are movable furnishings. Some items need to be out of children's reach; for example, the TV, the first aid kit, and a minimal kitchenette for snack preparation and beverages. A restroom with child-sized fixtures and a changing area is needed. A storage closet is essential. The teacher's desk and computer need not be in a separate space; but it does need to be inaccessible to the children. A direct link to the playground outside and kiddy pool area is logical.

CHAPTER 12
DINING

Dining and drinking while overlooking a recreational venue is a popular pastime. In golf, doing so in view of the 18th green is characterized as part of the game, and thus called the 19th hole. In skiing, this postskiing activity is termed après ski.

The essence of designing for dining at recreational venues is positioning the diner to overlook the activity and the natural vista. The challenge in planning the dining facility is to capture the view while avoiding circulation conflicts between diner access and kitchen service.

There are five basic planning relationships linking kitchen service and dining with a view:

- Dining room with a corner kitchen
- Multiple dining rooms with an island kitchen
- Vertical separation with entry above the kitchen
- Vertical separation with a banquet and function room above
- Divisible function space

▼ Old Overton Club, Birmingham, Alabama, dining room. Drawing by E. Addison Young.

SINGLE DINING ROOM WITH A CORNER KITCHEN

A main dining room oriented to the view, with its kitchen, deliveries, and receiving area at the same level, is possible without conflict between staff and diner access through planning.

An additional private dining room, porch, or bar lounge may work acceptably if accessed or served through the main dining room.

Planning a second dining room with the same view and requiring a separate entrance, however, will result in cross-traffic conflicts between diner access and service from the corner kitchen.

▶ *Corner Kitchen I diagram. Diedrich LLC.*

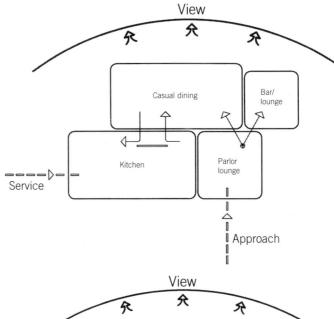

▶ *Corner Kitchen II diagram. Diedrich LLC.*

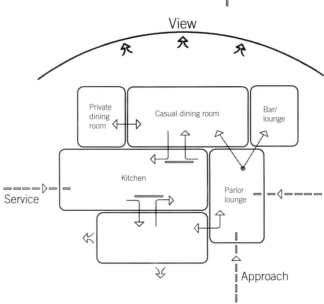

▲ *North River Yacht Club, Tuscaloosa, Alabama, exterior of view-oriented club-house. Diedrich Niles Bolton & Associates, architect. Photo by Gabriel Benzur.*

▶ *North River Yacht Club, Tuscaloosa, Alabama, interior view from dining room. Diedrich Niles Bolton & Associates, architect; Image Design, Inc., interior design. Photo by Gabriel Benzur.*

MULTIPLE DINING ROOMS WITH AN ISLAND KITCHEN

A solution to serving food in multiple rooms oriented to a particular view may be developed with an island kitchen, that is, a kitchen that serves as an island hub between the dining rooms. Receiving and servicing of the island kitchen is done from below; this allows diners to access the dining rooms, which may then be arrayed around the kitchen. Servers may radiate from the kitchen without conflicting with diners entering the two main rooms.

Additional dining rooms with a view may be planned, accepting service or user access through the main dining room. At Cherokee Country Club in Atlanta, Georgia, diners may enter the more for-

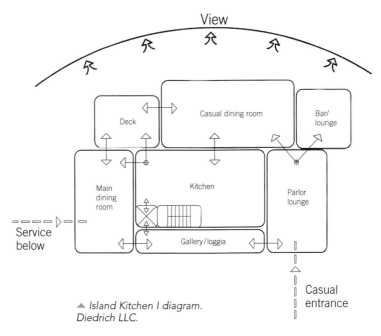

▲ *Island Kitchen I diagram. Diedrich LLC.*

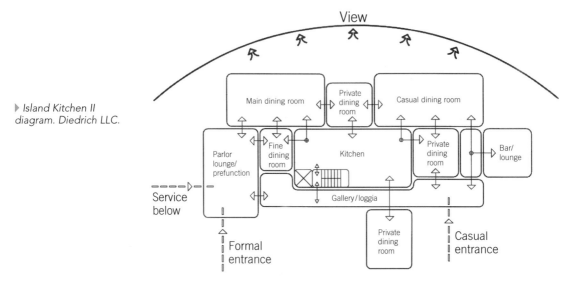

View

▶ *Island Kitchen II diagram. Diedrich LLC.*

Main dining room

Private dining room

Casual dining room

Parlor lounge/prefunction

Fine dining room

Kitchen

Private dining room

Bar/lounge

Service below

Gallery/loggia

Formal entrance

Private dining room

Casual entrance

▲ *Cherokee Country Club, Atlanta, Georgia, golfside view. Diedrich Architects. Photo by Dennis Portwood.*

mal entrance through the porte cochere and main lobby, to access directly either the mixed grill dining room or the function rooms. Both the dining and function rooms overlook the golf course. Service from the kitchen to the function rooms, however, is through the mixed

grill dining room. Service for an event, like a buffet in the function room, may be set up before the dining room is opened. Meanwhile, at the other end of the clubhouse, golfers may enter the men's grillroom through a separate entrance. This more casual dining area and card room also has a view of the golf course. Food service comes from the same kitchen that serves the more formal spaces at the opposite end of the clubhouse.

VERTICAL SEPARATION WITH ENTRY ABOVE THE KITCHEN

Another solution may be generated on a hillside location where the diner arrives at an upper level with an overlooking view but still may have a vista if the dining rooms are located on a lower level. The solution entails placing the arrival lobby above the kitchen, with diners circulating down to an assortment of dining areas arrayed around the kitchen, one level below. All dining rooms may be view oriented and serviced from a central, internal kitchen. Multiple rooms

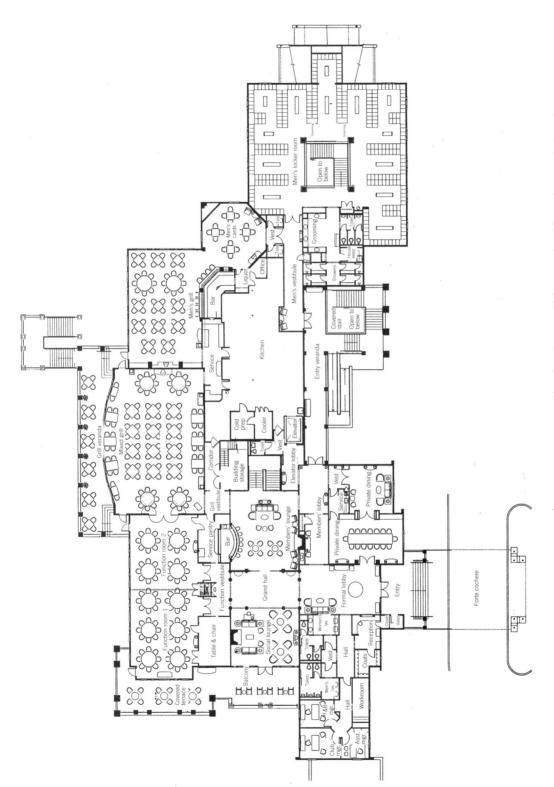

▲ Cherokee Country Club, upper level floor plan. Diedrich Architects.

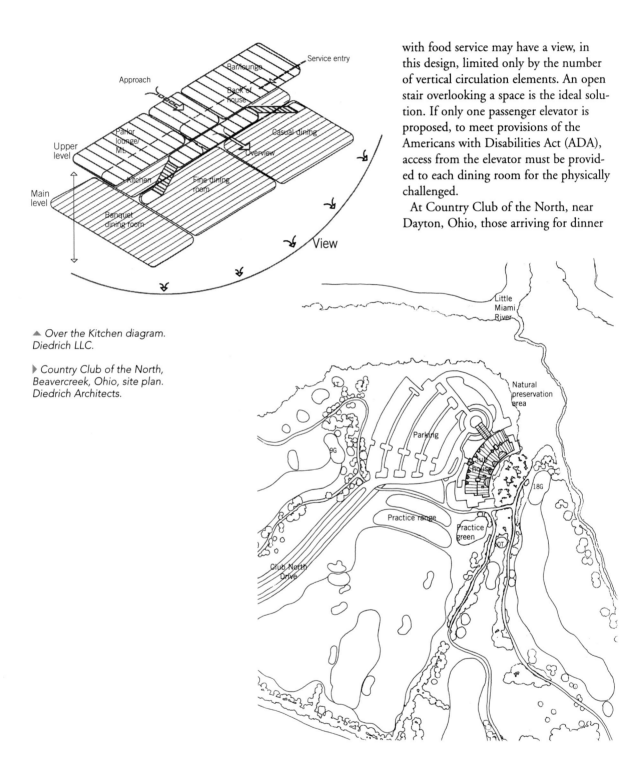

with food service may have a view, in this design, limited only by the number of vertical circulation elements. An open stair overlooking a space is the ideal solution. If only one passenger elevator is proposed, to meet provisions of the Americans with Disabilities Act (ADA), access from the elevator must be provided to each dining room for the physically challenged.

At Country Club of the North, near Dayton, Ohio, those arriving for dinner

▲ Over the Kitchen diagram. Diedrich LLC.

▶ Country Club of the North, Beavercreek, Ohio, site plan. Diedrich Architects.

◀ *Country Club of the North, stair to grill room from lobby. Image Design, Inc., interior design. Photo by Gabriel Benzur.*

▼ *Country Club of the North, upper level floor plan.*

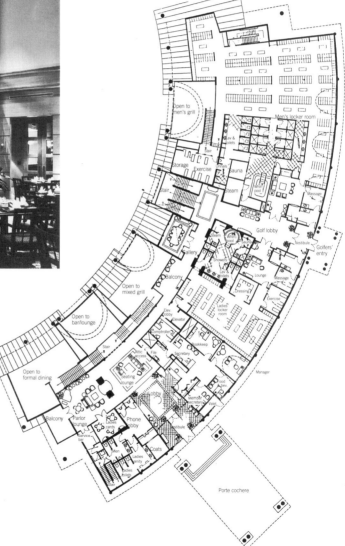

at the clubhouse enter through the porte cochere and the main lobby on the upper level. On the axis of the main entrance, an overlook enables members to enjoy the vista to the 18th green by looking through the two-story space of the bar and lounge on the level below. A member may then circulate to the lower level by taking one of two stairs or, meeting ADA code, an elevator. The stair to the left accesses the more formal main dining room below, which overlooks the golf course and has an adjoining terrace. The stair to the right leads to the casual grill-room, adjacent to the bar and lounge, and also provides direct views to the finishing hole of the golf course. With the bar between the dining rooms, beverage service associated with dining in either space may be served from one bar.

Food service for all three rooms comes from the main kitchen on the interior of the building, behind the stairs, lounge, and dining rooms. Thus there is no cross traffic between diner access and staff service from the kitchen. The kitchen, in turn, has receiving, back-of-the-house, support elements, and trash out at the same lower level.

▲ Country Club of the North, main dining room. Photo by Gabriel Benzur.

▶ Country Club of the North, lower level plan.

VERTICAL SEPARATION WITH A BANQUET AND FUNCTION ROOM ABOVE

To serve quality à la carte meals, the kitchen must be on the same level as the dining room, regardless of the menu. In banquet dining, however, where multiples of the same meal are served, hot carts and cold carts enable a quality banquet meal to be served from a main kitchen to a separate level. A banquet room is workable, therefore, for dining (or functions) with a view on a level separate from the kitchen. Usually the floor above has the better views.

In the DeBordieu clubhouse, serving a second-home community, members may use the main level for dining or socializing while a function takes place on the floor above without conflict between club members and function attendees. This approach also has the advantage of a vertical separation of the prefunction lobby.

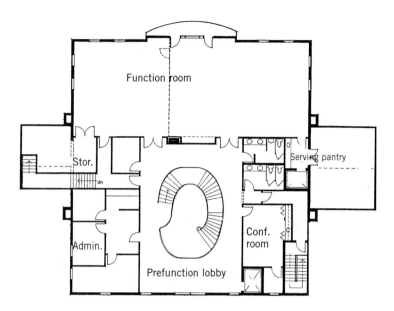

▲ *DeBordieu Club, Georgetown, South Carolina, upper level floor plan. Diedrich Architects.*

◀ *Above the kitchen diagram. Diedrich LLC.*

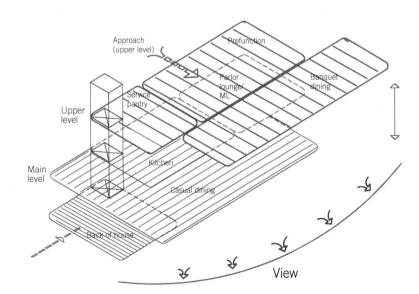

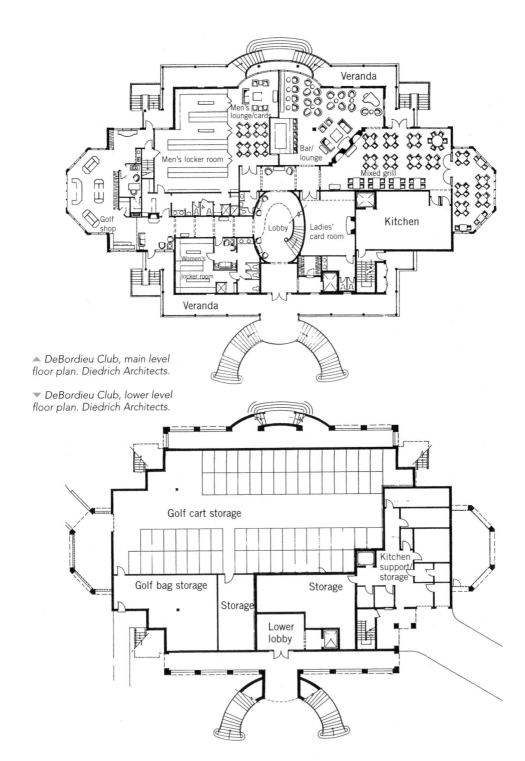

▲ *DeBordieu Club, main level floor plan. Diedrich Architects.*

▼ *DeBordieu Club, lower level floor plan. Diedrich Architects.*

Veranda

Men's lounge/cards

Bar/lounge

Mixed grill

Men's locker room

Kitchen

Golf shop

Lobby

Ladies' card room

Women's locker room

Veranda

Golf cart storage

Golf bag storage

Storage

Storage

Kitchen support/storage

Lower lobby

◀ DeBordieu Club, view-side exterior. Photo by Creative Sources Photography, Inc.

▼ Divisible Function Space diagram. Diedrich LLC.

DIVISIBLE FUNCTION SPACE

Flexibility for banquet or function rooms is often increased by the use of movable partitions. Assuming maintenance of the view, subdividing the banquet or dining rooms has the same effect on access and service as separate rooms. Secondary views may be used to expand the number of the view-oriented rooms without increasing access and service conflicts.

The main clubhouse at Mirasol, a recreational community in Palm Beach Gardens, Florida, houses a main dining room that seats over 500 for large events and overlooks the golf course. During high season, in winter, the whole room may be open for lunch with a bountiful buffet in the middle. There are many situations, however, when the room is subdivided to serve more than one function. For example, two-thirds of the room may be used for member dining while a mov-

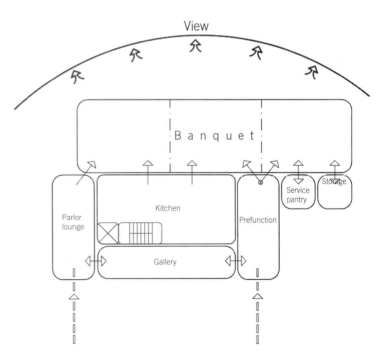

able partition defines a smaller room for a private function. Both rooms continue to have a view of the golf course. Each room is accessed by diners from the lobby around the island kitchen. Service from the kitchen to both rooms is provided without cross traffic.

If two partitions are closed, however, diner access to the center room is compromised. The view of the golf course and service from the kitchen still func-

tion as planned, but a diner has to move through another dining room to get to the center space. Although workable, it is not ideal. In common practice, it would be rare that all three spaces would be used by separate groups for dining at the same time. Most likely two rooms would work together for the same group, for instance, one for a stand-up reception and the other for sit-down dining.

▼ *Mirasol Country Club, Palm Beach Gardens, Florida, upper level plan. Diedrich Niles Bolton & Associates, architect; Jeff Ornstein, architect.*

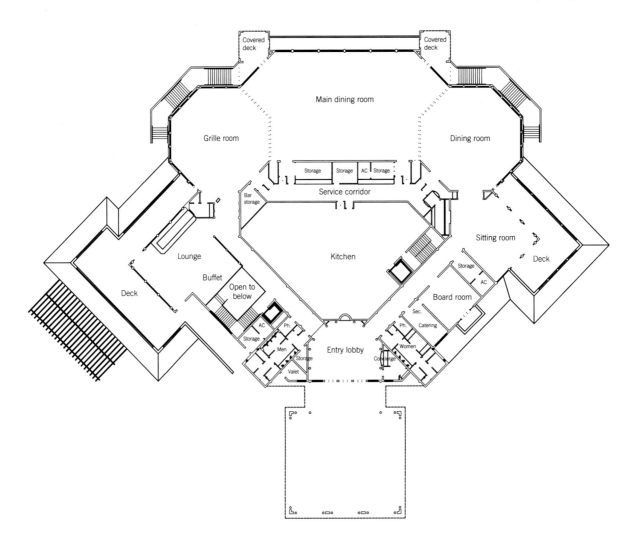

In clubhouses, as opposed to hotel and conference centers, folding partitions are an issue. Standard vinyl-fabric-finished folding partitions tend to clash with the warm, naturally finished and highly detailed millwork that is characteristic of a clubhouse. Even a contemporary interior suffers from the inherently modular nature of movable partitions. Some success has been achieved by modifying the panels, using acoustical fabric and millwork trim. An even greater difference may be achieved by using a French door panel with etched glass. Operation of the doors, however, may mar the millwork, and acoustical concerns with the glass may offset these aesthetic effects.

Terraces

Terraces replace the appeal of a vicarious view of activity through a window from a conditioned space, as the diner becomes part of the setting. In pleasant weather, a terrace, whether bordering the serenity of the sea or the activity of a marina, enhances the experience of dining.

Orienting terraces and balconies to the view is not as simple as merely extending the indoor space. The challenge is making sure the projected deck does not compromise or even block the view from the interior. Hard construction roofs, awnings, and the clutter of furniture on a deck may render a window seat second-rate. Of paramount concern is the railing, as the legal height is 42", which is

▲ Sanctuary Golf Club, view of alfresco dining. Photo by Gabriel Benzur.

▼ Sanctuary Golf Club, Sanibel Island, Florida, view showing folding partitions doors. Eric Brown Design Group, design architect; Richard Cramer, architect of record; Image Design, Inc., interior design. Photo by Gabriel Benzur.

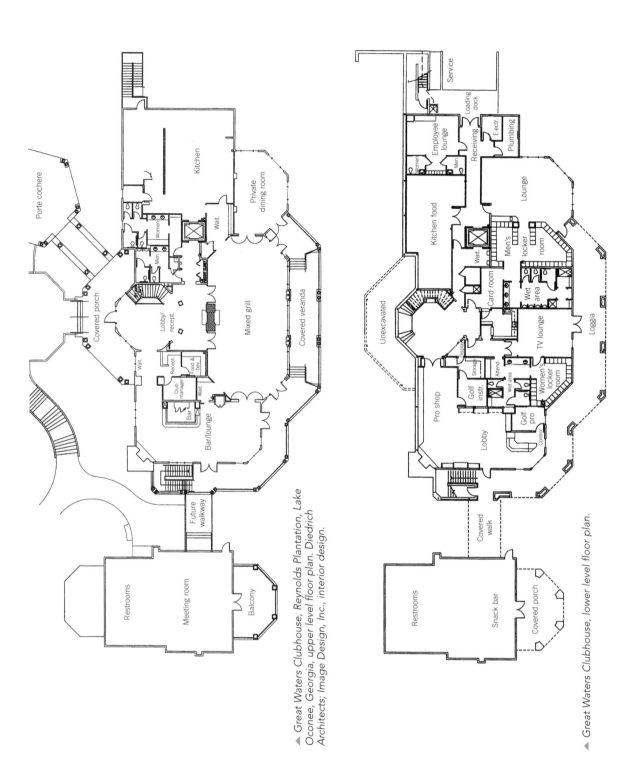

▲ Great Waters Clubhouse, Reynolds Plantation, Lake Oconee, Georgia, upper level floor plan. Diedrich Architects; Image Design, Inc., interior design.

▲ Great Waters Clubhouse, lower level floor plan.

Upper level floor plan labels:

Porte cochere
Kitchen
Covered porch
Women
Men
Wait.
Private dining room
Lobby/recept.
Recept.
Food & bev.
Club manager
Wait.
Bar
Bar/lounge
Mixed grill
Covered veranda
Future walkway
Restrooms
Meeting room
Balcony

Lower level floor plan labels:

Service
Loading dock
Receiving
Electr.
Plumbing
Employee lounge
Women
Men
Kitchen food
Lounge
Wait.
Men's locker room
Card room
Wet area
Unexcavated
TV lounge
Loggia
Attend.
Storage
Wet area
Women's locker room
Pro shop
Golf instr.
Golf pro
Control
Lobby
Covered walk
Restrooms
Snack bar
Covered porch

190

◀ *Great Waters Clubhouse, lakeside view. Photo by Dennis Portwood.*

basically eye level. This height obstructs the view if a person is looking out and down, as toward a golf course or the water. Solutions include moving the terrace to one side of the window wall. The terrace also may be lowered if cover and umbrellas do not conflict with sight lines. Access for the handicapped, however, may become an issue. A ramp is a space-consuming solution.

FORMS OF DINING

Dining may be a snack, casual (including in the card rooms), fine, or banquet.

Snack Bar

The snack bar may be in the form of a pool snack bar, a fitness juice bar, or a golf turnstand or halfway house. In a clubhouse, the snack bar represents club fast food, and it is the place to get the quickest and least-expensive meal. It is the most casual dining area and is, therefore, receptive to sport clothing.

In its prep area, the snack bar ranges from prepreparied food to menus demanding more cooking area. The biggest impact on the facilities design is whether the amount of grilled and deep fried cooking (i.e., hamburgers and french fries) requires a hood. The grill hood and its exhaust system is a significant mechanical device. Its exhaust element should be addressed architecturally. The hood also requires structural analysis to support its significant weight.

Casual Dining

When linked with leisure and recreational activities, dining is predominantly casual. Even in clubhouse dining, the strong trend is away from formal to more informal dining, toward a relaxed meal. Clubs are separating adult and families-with-children dining to make each group comfortable.

Actual layout of tables and chairs show that 20–25 sq ft per seat is a realistic program area for casual dining. In a smaller club dining room (under 50 seats), with large tables and chairs, and the desire of diners for uncrowded and quiet dining,

▲ Clubhouse casual dining, Delray Beach, Florida. Image Design, Inc., interior design. Photo by Gabriel Benzur.

▼ Old Overton Club, Birmingham, Alabama, view of main dining room overlooking the golf course. Diedrich Architects; Image Design, Inc., interior design. Photo by Gabriel Benzur.

ample spacing requires 25–30 sq ft per seat.

Card rooms

Card rooms often also serve as private dining rooms in a clubhouse. If that is the case, it is useful to provide a wait service station nearby and a buffet or counter for beverages and light fare.

As card rooms, however, some other issues should be noted. Serious card players want to concentrate; therefore, a room should have appropriate separation from distractions and noise. For example, a men's card and locker room lounge may be adjacent, and the open doors between would encourage camaraderie. If a serious card game is going on, however, the card

players need to be spared the sounds of the television. In like manner, card players concentrating on bridge and those playing mah-jongg (e.g., clicking tiles) cannot be housed in the same room. Card rooms need good lighting at the table level (100 footcandles), but lighting fixtures should allow dimming for dining. Card tables should have glass holders or separate corner tables for beverages.

Fine Dining, Gourmet Dining, and Wine Cellars

Some club venues require fine dining for special occasions or gourmet meals. Wine display and storage are an important aspect. Clubs have even created a private dining room in a wine cellar. Although a wine room is kept cool (54°F), the solution to comfort is to turn off the cooling a few hours before an event. The heat generated by the occupants then tempers the room. Such temperature fluctuations are not acceptable for the finest wines, however.

Fine dining in a club is usually in a smaller, more intimate, high-décor room. The same room is also used for private dining and receptions. Since gourmet dining is usually an evening meal, the view may not be paramount except to see the lights of a city if of interest.

Banquet, Function, and Event Dining

Banquet, function, and special event dining fit in well with group recreation; witness the golf outing or member-guest

▲ Mediterra Clubhouse, Naples, Florida, view of grillroom overlooking the golf course. Diedrich/NBA, architects; Image Design, Inc., interior design. Photo by Gabriel Benzur.

◀ Sherwood Clubhouse, Thousands Oaks, California, interior of wine cellar. Zmitkowski & Associates, architect; Image Design, Inc., interior design. Photo by Gabriel Benzur.

▲ *Old Overton Club, Birmingham, Alabama, view of outing pavilion. Diedrich Architects. Photo by Gabriel Benzur.*

floor, a dais, portable bars, and banquetware such as chafing dishes must be provided. The prefunction area also includes space for a sign-in table, coat storage, restrooms, and a phone booth.

Seating area ranges from 12.5 sq ft per seat for a large room (150 plus people) with 10-seat, 72" in diameter tables to 15 sq ft per seat with 8 seats per round table. To that must be added area for a dance floor, band entertainment, and a head table. A buffet line may also be part of a function.

ACOUSTICS

Acoustics is a particular challenge in designing an indoor dining space as part of a recreational facility. Inherent in the view orientation to the recreational venue are glass walls. Acoustical reverberation from these walls may be a problem, particularly in dining spaces where quiet conversation is expected to be a part of the meal. Treatment of the other surfaces in the room with acoustically absorbent material may alleviate the potential problem. Floors are often carpeted; tables may be padded and dressed with cloths; and chair backs may be upholstered. A direct solution is an acoustically treated ceiling coupled with carpeted floors. In upscale spaces, however, the architect or interior designer may reject the typical acoustical tile ceiling for aesthetic reasons and use a simpler drywall surface, creating another source of reverberation. Recently, larger ceiling panels covered in fabric and acoustically absorbent have become available, but at a price.

Given the glass wall at the view orientation, another solution is to treat acoustically the opposite interior wall with absorbent material, such as a fabric-upholstered wall. Cost and mainte-

event. In food and beverage, hoteliers and club managers recognize group business as a lucrative approach when compared to à la carte dining.

A reception and prefunction area is an essential place for groups to gather. A permanent bar opened and staffed for the event, or space for portable bars, must be provided. Convenient chair and table storage is required to meet the seating demands of various events. Stack chairs and folding tables stored on carts are typical. Storage of a portable dance

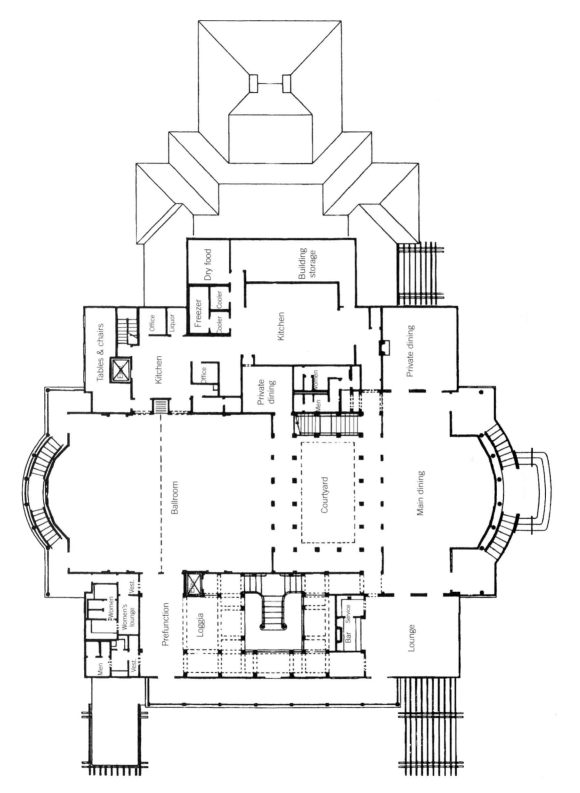

The labels within the floor plan, reading from top to bottom and left to right:

Dry food

Freezer

Building storage

Office

Liquor

Cooler

Cooler

Kitchen

Tables & chairs

EL.

Kitchen

Office

Private dining

Private dining

Women

Men

Ballroom

Courtyard

Main dining

Women's lounge

Vest.

Prefunction

EL.

Loggia

Bar

Service

Men

Vest.

Lounge

▲ *English Turn Country Club, New Orleans, Louisiana, upper level floor plan. Diedrich Architects.*

nance may be an issue in this solution, however.

Location of mechanical equipment and its sound isolation should be addressed. The kitchen itself should be separated from the dining room by sound-insulating walls. The service connection to the dining area should be an acoustically treated vestibule to absorb kitchen sounds and to screen the commercial lighting.

Considering the above, the most prudent design approach is to have a significant dining space in a clubhouse, for instance, checked by an acoustical consultant before finalizing selection of materials for interior surfaces.

KITCHENS

Commercial kitchens are sized based on the menu and the volume of meals served. Rules of thumb commonly used

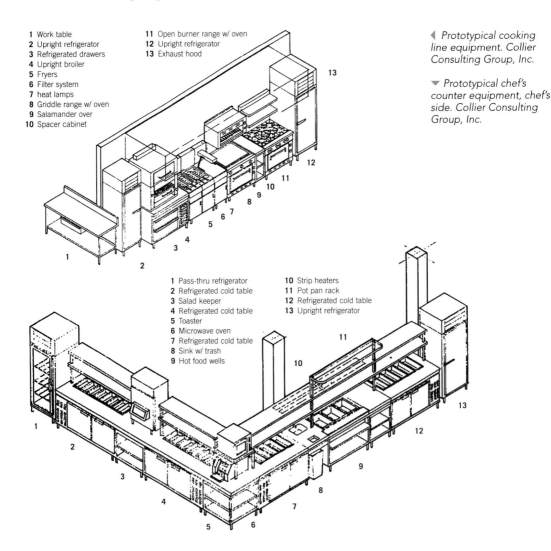

1 Work table
2 Upright refrigerator
3 Refrigerated drawers
4 Upright broiler
5 Fryers
6 Filter system
7 heat lamps
8 Griddle range w/ oven
9 Salamander over
10 Spacer cabinet
11 Open burner range w/ oven
12 Upright refrigerator
13 Exhaust hood

◀ Prototypical cooking line equipment. Collier Consulting Group, Inc.

▼ Prototypical chef's counter equipment, chef's side. Collier Consulting Group, Inc.

1 Pass-thru refrigerator
2 Refrigerated cold table
3 Salad keeper
4 Refrigerated cold table
5 Toaster
6 Microwave oven
7 Refrigerated cold table
8 Sink w/ trash
9 Hot food wells
10 Strip heaters
11 Pot pan rack
12 Refrigerated cold table
13 Upright refrigerator

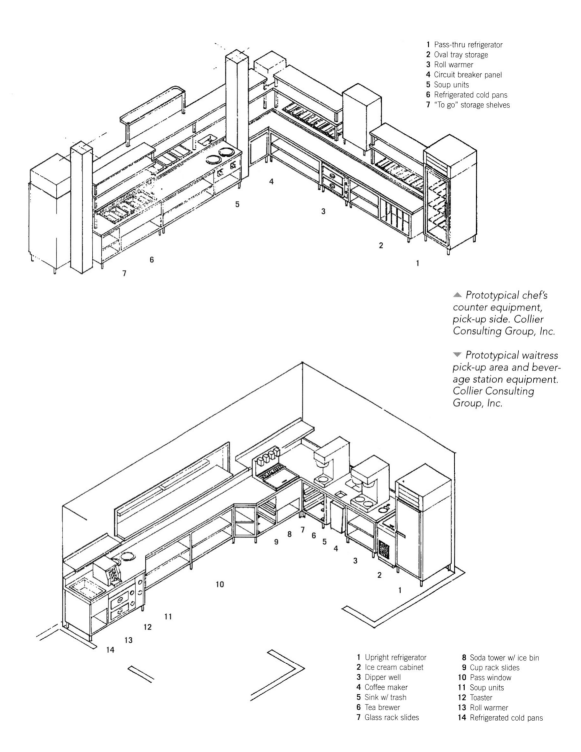

1 Pass-thru refrigerator
2 Oval tray storage
3 Roll warmer
4 Circuit breaker panel
5 Soup units
6 Refrigerated cold pans
7 "To go" storage shelves

▲ Prototypical chef's counter equipment, pick-up side. Collier Consulting Group, Inc.

▼ Prototypical waitress pick-up area and beverage station equipment. Collier Consulting Group, Inc.

1 Upright refrigerator	8 Soda tower w/ ice bin
2 Ice cream cabinet	9 Cup rack slides
3 Dipper well	10 Pass window
4 Coffee maker	11 Soup units
5 Sink w/ trash	12 Toaster
6 Tea brewer	13 Roll warmer
7 Glass rack slides	14 Refrigerated cold pans

FOOD-SERVICE SPACE REQUIREMENTS		
MENU	KITCHEN (sq ft)	FOOD & BEVERAGE SUPPORT (sq ft)
Snack bar	200–300 (assumes paper service)	Included with kitchen
Limited grill–à la carte	1200–1400	500–800
Full à la carte	1600–2000	1200–1500
À la carte & banquette	2000–2400	1500–2000

for the ratio of kitchen to dining space may be misleading. In recreational facilities, such as clubhouses, the menu is the most important factor in sizing the kitchen and food and beverage support facilities.

Areas listed in the table above are to be used for initial programming and planning purposes. The space for the kitchen layout and support facilities needs to be confirmed by a kitchen consultant's preliminary layout of equipment as early in the planning process as possible. Kitchen space indicated includes the main cooking lines, chef's counter, cold food preparation, dishwashing, and pot-and-pan cleanup area. Also necessary is easily accessible food storage.

In addition to the indicated areas, there may be specialty preparation spaces such as bakeries for desserts and breads or the cold kitchen for salads, chilled feature foods, and ice sculptures. The food and beverage support area includes bulk storage such as walk-in coolers and freezers; storage of dry-goods; beer, wine, and liquor; banquet serving-pieces; stack chairs and folding tables; receiving area; and employee facilities, including break room, restrooms, and lockers.

The total food and beverage area is also affected by whether the facilities are concentrated in one area or on different levels. Separate kitchens may duplicate some elements of food and beverage equipment. The goal in planning is to serve from one main kitchen to save on space, equipment, and, above all, personnel.

BARS

Bar-served beverages are typical in recreational facilities. Wine is increasingly outselling mixed drinks. Wine may be stored in a featured display. For clubhouses, bars may sometimes be handsome millwork pieces that function as service bars with little or no seating.

SERVICE AREAS

Service areas for dining are a particular challenge for architects and landscape architects. The golf and country club clubhouse may be surrounded by the golf course and related golf areas, tennis courts, aquatics center, and arrival and parking areas. To this building, with no place for a back door, the architect must provide access for deliveries-in and trash-out. The typical country club clubhouse requires delivery by trucks, including small semitrailers. Access is also required for trash trucks to dumpsters or compactors. Closed compactors hauled away with the contents disposed of elsewhere are preferred, particularly where food and beverage are served outdoors.

PART IV

FEASIBILITY AND SUSTAINABILITY

Previous page: *Rancho La Puerta, Tecate, Mexico. Photo by John Durant.*

CHAPTER 13
FEASIBILITY

RALPH STEWART BOWDEN

Recreational development is pursued for myriad reasons that are as varied as the range of types of facilities in this book. Some forms of recreational development are freestanding commercial ventures that are expected to pay for themselves and to produce a profit. Other forms of recreational development represent facets of a larger development concept and contribute or transfer value to the concept by enhancing an overall experience.

Feasibility has many meanings and is relevant to numerous points in the development process. It may be legal and political with respect to zoning and permitting. Market feasibility focuses on whether there is adequate demand to support a recreational activity and the associated facilities. Physical feasibility centers on the capacity of a particular site to accommodate a facility. Economic or financial feasibility is about recapturing the capital costs of development and operating at a profitable or sustainable level. All of these types of feasibility need to be addressed. The results of these analyses will determine if a facility can be built and supported, and whether it can be financed. The type of feasibility most frequently discussed is financial.

▼ *Marlborough Community, Marlborough, Connecticut, view of dining area. Diedrich, LLC. Drawing by E. Addison Young.*

RECREATIONAL FACILITY FEASIBILITY

There are eleven categories, along with several subcategories, of recreational facilities discussed in these chapters. This chapter is not intended to be a manual on how to perform feasibility studies for each type of facility. Rather, it is intended to provide a context in which to consider feasibility. Accordingly, the principles of determining financial feasibility will be presented and followed by a discussion of how facilities that are not individually financially feasible contribute to a greater goal.

For freestanding structures, once legal, physical, and market feasibility has been determined, financial feasibility may be addressed. First, the capital costs of land, design and permitting fees, and infrastructure and facility construction need to be estimated. Capital costs are recaptured by selling the facility at some point in the future, or by selling memberships that then provide either access or ownership and are priced to cover capital costs and produce a profit. Second, operating costs need to be determined, accompanied by a strategy to cover those costs with operating revenues, and (if appropriate) produce operating profits. Both capital requirements and operating requirements need to be covered for a facility to be deemed "financially feasible."

When recreational facilities are part of a larger development, such as a country club community or a resort, they must be viewed in the context of what they contribute to the overall development. While many recreational facilities may be legally and physically feasible, they may not be financially feasible when viewed as an independent operation. In situations such as these, it is important to examine their contribution to the feasibility of the entire development, whether it is a resort or a country club.

The determination of feasibility begins with the consideration of demand. Evaluating demand is sometimes characterized by the complex question — "How often will how many of whom pay how much for what?" The answer to this question may be very broad or very narrow. For example, daily-fee golf courses rely on public participation. In the case of a daily-fee golf course, one needs to estimate what portion of the population in the local market area is old enough, has enough available time, has enough discretionary income, and is not adequately served by current supply to be considered candidates to use the golfing facilities.

Assuming that there is adequate demand to justify consideration of building a new course, new opportunities may emerge that will make the golf facility more productive. Golf courses are used during the daytime. How might these facilities be used during evening hours to make them more productive? Since most courses have some form of food and beverage operation, it may be logical to consider how the club house and parking lot may be put to productive use by expanding the food and beverage operation into catering for banquets and weddings. This new consideration now calls for an additional dimension of demand analysis. In this case, questions pertaining to how much unsatisfied demand exists for the services being considered and how much revenue can the operation generate must be addressed and answered.

Private facilities represent the other end of the range of demand. Rather than being broadly inclusive, private facilities are by definition narrowly inclusive, that is, exclusive. Private facilities depend on relatively small demand groups that are highly qualified with respect to their ability to pay for the continuous availability of the services they desire, whether they use them regularly or not. Due to the restricted utilization of private facilities, they are frequently established as not-for-profit organizations. In these cases, the measure of feasibility is sustainability rather than profitability and how the facilities contribute to the value of other products being offered, whether the product is a meal, a tennis racquet, or real estate.

Timing is another component of feasibility. For example, recreational facilities in master-planned communities, whether public or private, are initially planned as components of the lifestyle that the community has to offer. The primary goal of the community developer is to sell real estate. The recreational amenities serve to position the community in the marketplace and in some cases to differentiate the community from its competitors.

At the beginning of the development, however, such facilities frequently operate at a loss. Initially, the role of amenities is to attract prospective buyers, rather than to independently generate profits. As marketing tools, recreational amenity facilities serve to transfer value to other elements of the community, particularly the value of the real estate. As the recreational community advances through the sales process, the importance of the amenities starts to transfer from the developer to the property owners.

At the end of the sales process, the importance of the amenity to the developer as a marketing tool has been exhausted, and continued ownership of the amenity might actually become a liability for the developer's business. Simultaneously, the community recreational amenities have become increasingly important to the residents of the community. The facilities become the basis for a lifestyle and an important part of the foundation of the value of their residential or resort property.

In such situations, individual recreational facilities may not appear to carry themselves. However, when the benefits of higher real estate prices and accelerated absorption are taken into consideration, apparent losses may turn into positive financial impacts.

Since feasibility analysis deals with future events, it is really an estimate of probability. A variety of assumptions may be made and tested within a feasibility analysis. Frequently, initial feasibility studies will conclude that a particular endeavor is not feasible, based on the assumptions employed. One of the benefits of feasibility studies is that such shortcomings may be recognized and addressed before buildings are built and operations started. New assumptions may be formulated and incorporated into the financial model. Such exercises are called sensitivity analyses, measuring the impact that various assumptions have on the viability of the proposed operation. Ultimately, these exercises will reveal the factors necessary for success; or they will reveal the reality that the facility should not be built or that the facility will need to be subsidized by other, more productive operations.

While the feasibility of recreational facilities may be estimated on a spreadsheet, success is measured by how much utilization of the facilities exceeds expectations. There is a technological analogy in the recreational development business that equates facilities with hardware and programs or operations as software. The best-designed facilities (hardware) will fail if the activities (software) that are conducted in them are not vital and appealing. An important component of feasible recreational facilities is enthusiastic management that keeps the software fresh and appealing and provides people with reasons to participate that add to the quality of their lives.

CHAPTER 14
ENVIRONMENTALLY SUSTAINABLE DESIGN

MARK A. DIEDRICH

According to the United States Green Building Council (USGBC), buildings in the United States consume more than 30 percent of the total energy and 60 percent of the total electricity produced annually. Nearly 75 percent of the energy is produced through the use of fossil fuels such as coal and oil. Buildings also withdraw approximately 340 billion gallons of fresh water per day from rivers, streams, and reservoirs to support residential, commercial, industrial, agricultural, and recreational activities.

Construction and demolition wastes comprise about 40 percent of the total solid waste produced in the United States. Furthermore, buildings account for use of 40 percent of raw stone, gravel, and sand and 25 percent of virgin wood, as well as other natural resources.[1]

From design to construction to occupancy, the buildings we create have a tremendous impact on our environment.

[1]LEED Reference Guide Version 2.0 (Washington, D.C.: U.S. Green Building Council, 2001).

▼ Riverfront club conceptual sketch. Diedrich Architects. Drawing by E. Addison Young.

Spurred by energy crises created in various regions of the United States in recent years, groups such as the USGBC now have an audience to assist them in seeking ways to conserve resources now and for future generations.

APPLICATION OF SUSTAINABLE DESIGN PRINCIPLES

Realizing the need for a written set of guidelines for sustainable principles to assist designers and developers, the USGBC introduced the Leadership in Energy and Environmental Design (LEED), the green building rating system. The rating system allows for a life-cycle evaluation of green building criteria for new and existing buildings based on five environmental categories: sustainable sites, water efficiency, energy and atmosphere, materials and resources, and indoor environmental quality. For more information on LEED certification requirements, as well as a checklist of sustainable design principles, visit the LEED website.[2]

The United States government, at many levels, has mandated green design—also known as sustainable design—in its buildings for years. Now many real estate developers are realizing that there are distinct advantages to creating a product that can be marketed as "green." Many are finding that when green building principles are considered early in the design process, provisions can be made that do not significantly affect the up-front building costs, but do reduce life-cycle costs. When green design principles are employed, everyone can benefit, from developer to users and to future generations.

[2]http://www.usgbc.org/

GREEN CONSIDERATIONS FOR RECREATIONAL FACILITIES

Understanding the simplicity of many sustainable design approaches, more and more developers (and other organizations that build) are helping to create a sustainable building environment by taking the initiative to conserve resources and to put into practice green building principles in recreational facilities. Many examples of green recreation buildings exist today, and the number is growing. Below is a summary of considerations specific to each building type.

Golf Support Facilities

The golf club developer should involve both a sustainable design professional and an architect during the land planning and site selection process. Just as locating the clubhouse to take advantage of the finishing holes is important, so too is its orientation to the sun and other environmental factors. Taking building orientation into consideration early in the design process allows designers to plan for a building that provides glazing and views to the finishing holes, whether facing toward the north or south, to take advantage of passive solar (i.e., daylighting) and active solar (photovoltaic panels) heating and illumination. Planning for a smaller building footprint reduces site disturbance, and the decision to locate golf cart parking under the clubhouse is a green consideration. An example of this can be found at the Old Greenwood Golf Pro Shop in Truckee, California.

Locating the cart parking under the building, however, calls for a mechanical ventilation system that is not required for free-standing, open cart barns. A green strategy for resort courses would be to allow for bag storage, thereby encouraging

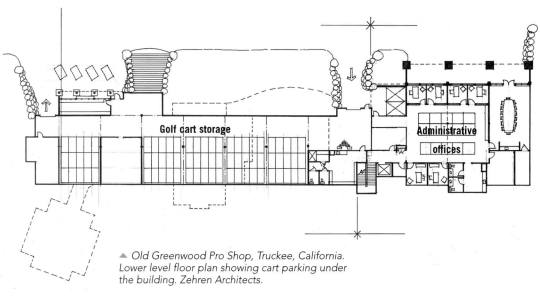

▲ *Old Greenwood Pro Shop, Truckee, California. Lower level floor plan showing cart parking under the building. Zehren Architects.*

▼ *Old Greenwood Pro Shop, upper level floor plan.*

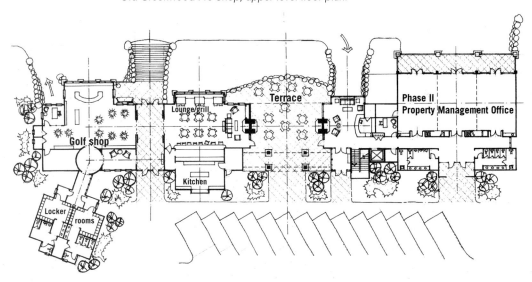

golfers to walk, ride a bike, or shuttle to the clubhouse for a round of golf. At clubs with capacity for large special events, such as weddings, paved parking lots can be reduced by providing overflow parking on designated grass areas. This measure reduces the need for paved parking and therefore reduces site runoff by providing more pemeable land on the site.

In the Old Greenwood Golf Pro Shop for East-West Partners, Zehren Architects of Vail, Colorado, reduced water consumption by planting drought-resistant native plants on the site. Within the building, East-West Partners required the use of low-flow fixtures activated by infrared sensors. Energy conservation measures include the ample use of daylighting, exclusive specification of Energy Star–rated fixtures and appliances, and design of operable windows for ventilation. Energy Star is a voluntary labeling program of the U.S. Environmental Protection Agency (EPA) and the U.S. Department of Energy (DOE) that identifies energy-efficient products.

Materials specified for the pro shop at Old Greenwood are sustainable as well. Typical materials are either recycled or readily renewable and contain low amounts of volatile organic compounds (or VOCs). VOCs are chemical compounds that contribute to air pollution, including ground level ozone, in the way that they react with sunlight and nitrogen. They are considered a detriment to human health, agriculture, and the environment. Scheduled for completion

in summer 2004, the pro shop at Old Greenwood is one of the first of its building type to be registered for LEED certification.

Green building considerations may also be made for golf outbuildings such as course shelters and toilet facilities. Measures include the use of skylights and clerestories in lieu of light fixtures, natural ventilation for supplemental conditioning of the facility, and solar power to operate exhaust fans, as well as installation of composting toilets and urinals over traditional forms. Many golf clubs already incorporate these measures without viewing them as green but, rather, because they eliminate the need to run power and plumbing services to remote buildings.

Aquatics

When the city of Boulder, Colorado, embarked on a project to renovate and

▼ North Boulder Recreation Center, Boulder, Colorado, floor plan. Barker Rinker Seacat Architecture.

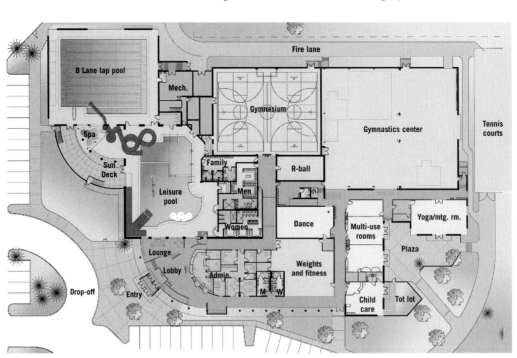

expand its North Boulder Recreation Center (NBRC), which includes two indoor pools, it elected to do so with the goal of being the first silver-level LEED certified building in the state.

To achieve this goal, the Parks and Recreation Department identified three major steps:

- Reduce the amount of landfill waste generated by the renovation and expansion

- Reduce the consumption of natural resources used in the project

- Improve the energy efficiency of the building.

According to green building consultant, the Architectural Energy Corporation, over 75 percent of the construction waste was diverted from landfills during the renovation. Salvaged materials from the existing building were reused at this and other facilities, and existing trees removed from the site were relocated to local parks. Additional efforts included the reuse of refurbished air conditioning units, doors, and flooring materials.

Meeting the goal of reducing natural resource consumption required researching materials that are made from recycled products or from readily renewable natural resources such as bamboo and cork. Conservation measures at North Boulder Recreational Center (NBRC) included the use of recycled content building materials, such as lockers and benches made of recycled plastic as well as carpet binding fabricated from recycled materials.

Energy efficient design at the NBRC began with what is regarded as the largest flat plate solar unit installed in the United States in twenty years.

The 6,000 sq ft of panels are used to preheat the water for two swimming

▲ North Boulder Recreation Center, view of rooftop solar heating panels. Photo by Michael Shopenn.

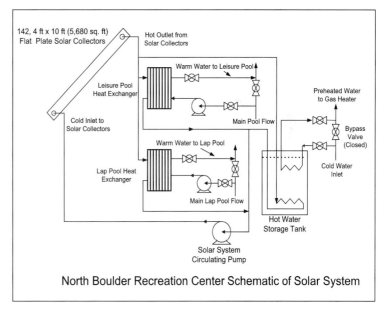

North Boulder Recreation Center Schematic of Solar System

▲ North Boulder Recreation Center, Boulder, Colorado. Schematic diagram of solar water heating system. Architectural Energy Corporation, designer.

pools in the center. In this system, water is pumped through the solar panels to raise the water temperature prior to being heated by boilers. This process is said to reduce the natural gas consumption by 50 percent. The above illustration shows how the solar water heating system operates. In addition, Barker Rinker Seacat Architects incorporated daylighting throughout the NBRC building to reduce energy costs needed for lighting. They also used low-emission (low-E) insulated glass to reduce solar heat gain and thus reduce cooling costs. Finally, the building was equipped with a carbon dioxide monitoring system that adjusts the amount of outside air used in the air-conditioning system according to the number of occupants in the facility at a given time. Reducing the amount of outside air during off-peak hours saves energy by recycling more of the preconditioned air already within the building. Energy modeling for the building estimated that the energy saving principles used in the NBRC will reduce the energy costs by an estimated $56,000 annually.

Boating

Boating facilities consist of many different building types, including yacht clubs, ship's stores, dry-stack storage, and crew houses. Consisting of dining, locker, administration, and retail facilities, yacht clubs and ship's stores are

▶ University of Wisconsin Crew House, Madison, Wisconsin. Elevation view of crew house. Vincent James Associates Architects in association with KEE Architecture.

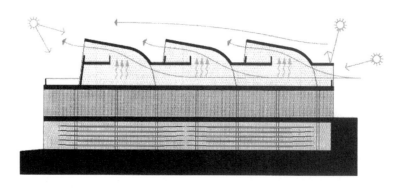

▶ University of Wisconsin Crew House, building section.

◀ *Princeton University Boathouse, Princeton, New Jersey. Interior photo demonstrates use of daylighting and glue-laminated wood trusses. ARC Architects. Photo by Nick Wheeler.*

similar in green tactics to golf clubhouses; but crew houses and dry-storage buildings challenge sustainability. Due to their typical proximity to water, efforts should be made to locate dry-stack storage and other boating buildings at least 5 ft above the one-hundred year flood plain, as defined by the Federal Emergency Management Agency (FEMA), and at least 100 ft from local wetlands to avoid eventual contamination of the water.

The typical large expanse of roof in this building type lends itself to taking advantage of the sun and wind. At the University of Wisconsin Crew House in Madison, Wisconsin, Vincent James Associates Architects (VJAA) oriented the building to take advantage of

clerestories to provide both daylighting and natural ventilation to reduce energy costs. The unique building design permits natural-stack ventilation to reduce cooling demand. It allows cooler air to be drawn into the building at a lower elevation as warmer air is exhausted through clerestory roof forms.

The use of natural light is evident at the Princeton University Boathouse in Princeton, New Jersey, and the building is an example of the use of sustainable materials. ARC Architects of Boston chose glue-laminated trusses to create the building's long span. This and other crew houses typically include fitness facilities, lockers, offices, and other spaces whose sustainability issues are discussed elsewhere in this chapter.

Racquet Sports

Indoor tennis buildings are large, open buildings that have the potential to consume an abundance of energy and natural resources if green considerations are not taken. Orienting the building in an east-west direction, such that the long walls have exposure to the north and south, takes advantage of daylight and reduces the need for lighting. Artificial lighting is typically achieved through the use of high-intensity discharge (HID) fixtures. Due to their efficiency, the lamps for these fixtures not only save energy but last a long time. The long lamp life also reduces the frequency of changing the lamps, which are typically in inconvenient locations.

Operable windows and louvers will also allow for fresh air ventilation and eliminate the need for cooling. Tennis facilities typically do not use air-conditioning, because the sport is typically played outdoors during warm summer months. Radiant heat is often used and is considered energy efficient as the system involves heat transfer directly from the source to an object, such as a person, and thus does not require the fans and ventilation of an air-handling system.

Consideration for sustainable materials can have a significant impact on natural resource conservation due to the large building size and resulting quantities of materials needed in racquet facilities. Most of these buildings consist of long-span steel structures, and most steel today is recycled. Corrugated steel exterior finishes are also prevalent due to the low relative cost and may also be considered a green product. Sustainable products, such as recycled rubber, clay, or concrete (with a fly ash admixture), should be considered in lieu of asphalt or virgin rubber athletic surfaces for the court surfacing. Fly ash is a postindustrial byproduct that has cementitious properties and may be used to replace a percentage of cement as a concrete admixture. Water conservation measures in racquet facilities are similar to those discussed above in golf clubhouses because of the large amount of water consumed in locker rooms.

Skiing and Winter Sports

The design team should consider harvesting water from rain or melted snow for storage and use as gray water in the building's heating, ventilating, and air-conditioning (HVAC) and plumbing systems. In addition, locating the building to take advantage of solar heat gain in the winter, as well as scenic vistas, should be a consideration. As mentioned earlier, this is achieved through the use of south facing glass walls.

At Northstar Village, the latest development at the Tahoe Mountain Resorts in California by East-West Partners, OZ Architects elected to minimize site disturbance by locating the skier service facilities underground, beneath the landing area at the base of the mountain. The ice rink at Northstar Village (see page 97) includes a translucent retractable roof that uses daylighting for illumination, whether open or closed. The other sustainable measures used in the village include exclusive use of low-flow plumbing fixtures, operable windows, low-E glass, and Energy Star–rated fixtures and appliances. Northstar Village is designed to be a LEED-certified building upon its completion.

Equestrian Sports

Equestrian facilities consist of several

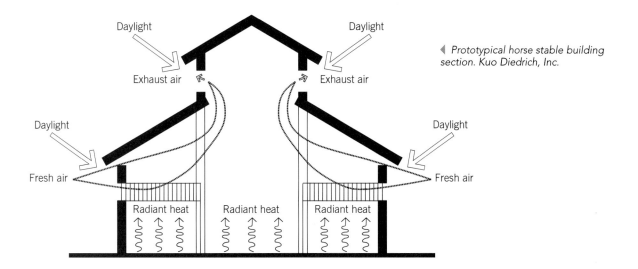

Daylight

Daylight

◀ *Prototypical horse stable building section. Kuo Diedrich, Inc.*

Exhaust air

Exhaust air

Daylight

Daylight

Fresh air

Fresh air

Radiant heat

Radiant heat

Radiant heat

building types that include stables, equestrian centers, and riding arenas. Some equestrian centers are programmed similar to typical clubhouses and include dining, lockers, administration, and retail facilities. Green building principles, therefore, are similar to those discussed earlier for golf clubhouses and yacht clubs.

Similar to dry-stack storage buildings for boats as well as tennis centers, the size and configuration of horse stables and riding arenas typically lend themselves to taking advantage of natural wind and sunlight. As was discussed in Chapter 7, the thermal comfort range for horses is between 45°F and 75°F. Such a range, combined with the necessity for good ventilation, often determine the shape of the building. Cupolas and clerestories in stables and arenas should serve the dual purpose of providing natural light as well as ventilation.

Radiant heat in the floor will also help promote stack ventilation during cold weather and can be very energy efficient.

An additional benefit of these green design approaches is that when the use of electricity is minimized so is the risk of fire.

When sustainable principles are applied to the material selection for the building, resources can be conserved while the costly investment in horses is protected. Steel is both a recycled material and a noncombustible product and may be used for the structural system, roofing, insulated wall panels, and stall gates. If wood is used, especially on the exterior, it should be recycled and refurbished paneling or certified woods. Certified woods follow the Forest Stewardship Council Guidelines for sustainable growing and harvesting of woods. In addition, treated woods, such as those treated for fire and moisture resistance, should be kept out of reach of the horses due to their tendency to nibble on the potentially toxic wood. When paints and stains are needed, low-VOC materials will allow the horses to breathe healthier, cleaner air and reduce the risk of illness.

Fitness and Wellness Facilities

Where fitness facilities are for the use of a neighborhood or community, choosing a central location with easy access to alternative means of transportation is important. In general, designing a sustainable fitness building raises special concerns for conserving water, due to locker room and pool use, and for conserving energy by taking advantage of natural light to illuminate the larger spaces usually programmed in such facilities.

At the Mannington Mills Fitness center in Salem, New Jersey, the owner is a flooring manufacturer with an emphasis on recycled content flooring, as well as a dedication to managing the environment, both within and around the manufacturing facilities. When expanding the fitness center used by their employees, Mannington made the decision to apply for LEED certification for the new building.

The Mannington Mills Fitness Center addition is oriented to allow the greatest exterior wall exposure in the north and south directions. This configuration allowed architects from Moeckel Carbonell Associates to take advantage of both passive and active solar sustainable design opportunities. As is the case with many sustainable buildings today, use and installation of photovoltaic (PV) panels will be suspended until more efficient panels reach the point at which the initial cost is covered by an acceptable payback period, resulting from reduced energy costs. Photovoltaic panel design is an ever-improving technology, making their use more realistic every year. A more efficient use of the sun is for solar water heating. The fitness center used evacuated tube technology to preheat hot water for the showers. Evacuated tube collectors use a series of parallel glass tubes, each with an inner (coated) and outer (clear) tube. The inner tube absorbs heat and transfers it to either water or heat transfer fluid, while the vacuum formed between them inhibits heat loss.

Site design ideas at the Mannington Mills fitness center include the use of native and drought-resistant plants and trees and a plan to harvest rainwater for use in the domestic water closets. Gray water from the showers is also collected and used for irrigation. Water conservation measures at Mannington also include the specification of automated low-flow plumbing fixtures, activated by infrared light

Attention to energy conservation was a driving force behind the unique shape of the building. Exterior solar shading devices are located at the windows, which are specified with low-E glass, to reduce heat gain from solar radiation. The shape of the roof and interior spaces allows for natural-stack ventilation to reduce cooling demand, as well as provides for daylighting to illuminate the interior spaces and thereby reduce lighting loads.

Energy efficient fluorescent fixtures were also specified to reduce energy consumption. Radiant floor heating will supplement the energy efficient HVAC equipment and help to ensure maximum occupant comfort for the building.

As a flooring manufacturer, Mannington mandated the use of sustainable materials for flooring and other applications. The first step was to recycle the existing fitness facility during the expansion. A focus was also placed on recycled content materials to reduce the

▲ *Mannington Mills Fitness Center, Salem, New Jersey, north side view. Moeckel Carbonell Associates, architect.*

▲ *Mannington Mills Fitness Center, building section. Moeckel Carbonell Associates, architect.*

demand for harvesting natural resources. As a flooring manufacturer seeking to develop a niche in recycled content flooring, the Mannington Mills Fitness Center serves as a demonstration tool for the environmentally conscious company as well as a state-of-the-art fitness facility that improves the comfort and morale of its employees.

Spa and Salon

Spa facilities are typically complex buildings or campuses, consisting of many different environments, activities, and sizes and shapes of spaces. Helping to facilitate a healthy lifestyle, many offer treatments and procedures that utilize natural plants and minerals. In taking consideration for the ecology of the site, programming the spaces to reduce the building footprint is an early and beneficial step. Consideration should be given for using a room for dual purposes, such as both massage treatments and facials. In addition, orienting the building to take advantage of natural light will both enhance the spa experience and reduce energy costs. At Rancho La Puerta in Tecate, Mexico (see Chapter 10), native and drought-resistant plant materials were used in the natural landscape.

Because of the large volume of water required in spa facilities, consider use of solar water heaters and the recycling and

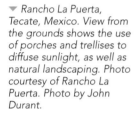

▼ *Rancho La Puerta, Tecate, Mexico. View from the grounds shows the use of porches and trellises to diffuse sunlight, as well as natural landscaping. Photo courtesy of Rancho La Puerta. Photo by John Durant.*

storage of gray water harvested from the building and site. At Rancho La Puerta, a biological swamp on the site is used to recycle gray water for reuse. Gray water is water that is recycled and partially treated for nonpotable uses, such as flushing toilets and irrigation. Both gray water and harvested rainwater are typically stored on the site in large cisterns. In a spa gray water is readily available from showers and bath areas.

Energy conservation measures should include the use of daylighting, low-voltage fixtures, natural ventilation, and high-efficiency mechanical systems and appliances. At Rancho La Puerta, trellises, balconies, and loggias help prevent direct solar heat gain.

The wide variety of uses within spa facilities calls for indoor environmental quality (IEQ) measures for sustainability. Such measures include zoned HVAC controls, increasing ventilation, and using low-VOC emitting materials. In addition, material selections should include recycled content materials such as bath tiles, local and regional materials such as local stones and masonry, and rapidly renewable materials such as bamboo flooring. If done properly, implementing sustainable principles into the spa building design can help enhance a healthy lifestyle for those who visit.

The owners of Rancho La Puerta have taken sustainability to the next level in establishing their own organic garden. As a result, only organically grown fruits and vegetables are served at the spa. The spa has also created and funded the Las Piedras Environmental Education Center to give back to the Tecate community. The center serves to educate schoolchildren on the environment. Combining the spa experience with the environment at Rancho La Puerta helps to treat the "mind, body, and spirit."

Lifelong Learning and Enrichment Centers

Where enrichment or interpretive centers are planned as part of a nature preserve, sensitivity to the local ecosystem takes precedence. The Virginia Hand Callaway Discovery Center is a 35,000 sq ft interpretive center for Callaway Gardens, a resort and recreation destination located an hour from Atlanta, Georgia.

The discovery center is unique in that it preceded the LEED 2.0 certification process. The team, led by Hart Howerton Architects of New York, however, was no less dedicated to design principles that included sustainable sites, water efficiency, energy and atmosphere, indoor environmental quality, and materials and resources.

Located in the heart of a natural recreation area, site considerations were the driving force behind much of the project. To prevent silt from entering an adjacent lake during the reshaping of the cove, a temporary dam was installed. Roads and walking paths were designed to minimize the disruption of the existing landscape, preserving existing large trees when possible. Trees that were removed were chipped and stockpiled for use as mulch in the gardens. Perhaps the most innovative green building principle used in the project is the use of the adjacent lake to heat and cool the center. Water from the lake is circulated in tubes from the lake bottom to tubes embedded in the floor of the building. In the summer, the cool water at the bottom of the lake cools the concrete floor, which in turn cools the air that circulates through the commons area.

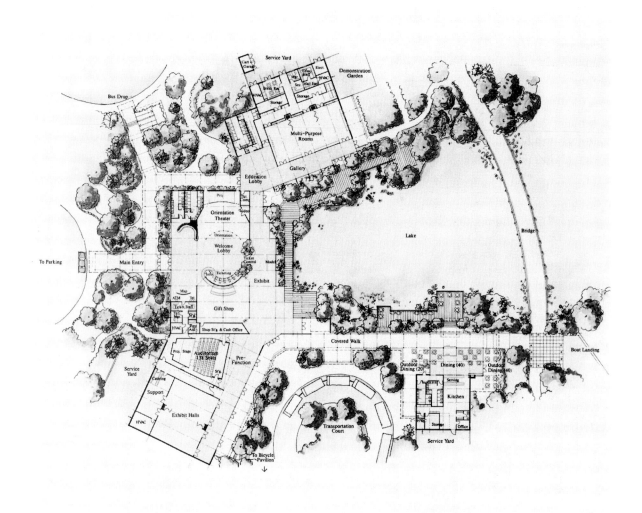

▲ Virginia Hand Callaway Discovery Center at Callaway Gardens, Pine Mountain, Georgia. Main level floor and site plan. Hart Howerton, architect.

In the wintertime, the lake water's consistent temperature is typically warmer than the outside temperature and works in the same way to preheat the building. To supplement the system, a digital HVAC control system and heat pump optimizes energy use while controlling fresh air intake and humidity levels. Heat recovered from the heat pump sys-

tem is in turn used to provide hot water for the restrooms. Water conservation is also addressed through the use of low-flow toilet fixtures equipped with motion sensors. In addition to the HVAC system described above, indoor air quality measures include carbon dioxide sensors, provisions for indoor plants, and the use of low-VOC emitting materials in the selection of paints and carpet glues.

Local materials were selected for the project when possible to reduce the energy needed for transportation. The center's floor is bamboo, a rapidly renewable substitute for wood flooring. Glue-laminated beams were used as structural supports. The beams were fabricated using new-growth softwoods and are locally supplied and manufactured. Like bamboo, the trees used in this process are rapidly renewable and save larger trees from being used to produce the necessary large beam sizes.

The Discovery Center at Callaway Gardens provides an excellent example of how a building may be designed to coexist in a natural environment. The center serves as an educational tool for those seeking to discover nature and to understand the principles of sustainable design.

Dining

When developer East-West Partners set out to create the restaurant Wild Goose, one of the first in a series of sustainable buildings at Tahoe Mountain Resorts, it did so with green considerations for design, construction, and restaurant menu selection in mind. The restaurant, which opened in 2003, was a renovation project that involved a small expansion to an existing building on the shores of Lake Tahoe.

Architect Cass Smith of CCS Architecture set out to create a restaurant reminiscent of the lake cruisers of the 1920s and meeting the owner's desire for a green building. Meanwhile, executive chef John Tesar set out to establish a menu that used seasonal and organically grown ingredients. The project became

the first to enroll in the LEED Commercial Interiors certification pilot program and is expected to obtain a LEED silver rating.

Under the direction of Aaron Revere, East-West Partner's director of environmental initiatives, the design team created a renovation project that ensured preservation of the existing trees and protection of the natural habitat. Parking for the restaurant is shared with the neighboring marina to reduce the number of

▲ *Virginia Hand Callaway Discovery Center at Callaway Gardens. Interior gallery view demonstrates use of bamboo flooring, glue-laminated framing, and other sustainable materials. Design Continuum, Inc., interior design. Photo by FCharles Photography.*

additional parking spaces needed. In addition, the team used the design opportunity to stabilize the shores along the lake and add drought-resistant and native plants, while adding new trees to support the local wildlife and enhance the overall site.

The architect and engineers were able to conserve water by applying both site and building principles. While the native plants reduced the need for watering, the necessary watering of plants was achieved through an efficient drip-irrigation system. Within the building, low-flow toilet fixtures, with infrared flush sensors, were specified.

CCS Architecture was able to reduce energy use by including operable windows, eliminating the need for an air conditioning system. Daylighting measures were also used to reduce the need for lighting during the daytime, while high efficiency appliances and fixtures were specified throughout. In addition, 50 percent of electricity used is purchased through "green certificates," provided by Bonneville Environmental Foundation, which supports power

▼ *Wild Goose Restaurant, North Lake Tahoe, California. Lakeside dining terrace. Cass Calder Smith Architecture. Photo by Eric Laignel.*

production through alternative means such as wind energy. Such green certificates cost the owner about a 5–10 percent premium over traditional energy providers, but they give East-West Partners the peace of mind that they are helping to solve the energy crises that persist on the west coast of the United States.

Within the building, designers sought materials that were locally sourced, rapidly renewable, recycled content, or otherwise sustainable. These materials included building insulation made from recycled denim blue jeans, certified sustainable lumber and woods, recycled wood paneling, bathroom and kitchen tiles made from recycled glass and ceramic, kitchen walls and bar back-coating made from recycled milk jugs, and low-VOC paints and stains.

With the construction of Wild Goose restaurant, as well as several other projects throughout the Tahoe Mountain Resorts development, East-West Partners has proven to be a pioneer in proving that green building principles can be a successful marketing strategy, as they help to ensure that their development will be there for future generations to enjoy.

As did East-West Partners, restaurant owners should consider reusing an existing building instead of building new when possible. Many different building types, from old train stations to factories and farmhouses lend themselves to creating a unique environment for a restaurant, and building conversions keep unwanted construction waste out of our landfills.

CONCLUSION

Studies show that the earlier green building principles are brought into the design process, the lower the up-front cost impact tends to be. In a 2003 study by Capital E, in partnership with the USGBC, a survey of 33 completed green buildings from across the United States concluded that the average premium paid was less than 2 percent.[3] Since these

▲ Wild Goose Restaurant. Interior stair shows recycled wood paneling. Photo by Eric Laignel.

[3]Gregory H. Kats, "Green Building Costs and Financial Benefits" (Washington, D.C.: U.S. Green Building Council and Capital E, 2003).

premiums typically equate to around $3–$5 per sq ft, the payback period due to reduced energy and utility costs usually takes about 7–10 years.

Successful green building design involves the commitment of all parties in the building process, from the design team (owners, architects, and engineer) to the construction team (contractors, suppliers, and waste collectors) to the building occupants and operators. Through environmentally sustainable design, the project team can help to ensure that future generations are able to enjoy activities such as golf, skiing, hiking, and other outdoor fitness and activities that this generation often takes for granted.

AMENITY FACILITY PROGRAM OUTLINE

MARKET SERVED	
Type of Community	
Primary homes	
Secondary homes	
Resort: hotel, villas, guest suites, fractional ownership	
Market	
Market range	
Age group	
Public amenities	
Private amenities	
Initial owner	
Ultimate owner	

RECREATIONAL ACTIVITIES OFFERED			
Activity	**Number of Members**	**Activity**	**Number of Members**
Golf		Sports, limited golf, swim, tennis	
Fitness		Boating	
Tennis		Guest rooms	
Aquatics		Enrichment center	
Dining/social		Other	

GOLF COURSE FEATURES	
	COMMENTS
Number of Nines Planned	
Phased	
Tournament Use	
Membership Program	
Full golf memberships	
Corporate	
Other levels of membership	
Resident members	
Outside members	
Resort use	

GOLF SHOP		
FACILITIES	**AREA**	**COMMENTS**
Sales Area (includes control/desk)		
Changing Rooms		
Director of Golf Office		
Membership Director Office		
Indoor Teaching Facilities		
Storage Area		
Total		

LOCKER ROOM, MEN						
FACILITIES	**ELEMENTS**				**AREA**	**COMMENTS**
Number of Lockers						
Members						
Guests						
Size of Lockers						
Locker Area						
Junior Locker Room						
Locker Room Amenities						
Card room						
Television lounge						
Food service						
Beverage service						
Attendant						
Wet area	shwr	wc	urn	lav		
Nonmember Changing Area						
Steam Room						
Steam Room Equipment						
Sauna						
Massage						
Exercise Equipment						
Billiards						
Total						

LOCKER ROOM, WOMEN				
FACILITIES	**ELEMENTS**		**AREA**	**COMMENTS**
Number of Lockers				
Members				
Guests				
Size of Lockers				
Locker Area				
Junior Locker Room				
Locker Room Amenities				
Card room				
Television lounge				
Food service				
Beverage service				
Attendant				
Wet area	shwr	wc	lav	
Nonmember Changing Area				
Steam Room				
Steam Room Equipment				
Sauna				
Massage				
Exercise Equipment				
Billiards				
Total				

CART STORAGE		
FACILITIES	AREA	COMMENTS
Cart Storage		
Cart Maintenance Area		
Private Carts		
Cart Power		
Cart Barn or Main Clubhouse		
Storage and Circulation		
Total		

BAG STORAGE		
FACILITIES	AREA	COMMENTS
Bags to be Stored		
Storage System		
Caddy Area		
Total		

GOLF OUTBUILDINGS		
FACILITIES	AREA	COMMENTS
Bag Drop		
Starter House		
Range House		
Golf Shelters		
Restrooms		
Cart area		
Turnstand		
Restrooms		
Cart area		
Permanent Scoreboard		
Total		

DINING AND SOCIAL			
FACILITIES	**SEATS**	**AREA**	**COMMENTS**
Mixed Grill			
Bar and Lounge			
Main Dining Room			
Banquet Space			
Terrace Area			
Parlor Lounge			
Private Dining Rooms			
Women's Cards			
Chair and Table Storage			
Prefunction Space			
Snack Bar, Areas Served			
Pool			
Tennis			
Indoor seating			
Terrace seating			
Golf Halfway House			
Kitchen			
Confirmed with kitchen consultant			
See Back of House for Kitchen Bulk Storage and Support Areas			
Total			

LOBBY AND RECEPTION AREA		
FACILITIES	**AREA**	**COMMENTS**
Porte Cochere		
Valet Closet		
Airlock		
Lobby		
Reception		
Coats		
Phones		
Restrooms		
Meeting Rooms		
Prefunction Lobby		
Reception		
Coats		
Phones		
Restrooms		
Sports Lobby		
Total		

ADMINISTRATION		
FACILITIES	**AREA**	**COMMENTS**
Club Manager		
Assistant Manager		
Food and Beverage, Catering Manager		
Membership Director		
Activity Director		
Financial		
Comptroller/accountant		
Bookkeepers		
Property Owners Association Office		
Project Office		
Receptionist		
Secretaries		
Work Area and Files		
Computer Equipment Room		
Staff Break Room		
Staff Restroom		
Total		

FITNESS						
FACILITIES	**NO. IN CLASSES OR STATIONS**			**AREA**	**COMMENTS**	
Aerobics						
Strength Equipment						
Cardiovascular Equip.						
Multiuse Court and Gym						
Women's Lockers	w	h	d			
	No. @					
Women's Wet Area	shw	wc	lav			
Men's Lockers	w	h	d			
	No. @					
Men's Wet Area	shw	wc	ur	lav		
Attendant						
Reception						
Retail						
Staff						
Storage						
Total						

CHILD-SITTING		
FACILITIES	**AREA**	**COMMENTS**
Play Area		
Staff		
Storage		
Restroom		
Total		

SPA		
FACILITIES	**AREA**	**COMMENTS**
Massage Rooms		
Treatment Rooms		
Women		
Steam rooms		
Steam equipment		
Sauna		
Whirlpool		
Lockers		
Wet area		
Men		
Steam rooms		
Steam equipment		
Sauna		
Whirlpool		
Lockers		
Wet area		
Salon		
Hairdresser		
Facial		
Manicure		
Pedicure		
Staff		
Storage		
Reception		
Retail		
Total		

AQUATICS							
FACILITIES	**AREA**						**COMMENTS**
Outdoor Pool							
Competition/ diving well/laps/ sculptural							
Outdoor deck							
Shaded area							
Indoor Pool							
Lap Pool							
Aerobics Pool							
Deck							
Handicap Ramp to Pool							
Adult Area							
Children's Pool							
Spa and Whirlpool							
Cabana Facilities (check local health code)	men/boys			women/girls			
	wc	ur	lav	shw	wc	lav	shw
Attendant							
Snack Bar							
Equipment							
Inside seating							
Outside seating							
Pool Equipment							
Total							

TENNIS AND RACQUET SPORTS		
FACILITIES	**AREA**	**COMMENTS**
Number of Courts		
Surface		
Lighted		
Indoor Courts		
Tennis		
Racquetball		
Squash		
Handball		
Tennis Shop		
Retail		
Office		
Changing room/restrooms		
Storage and stringing		
Shelters		
Maintenance Equipment		
Total		

SUPPORT AREA, BACK OF HOUSE		
FACILITIES	**AREA**	**COMMENTS**
Building Storage		
Maintenance Office		
Staff Facilities		
Break room		
Toilets		
Lockers		
Laundry		
Housekeeping		
Steward's Office		
Receiving		
Trash System		
Service Elevator		
Equipment room		
Kitchen Support		
Cooler		
Freezer		
Dry storage		
Beer storage		
Wine and liquor storage		
China and banquet storage		
Soda System		
Total		

SUMMARY: FITNESS, AQUATICS, TENNIS					
FACILITIES	AREA	PHASE			NOTES
		I	II	III	
Fitness					
Multiuse aerobic area					
Exercise equipment					
Gym					
Women's locker room					
Men's locker room					
Attendant					
Staff and reception					
Retail					
Storage					
Subtotal, Fitness					
Baby Sitting					
Spa					
Massage and treatment					
Steam, sauna, whirlpool					
Salon					
Staff and reception					
Storage					
Subtotal, Spa					
Aquatics					
Cabana facilities					
Attendant					
Snack bar					
Pool equipment					
Subtotal, Aquatics					
Tennis/Racquet Sports					
Retail					
Office					
Changing rooms and restrooms					
Storage					
Maintenance equipment					
Subtotal, Racquet Sports					
Total					

FACILITIES	AREA	PHASE		
SUMMARY				
		I	II	III
Golf Shop				
Men's Locker Room				
Women's Locker Room				
Dining and Social: À la carte				
Banquet				
Lobby and Reception: Member				
Banquet				
Administration				
Fitness, Child-Sitting, and Spa				
Support and Back of House				
Subtotal				
Circulation				
Subtotal, Conditioned				
Golf Cart Storage				
Bag Storage				
Golf Buildings: Turnstand and range house				
Golf shelters				
Aquatics Tennis				
Subtotal Cart Barn Range House and Turnstand				
Total				

GLOSSARY

ABC type fire extinguisher: extinguishers that employ a nontoxic monoammonium phosphate dry chemical agent, which is highly effective against A, B, and C class fires.

event business: food and beverage business based on an event such as a wedding or anniversary or a created event like a wine-tasting and dinner.

golf cart: technically, in golf, a hand-pulled, two-wheel carrier for a single bag as opposed to a golf car, which is a two-seat two-bag gas- or electrically-powered vehicle. In common usage, however, and in this book, golf cart is the term used for the latter.

group event: in golf, an outing in which a number of players start at the same time on different holes, play through 18 holes, finishing at essentially the same time, which is usually followed by a group meal.

hydraulics: artificially created waterway and rapids for white-water kayaking.

lifelong learning: continued education or ongoing search for knowledge beyond traditional school age and in other than a traditional educational setting.

lofting space: area for sewing, repairing, or storing sails.

logo-ware: clothing such as a golf shirt, robe, visor, etc., that is embroidered with the logo (brand symbol) of the resort or club.

outing pavilion: a shelter, often with partially open sidewalls, where a golf or group event (an outing) convenes and ends, usually with a meal.

participation rate: percent of adult population (over age 16) participating in a particular recreational activity.

party barn: a large, open structure or pavilion that is relatively rustic or unfinished and that may be used for group events or parties.

ranger: a representative of the golf course management who keeps order on the golf course, usually from a golf cart.

recreational communities: master-planned communities that include recreational amenities, for example, golf, aquatics, tennis, walking trails, etc.

rounds per occupied room: in a golf resort, the ratio of the total number of golf rounds per occupied hotel room over a designated period.

shotgun outing: named because players spread throughout the golf course and start on different holes. See "group event."

snowboard terrain park: an in-bounds obstacle area catering to snowboarders.

snowboard pipelines: large "U" shaped, sloping pipes cut in half (half-pipes) covered with snow or ice as a venue for snowboarding.

snowcats: tracked vehicles able to navigate snow-covered mountainous terrain and used to manage and maintain ski slopes.

soft tennis courts: courts surfaced with clay or artificial granular material as opposed to cushioned asphalt surface known as "hard courts."

GLOSSARY

structured programmed activities: planned and supervised activities for teenagers as opposed to casual interaction and spontaneous play.

venue: setting where some event or activity takes place; for sports, the playing field or course is the venue.

wet areas: the area of a locker room that houses fixtures that use water—such as sinks, toilets, showers—and is usually finished in surfaces resistant to moisture.

zero entry: gently sloping swimming pool entry as at a beach, without a wall or step.

BIBLIOGRAPHY AND REFERENCES

Atkinson, William. 2003. "Design Fitness/Spa." *Hotel and Motel Management Magazine.* April 7, 32.

Barnes, Brooks. 2003. "Pool Wars." *Wall Street Journal,* June 13.

Binkley, Christina. 2003a. "Shooting for Stars, Hotels Add Spas, Spitzers, Umbrellas." *Wall Street Journal,* October 17.

———. 2003b. "Hotels Pump Up Their Gyms to Lure Execs Seeking Pecs." *Wall Street Journal.* November 13.

Birchfield, John C., and Raymond T. Sparrowe. 2003. *Design and Layout of Foodservice Facilities.* 2nd ed. Hoboken, N.J.: John Wiley & Sons.

Blais, Peter. 2002. "A Mountain of an Amenity." *Urban Land Magazine,* August., 98–106.

Bodo, Peter. 2003. "Hardball for Bluebloods." *Wall Street Journal,* September 26.

Bordeau, Topher. 2003. "This Old Boathouse." *Rowing News,* June 1, 30–35.

Bowden, Ralph Stewart. 2001a. "So What Do Boomers Want Now?" *Bowden's Market Barometer,* December.

———. 2001b. "The Golf Gallery." *Bowden's Market Barometer,* December.

———. 2003a. "The Spa The New 'It' Amenity." *Bowden's Market Barometer,* June/July.

——. 2003b. "Ancillary Amenity Assessment." *Bowden's Market Barometer,* June/July.

Bowker, J. M., Donald B. K. English, and Ken H. Cordell. 1999. "Projections of Outdoor Recreation Participation to 2050." In *Outdoor Recreation in American Life: A National Assessment of Demand and Supply Trends,* ed. H. K. Cordell and Susan M. McKinney. Champaign, Ill.: Sagamore Publishing.

Buckley, Bruce. 2003. "Shops Tackle Tough Market Reality." *Golf Inc. Magazine,* September, 17.

Bruns, Rick. 2000. "Design for Wine." *Lodging F&B,* November.

Burke, Monte. 2004. "Out Front X-treme Economics." *Forbes,* February 2.

Conde Nast Traveler. 2003a. *Top Spas 2003,* April.

———. 2003b. *Readers Poll 50 Top Ski Resorts,* December.

Cordell, Ken. 2003. "Staying in Touch with the American Public, People and National Forests: NSRE Results on Recreation and Forest Values." Presentation at the Junior Forest Ranger Program Meeting, Washington, D.C., FS Research, Athens, Ga., February 4.

Cordell, Ken H., Carter J. Betz, J. M. Bowker, Donald B. K. English, Shela H. Mou, John C. Bergstrom, R. Jeff Teasley, Michael A.. Tarrant, and John Loomis. 1999. *Outdoor Recreation in American Life: A National Assessment of Demand and Supply Trends,* ed. Susan M. McKinney. Champaign, Il.: Sagamore Publishing.

Falbey, Wayne. 2002. "Market News." *Urban Land Magazine,* August.

Finan, Teri. 2000. "Survival of the Fittest: Industry Professionals Predict Trends in Fitness Programs and Equipment." *Club Management,* October.

Gartner, William C., and David W. Lime. 2000. *Trends in Outdoor Recreation, Leisure and Tourism.* CABI Publishing

Gimmy, Arthur E., and Brian B. Woodworth. 1989. *Fitness, Racquet Sports, and Spa Projects: A Guide to Appraisal, Market Analysis, Development, and Financing.* Chicago, Il.: American Institute of Real Estate Appraisers.

Golf Business Magazine. 2002. "Golf 20/20 Publishes First Industry Report." September.

Green, Gary T., Ken Cordell, and Becky Stephens. 2003. "Boating Trends and the Significance of Demographic Change." Presented at the International Boating and Water Safety Summit in Las Vegas, Nev., April 15–17. Available on the Internet: www.srs.fs.usda.gov/trends/NASBLALV.pdf

Higley, Jeff. 2002a. "Making Waves." *Hotel and Motel Management Magazine,* August.

———. 2002b. "Building Costs, Time Important to Consider When Diving into Hotel-Waterpark Business." *Hotel and Motel Management Magazine,* August.

———. 2002c. "Operators Need Education Before Developing Waterparks." *Hotel and Motel Management Magazine,* August.

———. 2003. "Luxury Hoteliers Play to a Different Crowd." *Hotel and Motel Management Magazine,* October 6.

Jackson, Richard J. 2003. "Physical Spaces, Physical Health." *AIA Journal,* December.

Leccese, Michael. 2002. "Market News 'Resort Rebound.'" *Urban Land Magazine,* August.

Levere, Jane L. 2003. "Spa Luxuries for Less Money." *New York Times,* December 7.

Muirhead, Desmond, and Guy L. Rando. 1994. *Golf Course Development and Real Estate.* Washington, D.C.: The Urban Land Institute.

National Golf Foundation. "Industry Report. Golf 20/20." Available on the Internet: http://www.ngf.org.

———. "Golf Participation by Age Group." Available on the Internet: http://www.ngf.org.

National Survey on Recreation and the Environment (NSRE): 2000–2002. 2002. The Interagency National Survey Consortium, coordinated by the United States

Department of Agriculture Forest Service, Recreation, Wilderness, and Demographics Trends Research Group, Athens, Ga., and the Human Dimensions Research Laboratory, University of Tennessee, Knoxville, Tenn. Available on the Internet: http://www.srs.fs.fed.us/trends/nsre.html

Nelson, Christina. 2002. "Sensory Design: Health and Fitness." *Archi-Tech Magazine,* Nov/Dec.

————. 2003. "Sensory Design: Health and Fitness. Part II" *Archi-Tech Magazine.* Jan/Feb.

O'Connor, Stefani C. 2003. "Hyatt Pumps Up Spa and Fitness Facilities, Plans Call for More Openings." HB, July 21–August 6.

Pearman, Hugh. 2004. "Bath Spa, Bath, England." *Architectural Record,* February.

Peers, Martin. 2004. "Buddy, Can You Spare Some Time?" *Wall Street Journal,* January 26.

Petersen, Andrea. 2003. "Home Is Where The Yoga Class Is." *Wall Street Journal,* September 30.

Phillips, Patrick L., and Urban Land Institute. 1986. *Developing with Recreational Amenities: Golf, Tennis, Skiing, and Marinas.* Washington, D.C.: The Urban Land Institute.

Pollack and Williams. 2000. "Health Tourism Trends: Closing the Gap between Health Care and Tourism." In *Trends in Outdor Recreation, Leisure, and Tourism,* eds. W. C. Garner and D. W. Lime. CAB International.

Potter, Rebecca Stapay. 2003–2004. "Colorado's Skiing Heritage." *Copper Mountain Magazine,* October.

Ramsey, Charles George, Harold Reeve Sleeper, and John Ray Hoke. 2000. *Ramsey/Sleeper Architectural Graphic Standards.* 10th ed. New York: John Wiley & Sons.

Raymond, Susan. "Stable Design". Available on the Internet: http://www.equiworld.net.

Riggs, Trisha. 2003. "A New Vision." *Urban Land Magazine,* September.

Sangree, David. 2002. "Real Estate Waterpark Resorts." *Hotel and Motel Management,* August.

Suchman, Diane R., and Urban Land Institute. 2001. *Developing Active Adult Retirement Communities.* Washington, D.C.: The Urban Land Institute.

Simon, Elaine Yetzer. 2003. "Spa Fast Becoming A Must-Have Amenity." *Hotel and Motel Management Magazine,* March 3.

Simonton, Stell. 2003. "Horses Pump $248 Million into the Economy of Georgia." *Atlanta Journal/Constitution,* September 15.

Sloan, Gene. 2003. "Nap in the Lap of Luxury." *USA Today,* December 5.

Taylor, Julie D. 2003. "Resorting to Retail." *Resort + Recreation,* February.

Tyson, Pat. 2002. "Las Piedras It's Magic!" *Baja Traveler,* 2002 edition.

Urban Land Institute. "Equestrian Developments, Selected References." Washington, D.C.: Urban Land Institute. InfoPacket No. 365.

Vic Davies Architect Ltd. "Aquatic Facility Design Trends in British Columbia." Available on the Internet: http://www.vicdavies.com/publications-5.htm

Wall Street Journal. 2004. "Spa Trek." February 6.

Warwick, Brook. 2003. "Trends in the Living and Recreating Place." Presented at Urban Land Institute Fall Meeting, San Francisco, November.

Weingarten, Tara. 2003. "TipSheet: Travel for Body and Mind." *Newsweek,* December 22.

Wheeler, Eileen Fabian. 2003. "Horse Stable Ventilation." In *Horse Facilities 7.* University Park, Penn.: The Pennsylvania State University Agricultural and Biological Engineering Extension. Available on the Internet: http://pubs.cas.psu.edu/freepubs/pdfs/ub039.pdf

Zajaczkowski, Jennifer Smith, and Eileen Wheeler. 2001a. "Fire Safety in Horse Stables." In *Horse Facilities 1.* University Park, Penn.: The Pennsylvania State University Agricultural and Biological Engineering Extension. Available on the Internet: http://pubs.cas.psu.edu/freepubs/pdfs/g100.pdf

———. 2001b. "Horse Stall Design." In *Horse Facilities 1.* University Park, Penn.: The Pennsylvania State University Agricultural and Biological Engineering Extension. Available on the Internet: http://pubs.cas.psu.edu/freepubs/pdfs/ub033.pdf

WEB SITES

Sports and Recreation

- National Survey on Recreation and the Environment (NSRE) 2000 — www.srs.fs.usda.gov/trends/ www.srs.fs.fed.us/recreation
- Sports Product Industry — www.sgma.com/reports/index.html
- SIRC: Sports Information — www.sirc.ca
- Americans with Disabilities Act (ADA) — www.doj.gov/crt/ada/adahom1.htm

Golf

- National Golf Foundation   www.ngf.org
- The United States Golf Association   www.usga.org
- Professional Golf Association   www.pga.com
- Ladies Professional Golf Association   www.lpga.com
- American Junior Golf Association   www.ajga.org

Aquatics

- Official Website of USA Swimming   www.usaswimming.org
- United States Masters Swimming   www.usms.org
- United States Water Fitness Association   www.uswfa.com
- Aquatic Exercise Association   www.aeawave.com
- World Waterpark Association   www.waterparks.org
- International Association of Amusement Parks and Attractions   www.iaapa.org

Boating

- United States Power Squadrons   www.usps.org
- National Marine Manufacturers Association   www.nmma.org
- Marina Operators Association of America   www.moaa.com
- International Marina Institute   www.imimarina.org

Handball and Racquet Sports

Handball

- United States Handball Association   www.ushandball.org

Racquetball

- United States Racquetball Association   www.racquetball.org

Squash

- United States Squash Racquets Association   www.us-squash.org
- World Squash   www.squash.org

Indoor Tennis

- United States Tennis Association   www.usta.com

Skiing and Winter Sports

- Snow Skiing — www.snowskiing.com
- Ski Central — www.skicentral.com
- Cross Country Ski Area Association — www.xcski.org

Equestrian Activities

- Equiworld — www.equiworld.net
- United States Equestrian Federation, Inc. — www.usef.org
- International Federation for Equestrian Sport — www.horsesport.org

Extreme Sports

- Extreme Sports Channel — www.extreme.com
- Extreme Sports — www.isportsdigest.tripod.com
- Streetboarding — www.streetboarder.com
- Skatepark — www.skatepark.org
- Skateboard Parks — www.skateboardparks.com
- EXPN — www.expn.go.com

Fitness

- American Alliance for Health, Physical Education, Recreation & Dance — www.aahperd.org
- American Council on Exercise — www.acefitness.org
- International Health, Racquet & Sportsclub Assoc — www.ihrsa.org
- Medical Fitness Association (MFA) — www.medicalfitness.org
- Club Industry Magazine — www.clubindustry.com

Spa and Salon

- International Spa/Fitness Association (I/SPA) — www.experienceispa.com
- The Association of Pool & Spa Professionals — www.theapsp.org
- The Spa Association — www.thespaassociation.com
- American Massage Therapy Association — www.amtamassage.org
- The Salon Association (TSA) — www.salons.org
- Day Spa Association — www.dayspaassocation.com

Enrichment and Lifelong Learning

- Anderson Ranch   www.andersonranch.org
- National Endowment for the Arts   www.nea.gov
- National Art Education Association   www.naea-reston.org
- American Craft Council   www.craftcouncil.org
- Potters Council of the
  American Ceramic Society   www.potterscouncil.org

Dining

- Club Managers Association of America   www.cmaa.org

Feasibility of Recreational Facility Projects

- Urban Land Institute   www.uli.org

Sustainability and Recreation

- US Green Building Council   www.usgbc.org

INDEX

BUILDING TYPE BASICS FOR RECREATIONAL FACILITIES:

1. Program (predesign)

What are the principal programming requirements (space types and areas)? Any special regulatory or jurisdictional concerns?
1–6, 9–16, 21–24, 26–40, 51–57, 60, 63, 68–70, 81–82, 101, 111–13, 116, 119–22, 124–25, 127–28, 132–36, 138, 142, 144, 146–47, 155–56, 159–60, 162–65, 168, 172, 177–80, 187–88, 191–92, 194, 198, 223–37

2. Project process and management

What are the key components of the design and construction process? Who is to be included on the project team?
6

3. Unique design concerns

What distinctive design determinants must be met? Any special circulation requirements?
21–24, 26–38, 41–48, 50, 55–57, 61–67, 71–74, 76–78, 82, 84, 86–87, 89–91, 94, 103–6, 109, 114–15, 121–23, 126–29, 131–32, 134–36, 138, 140–41, 148, 151, 157, 172, 174–75, 178–80, 185, 187–88, 191–94, 198, 224–29, 231–35, 237

4. Site planning/parking/landscaping

What considerations determine external access and parking? Landscaping?
17–21, 52, 57, 67, 82–84, 96, 101–2, 144, 158, 166, 169, 206–7, 209, 217, 220

5. Codes/ADA

Which building codes and regulations apply, and what are the main applicable provisions? (Examples: egress; electrical; plumbing; ADA; seismic; asbestos; terrorism and other hazards)
102–3, 182–83

6. Energy/environmental challenges

What techniques in service of energy conservation and environmental sustainability can be employed?
6, 99–100, 165, 205–22

7. Structure system

What classes of structural systems are appropriate?
24, 41, 47, 75, 96, 107, 211

8. Mechanical systems

What are appropriate systems for heating, ventilating, and air-conditioning (HVAC) and plumbing? Vertical transportation? Fire and smoke protection? What factors affect preliminary selection?
45, 48–50, 73, 75, 101–3, 107, 146, 159, 180, 182, 196, 211–14, 216–18

9. Electrical/communications

What are appropriate systems for electrical service and voice and data communications? What factors affect preliminary selection?
6